HARSENS ISLAND REVENGE

By

Karl Manke
Author of
Unintended Consequences
The Prodigal Father
Secrets, Lies, and Dreams
Age of Shame
The Scourge of Captain Seavey
Gone to Pot
The Adventures of Railcar Rogues
Available at authorkarlmanke.com

©2018 Curwood Publishing
All rights reserved

Dedicated to the memory of my longtime friend, Lyman Woodard.

Publisher: Curwood Publishing
Cover Design, book design and formatting: Jeffery Gulick
Editor: Kirsten Pappas
Copyright ©2018 Karl Manke/Curwood Publishing

All rights reserved.

Reproduction and translation of any part of this work beyond that permitted by Sections 107 and 108 of the United States Copyright Act without the permission of the copyright owner is unlawful.

ISBN-10: 0-692-11214-6
ISBN-13: 978-0-692-11214-4

The author and publisher have made every effort in the preparation of this book to ensure the accuracy of the information. However, the information in this book is sold without warranty, either express or implied. Neither the author nor Curwood Publishing will be liable for any damages caused or alleged to be caused directly, indirectly, incidentally, or consequentially by the information in this book.

The opinions expressed in this book are solely those of the author and are not necessarily those of Curwood Publishing.

Trademarks: Names of products mentioned in this book known to be or suspected of being trademarks or service marks are capitalized. The usage of a trademark or service mark in this book should not be regarded as affecting the validity of any trademark or service mark.

Curwood Publishing

All of Karl's books are available at authorkarlmanke.com

Karl Manke was born in Frankfort, Michigan. He has spent most of his life in the small Mid-Michigan town of Owosso, home to author and conservationist James Oliver Curwood. He and his wife Carolyn have twin daughters and five grandchildren.

A graduate of Michigan State University, the author has been a self-employed entrepreneur his entire working career. After discovering his inclination for telling a good story, he now spends much of his time fine-tuning the writing craft.

PROLOGUE

Somewhere in France and sometime after midnight on October 20, 1918, the clouds are causing a waning moon to create ominous shadows that give the area a disturbing sense of doom. Covered from head to toe in camouflage made up of rags and dried weeds, the soldier ever so slowly crawls across the open terrain while dragging a M1903 caliber .30-06 Springfield, five-shot bolt action sniper rifle. To an ordinary human, this kind of atmosphere is a lonely departure from what is considered normal, but this is where the young soldier finds meaning. He has spent countless hours in similar situations, only to have each encounter hone his expertise and ready him for another.

Soon, the night gives way to breaking morning light. This is the second day this specialist has spent moving inch by inch to get closer to a hidden group of Germanys' new A7V armored tanks, which are waiting for a fuel supply. These instruments of destruction are expected to advance the military edge of the Kaiser's army over the British, French, Russians, and Americans. On the other hand, these weapons that ominously stand as iron and steel sentinels are the targets of an ever-pursuing force hell-bent on destroying them.

He's been trained to notice things that don't fit, so he takes note that the birds of the forest are unusually quiet; it's as if they anticipate an interruption to their morning routine. The morning is cold, but he's used to that this time of year in his native Harsens Island, Michigan. To add to the cold, there's been a sprinkling of snow—enough to put in his mouth. The idea is to cool his mouth to keep his steaming breath from being seen.

He slowly crawls on his belly until he's a satisfactory distance from these behemoths. He stops and looks; there is no activity to be seen. He's convinced there are no posted guards. It's as if the beast itself is the sentry. The crew of each of these tanks is spending the night inside their enclosed walls for warmth and protection because they think there's little danger in leaving their posts.

He's within a hundred yards of his resting, armored adversary. He's been trained by military experts. He has been schooled in the interior and working positions of the seven-man crew for each of these Goliaths. The rehearsal is over and is now quickly becoming a live show. Wasting no time, he gets a little closer and positions himself behind the roots of a blown-up tree. In mind, body, and soul, he prepares himself to bring an end to the mission he began two days ago.

Readying his Springfield, he flips up his rear sight, aligns it with the iron front sight, and takes aim at the vulnerable track system that's used to move these monsters. The idea is to take out the legs of these tanks before they can reposition themselves to do him harm.

BANG! BANG! BANG! BANG! BANG! He hits all three tanks, wrecking the track system on each of them. Quickly releasing the empty magazine, he slams another five-shot ammo clip into the rifle.

The groggy crew's not sure what's hit them. Their first response is to peer through the tanks' viewing slots. Seeing nothing, they fire up the engines in the hopes of moving these war machines into a position that will ensure their protection. They soon discover the damage has been done; the wheels supporting the tracks only rip off more steel belts when they try to move in any direction.

The middle A7V is in a position to do this lone soldier the most harm. With the sight of an eagle, this trained assassin catches sight of the hatch door on the side barely cracking open; by reflex, he fires his sniper rifle again. The hand grasping the hatch door from inside immediately loses its grip, and the door closes on it. In a matter of seconds, the hand is pulled out by a fellow crew member. Experience tells the sniper that he's taken the top part of this man's head off, but more than likely, each tank has a full crew.

The sniper knows his cartridge can penetrate the tank's armor at this close range. He guesses a well-placed shot to the side plating of this impaired brute will penetrate and bounce around inside, causing unseen damage. With this expectation, he empties another clip into the sides of each of these prodigious machines. Wasting no time, he forces another magazine into the waiting slot of his rifle, which he believes will undo the stunned enemy soldiers.

As predicted, the hatch doors of each of these imposing apparatuses begin to open. The first of these produces an obviously seriously wounded soldier who's struggling to find a reprieve from the violence he's just undergone. Blood—maybe his, maybe others'—coats his hands and arms as he struggles to get out of what he'd thought of as a bulwark of protection, but is becoming a tomb. A shot rings out from the sniper's rifle, and the man crumples in a heap over the edge of the tank, sliding like a rag doll to the ground below.

Another shot finds its mark in the skull of another of the Kaiser's defensemen. Another meets the same fate; a fatal shot through the chest throws his entire body out of the top hatch, where it drapes over the mounted front cannon. It hangs there for a moment, then slithers to the ground. This appears to be an officer.

With the waiting eyes of a hawk ready to pounce and the heartbeat of a sprinter, the furtive sniper observes no more movement. His breathing is measured, and his hands are steady, as they have been through this entire ordeal. He and his rifle have once again become one. With a knowing grin, he lingers a moment. This simple moment of elation is a very short celebration compared to the time it took him to bring this mission to fruition.

The extra training these young sharpshooters have undergone is paying off in aces against the Triple Entente. One strategically placed expert shooter is worth a thousand lives. There might still be danger lurking inside of one or more of these machines. He cautiously makes his way to the closest one. Seeing the hatch side door open, he lobs a grenade inside.

BOOM! With that done, he moves to the next and then the next, until he's certain they are all compromised. Satisfied he has done the damage he came to do, the sixteen-year-old American sniper prepares to make a surreptitious exit. He slowly backs out with a wary eye glued on his disabled prey as though it's a wounded bear. Satisfied there is no perceptible peril, and guessing he's out of range of a standard Mauser, he gets to his feet and hastens his departure.

Six months ago, Frankie Morgansky lost his girlfriend. Along with several thousand other young patriots, he decided to enlist in the army and help "fight against the Kaiser." Because they were desperate for soldiers to fill the trenches in France, it had become common for recruiters to look the other way when they had the chance to induct underage boys into the armed services. Most of them were automatically placed into the infantry. Their training was hastened to speedily fill the vacuum produced by trench warfare's high death toll.

Frankie came from Michigan and had shown how his hunting skills could be readily turned into sharpshooting. Sufficiently impressing his instructors, he was chosen for "sniper training," which allowed him to avoid the infantry. He's a tall kid, and not deep-chested, but well-muscled and athletically built—the kind of kid who stands out in a crowd.

"Hell, that kid can shoot the eyes outta flies at a hundred yards! We can't waste him," said his Sergeant.

It didn't take long before Frankie's skills with a Springfield M1903 sniper rifle, along with his quick mind, brought him to the forefront of his class. He was eventually sent out on harrowing assignments, and always came back with stellar results.

By November of 1918, the Armistice was declared. It brought the war in Europe to a close. This also brought young men like Frankie back home to his family. Once he's back home, he finds things have changed drastically on Harsens Island, despite the short duration of the United States' involvement in the Great War. The entire state of Michigan has become a dry state; no alcohol can be legally bought or sold. Some social changes are determined to be for the better, but nonetheless, this piece of legislation remains very unpopular with all classes except a small group of Protestants. This small percentage of the nation's population enjoys this triumph, while others benefit the most monetarily. A bootleg business has sprung up. The hotspots for this activity are along the St. Clair and Detroit Rivers, along with Harsens Island. These usually amount to someone with a small fishing boat making a contact in Canada for a load of a few cases of liquor to pass on to a buyer in Michigan. In this business, there are those who are well aware of the potential for huge profits. This probability has created a subculture of lawlessness that is rapidly becoming more and more aggressive.

There is a faction forming among this very active and aggressive set by means of an agenda to bully those who are incapable of adequately defending themselves out of the business; typically, these are small cottage-industry people with a small boat—regular individuals trying to pick up a few bucks. Without a doubt, these small entrepreneurs are always much weaker individuals than their counterparts. This weaker group is always reduced into a submissive role of surrendering their cargo or being killed—or, at times, both. Members of Detroit's Purple Gang are the bullies.

This is how this story begins: one Frankie Morgansky gets fed up with this group of racketeers intimidating himself and his neighbors. He's willing to fight against these domestic terrorists as diligently as he did against the Triple Alliance in the Great War.

CHAPTER 1
FRANKIE

The glimmer is small. It has to be, because this indispensable lighting creates unwanted attention by creating a shimmer across the water. This kind of work has to be performed silently and quickly. The light is from a kerosene lantern that hangs from the stubby branch of a shoreline cedar on the Canadian side of the south channel of the St. Clair river. Its purpose is to stingily illuminate the workspace for several silent recruits.

A 1920 Ford truck is gingerly positioned with its rear bed as close to a waiting skiff as it can get without entering the water. With the kind of stealth that can only be perfected with a considerable amount of experience, the laborers quickly and silently pass a dozen crates from the truck bed onto the skiff's planking. The uneven glow of the lantern forces the workers to repeatedly reposition their heads so their eyes can refocus each time they move from truck to skiff. Men with less experience might have stumbled already and, in the process, destroyed a case of lucrative Canadian liquor. These men are not run-of-the-mill stumble bums, but well-disciplined and well-paid company men who get the job done, despite the conditions. Their arms and faces glisten with sweat in the dim glow of the lantern. The efficiency with which they perform the task instills a sense of professional pride in them. They hardly consider it the "Devil's work," as some do.

Canada had also gone dry during the war years, but had been unable to convince the provincial governors to repeal the prohibition act after the war's end. Various temperance groups had fought feverishly to suspend all liquor sales in the hope of ending its consumption, but a loophole to allow Canadian liquor companies to export remained. The United States was quickly becoming their largest patron.

On this particular night, the recipient of this covert cargo is Franklin "Frankie" Morgansky, a veteran of the Great War, hunter, and fisherman. Up until a week ago, he had been a deckhand on his father's Harsens Island commercial fishing boat, but because of his lackluster attitude toward the business, his father fired him in a fit of rage.

Frankie's interested in the liquor trade because of the pervasive public demand; the nation's thirst for booze begs to be quenched. (Despite the 1920 prohibition on alcohol, sales persisted not only in Michigan, but across the entire country.) There's quick and seemingly easy money to be made by those who are willing to assure their fellow citizens that despite the circumstances, they will continue to enjoy an ample supply of their favorite beverage. Frankie's earlier part-time job as a numbers runner for Miksa "Maxie" Ullman, a ranking member of Detroit's infamous Purple Gang, has only served to whet his appetite for this line of work.

Even though Frankie's home on Hasting Street is in the city, his father's fishing business is on the island. As a boy, Frankie spent much of his time playing and working around the island's waterways. It's the largest fresh water estuary in the entire country. Its marshes and hidden coves are abundant with fish and wildlife. At times, Frankie has made a seasonal side business of being a hunting and fishing guide for city people who come to the island. He knows the island like he knows the back of his hand, but he's brand new to this rum-running work.

Reaching deep into his front pocket, Frankie produces a wad of bills and quickly passes it to a short, thin, bespectacled man. This shoreline accountant quickly assesses the payment with the deft fingers of one who has performed this task many times.

"Good doin' business with ya, kid. When ya want another load, jus' give us a holler," says the bespectacled man, satisfied that he's gained another US customer who's willing to circumvent the Volstead act that prohibits the production, sale, and transport of intoxicating liquors.

So far, the transaction has gone smoothly—but then, the Canadian border people are willing to turn a blind eye to this transaction, since it doesn't violate any serious Canadian laws. It's illegal for Canadian distilleries to manufacture for Canadian consumption, but not for export. This exception to the law brings millions of American dollars into the Canadian economy.

The lantern is hastily taken down so its glow is immediately halted. Frankie's eyes struggle to adjust to the dark, moonless night. For this very occasion, he has outfitted himself with a state-of-the-art eighteen-foot skiff, powered by an Evinrude outboard motor. The lights dotting the shoreline are the only guides to help him find his way back through the channel to the American side. He's looking for one in particular: the inviting green signal light at the Riverside Hotel. Its only purpose is to make rumrunners aware that it's safe and that they and their shipment of Canadian liquor are expected.

What he sees next is not welcoming. It's the sudden burst of a spotlight followed by the roar of an engine. In a second, he knows it's one of two things—either the law, or what has become known as the Little Jewish Navy. This "navy" is the waterways division of the Purple Gang. Either way, they both take exception to his presence. The gang can typically be much more troublesome, and certainly more dangerous.

To get caught attempting to cut into a rum-running territory claimed by Detroit's infamous Purple Gang is asking for the throes of hell to come into one's life. The Purples control the majority of the illegal alcohol distributed throughout the United States, and much of that business has been forcibly taken from unsuspecting rumrunners like Frankie, who are attempting to make a quick buck on their own. In any case, the fate of these entrepreneurs is shaky at best.

A surge of adrenalin suddenly shoots through Frankie's entire system like a rocket. Flight mode kicks in. The thunder emanating from this interloper's engine and the prevailing spotlight tell him that this boat means to overtake him. Without a conscious thought, his wrist twists the handheld throttle of his outboard motor in an attempt to rid himself of this unwelcome marauder who's already hell-bent on dogging his course.

"Sons of—" Frankie says. He can feel a slight surge as his outboard motor attempts to push his skiff through the choppy waters. The sound of the boat's bottom slapping against the river's small waves gives him a false sense of speed. He experiences a moment of sheer panic when he realizes his motor is wide open and the stalker is gaining on him.

I gotta do somethin' fast. I gotta get out of this spotlight. Failure will, without a doubt, determine the course of the rest of his life. The steady expansion of the spotlight means this lurker is gaining on him.

Frankie's sniper training kicks in. He pushes the steer lever hard to the right, forcing the small craft into a 180-degree turn. In the next second, his head snaps to the side in time to see the pursuer's boat continue on a straight course. The immediate benefit of this maneuver is that it has swiftly taken him outside the perimeter of the pervasive searchlight.

Instantaneously, he has interrupted his antagonist's pursuit, returning him to the safety of the pitch black, moonless night. He takes a moment to relish this brief success. He's grateful for the bit of time he's gained but knows it's likely to be a temporary reprieve. Nonetheless, he hopes he can make this small success work for him. He needs this little bit of extra time to aim for a small lagoon that won't admit a craft as large as the one pursuing him.

Once again, he opens his Evinrude to its maximum speed. It's only moments before he hears the Doppler sound of the bigger boat turning to follow him. The angry sound of his pursuers' engines tells him the craft is much larger and faster than his. Craning his neck around, he sees their spotlight frantically swiveling to search for its lost prey. The pitch darkness of this moonless night is proving to be his only friendly companion.

Frankie's army training is continuing to serve him well. He's totally aware that panic would prove to be his undoing. Keeping his wits about him is paramount to survival. He keeps an eye on the shoreline to find his lost lagoon, and the other on his pursuers' course.

Setting aside Frankie's military record, there've been other times where he's found himself in a perilous situation. After he arrived in Detroit as the son of Russian-Jewish immigrants, Frankie soon found himself surrounded by other young immigrants from other countries. Most of these newcomers banded together in their own ghettoes, which were bound by common languages and traditions. The Italians made up much of the power structure in the neighborhoods and bullied the Johnny-come-latelys—especially the Jews and Irish.

As a young boy, Frankie chose to band together with other Jewish boys rather than risk struggling alone. After taking a beating by a group of Eastside Dagos, Frankie was approached by a group of likeminded Jewish neighborhood boys who referred to themselves as the Sugar House gang. Even then, he was inclined to take risks. His tenacity to succeed has always set him apart. Before long, he was initiated as a full-fledged member.

Along with Frankie, many of these young Jewish boys attended the Old Bishop School. It was as close to an old-time reform school as it could be without being obvious. Those young boys whose parents were able to get out of the ghetto and give their children some advantages also left the gang behind. On the other hand, the young men who lacked the skills to move on, often found themselves leaving the Sugar house gang and graduating to become a foot soldier (Purple Jr.) in the Purple Gang. Frankie was one of the latter. He found a job working for Maxie Ullman in the numbers game. It was small-time stuff compared to making a big hit in the liquor business.

For as long as Frankie can remember, he's wanted to be free of those who tell him how far he can go and how to run his own ship. This same personality trait made him the successful sniper he became for his country.

Frankie believes he needs to make this initial booze run a reality so he can become his own man. He figures if he plans well and plays his cards right, he can sneak a big-money booze run now and again without getting caught. *After all, I know this island better than any of these city boys; I'm a natural.*

Despite being Jewish himself, if he gets caught cutting in on the mob's territory, they'll hand him his ass packed full of concrete at the bottom of Lake St. Clair. Notwithstanding the risks, he figures he can outsmart any conditions that might come his way. Tonight, he's been handed an opportunity to test himself.

The boat behind him appears to be an inboard speedboat capable of running him down at will, providing they can keep him in their sights. It's become his prideful undertaking to remain the elusive target. The navigational skills and knowledge of this area he acquired as a young boy working on his father's fishing boat are being put to the test. As far back as he can recollect, he's rehearsed for this kind of showdown. What had been a moment of unease is turning into a resolve to show these "silk suit Kikes" who they're dealing with. Frankie knows these gangsters well enough to know they believe anyone from the island is a hick: "Reuben" or a "Rube." Now it's time to show his mettle. He's ready to march up to the cannon's mouth.

The higher-ups in the Purple Gang are the four Burnstein brothers. There are obvious reasons why they put out a "notice" on Frankie. Talk gets around. It seems Frankie's been asking around about the Canadian liquor contacts. Word always has a way of getting back. As far as the Burnstein Brothers are concerned, they should "nip this young punk's ideas of grandeur in the bud" now rather than later. Unbeknownst to Frankie, they've had him in their sights for some time.

Frankie urgently scans the shore line for the small lagoon he knows will offer the sanctuary he confidently seeks. The powerboat is no more than 300 yards behind him when the spotlight crosses him once again, and also reveals the opening to the lagoon. It's a narrow passage with a sandbar on one side and enough room to allow a small boat passage on the deeper side. With the spotlight behind him, Frankie quickly takes advantage of the illumination by swinging his small craft around to the side with a deeper current.

Having at last caught sight of their elusive prey, the powerboat crew are convinced there's no place left for this elusive prey to run. They figure his luck's run out, and they're determined to close the gap on this gangland reprobate once and for all. The powerboat pilot slams the throttle to the max with the full intention of making short work of this "Schmuck in a stinkin' rowboat thinkin' he can outrun us."

Frankie has safely made his way through the channel and into the deeper portion of the lagoon when he hears what can only be described as a dull *thud* and the cracking sound of the wood hull. He's surprised at how much the distance between them had shrunk. He can tell his pursuers had hit the sandbar at full throttle, abruptly bringing their craft to a dead stop and jettisoning its crew over the bow and into the water. The next sounds are the frantic curses of several men's voices as they try to rescue themselves from what only can be described as an event from hell.

It's dark. Frankie can't see clearly, but he can hear the gasping and choking of men who are unable to swim and struggling to survive clearly enough over the low purr of his own small motor. He remains at a comfortable, safe distance from his would-be tormentors until he no longer hears the anguished calls for help. When there's silence, Frankie makes his way back through the channel entrance and is careful not to strike any of those who might still be able to keep themselves afloat as he makes his way past the wrecked powerboat. The bottom is evidently compromised; the high-end luxury speedboat is taking on water.

There is still one lone figure along the shoreline struggling to free himself from the muck that's sucking his legs down. All Frankie can detect in the darkness is the man's arms flailing and a mumbled, desperate voice competing with the low tone of his almost idling boat motor. He feels compassion toward the man for a fleeting moment before he's slammed with a second thought that was instilled by his army training: kill or be killed.

Satisfied the danger is behind him, Frankie continues on his way to make his delivery.

CHAPTER 2
STELLA

With none the wiser about his past hour's encounters, Frankie soon locates the Riverside Hotel dock with his load. The dock has an assorted number of luxury yachts berthed in slips designed for up to forty-footers. The owners of these monster boats are big shots from Detroit. His eighteen-foot duck boat is conspicuous in its paucity.

"What the hell took ya so long?" asks a hotel employee wearing a white apron and slicked back hair.

Hardly ready to go into detail with this bartender, Frankie avoids the question with a pronouncement of his own. "Don't piss your pants 'til the water comes, hotshot! I'm here, ain't I?"

When they're both satisfied they've blown off enough steam, they get down to unloading the cargo. Young boys from the kitchen staff come down to carry the cases. Their expressions betray a certain longing fascination with Frankie, as each of these young men romanticizes his task and thinks, *I could do the same thing*. They each pensively study the supply, the skiff, and the skipper. Within minutes, Frankie's skiff is lighter. He has a fist full of cash, and the hotel has a few days' supply of Canada's best.

All that remains for this neophyte to the bootlegging racket to do is get back to the mainland and do a little celebrating. This first success has truly whetted Frankie's appetite for life in the fast lane. His thoughts turn to all the days he's spent working in his father's fishing business for peanuts. "Hell, I made more tonight than I did workin' for the ol' man for a month," he muses. For the moment, he finds it easy to set aside the values his father has attempted to instill in him about hard work and righteous living. As a young man, making big money like he's done tonight trumps any idealistic values his family might have.

Ditching his boat at his father's launch, Frankie cranks up his old Ford truck. His watch says 2:00am. *With a little luck, I can get to Squeaky's blind pig before all the broads get taken.*

On his way to the ferry landing he expects to take to the mainland, his headlights suddenly hit the lone figure of a man who's slogging down the road with his thumb out, hoping to hitch a ride. Frankie recognizes him as the lone survivor of the ill-fated boat crash back at the lagoon. His clothing appears to be wet and sagging. His right arm is holding a rumpled suit coat slung over his shoulder. His expensive black and white spectator dress shoes are covered in dark muck, and his previously white shirt has acquired a muddy patina. All in all, his demeanor is that of a very despondent, unhappy man.

Frankie slows enough to give the impression that he's taken pity on the droopy reprobate. To give the man some hope that he's at last getting a ride, Frankie stops some twenty feet down the road from the would-be passenger. Believing he's in luck, the man runs to catch his ride. Just as the man's hand clutches the car door handle, Frankie causes the truck to lurch forward, tearing the handle out of the poor sap's grasp. Repeating these hijinks several more times continues to leave the loser lost and despondent on the side of the road. Discovering he's still without help, this poor would-be evacuee's only recourse is to raise his fist and curse Frankie. Thoroughly enjoying this victory, Frankie flippantly and merrily makes his way down the road.

With Lady Luck once again smiling on him, Frankie makes it to the boat landing in time to catch the last ferry to the mainland. The hour ride into Detroit is mundane and agonizing. The road is the same road he's driven what seems like a thousand times before, but on this particular night, he has a pocket full of cash and a strong desire to celebrate his solo victory with others; he can't get to town fast enough.

Squeaky Schwartz owns a blind pig on Detroit's lower east side near Hamtramck. He's a Detroit transplant. Some twenty years ago, he had originally run a bordello in Frankfort, one of northern Michigan's port towns. It seems he had mistreated one of his working girls, and she found a way of getting even by giving Squeaky a severe beating. It turned out she was also a close friend of the Great Lakes' most notorious pirate, Captain Dan Seavey. When Seavey discovered how Squeaky had mistreated this poor soiled dove, he threatened to take Squeaky's beating to another level.

This turn of events caused Squeaky to leave town in pursuit of greener pastures. He made his way to Detroit, where he has family. It was a timely move for Squeaky, and because of the 1916 Michigan ban on alcoholic beverages and the recent federal ban, he's been running a blind pig along with his bordello. This could only happen because on his mother's side, he's related to the Purple Gang's Burnstein brothers, who have a stranglehold on Detroit's rackets, including prostitution and alcohol distribution. It's proven to be a much better gig than the Frankfort operation, despite the obscene percentage he pays out in "insurance" to his cousins who run the Purple Gang. This further strengthens the old adage "There is no honor among thieves."

It's after three in the morning when Frankie arrives at Squeaky's. After ringing the buzzer, the peephole opens enough for Frankie to recognize the familiar eye of the doorman, Louie Goldman. He has a distinct scar running down his forehead, across his eye socket, and parallel with his nose. Rumor has it he got the scar after he shot and killed his ex-wife's boyfriend; she went after him with a blade before he shot and killed her, too. Frankie has known Louie since they were kids attending the Old Bishop vocational school, but he's never had the nerve to ask if the rumor is true. In this world, it's best to let rumors be rumors.

Recognizing Frankie, Louie opens the door. "Hey, how ya doin', kid?"

"Good. How you doin', Louie?" asks Frankie. Not waiting for an answer, he continues his probing. "Got anything left that ain't been slobbered all over by these downtown big shots?"

What Louie lacks in personality, he gains back in his lack of scrupulosity. He's a big man with a reputation for doing a hit if the price is right. He works for Squeaky as a bouncer, bodyguard, and doorman. He knows exactly what Frankie is asking about without any further questioning.

"Yeah, Squeaky got a new bunch he's breakin' in. One named Sasha or Stella or somethin' like that. She got a set of jugs that don't quit. If that girl ever fell down, she'd play hell standin' back up again." Louie states all this with the same blank expression he'd use while telling someone how he puts his shoes on in the morning.

Not being the least bit timid about his new good fortune, Frankie doesn't hesitate for a moment to show off his wad of bills. Peeling out a ten-dollar bill, he folds it into Louie's hand. "See what you can do for me, will ya, Louie? I'll be at the bar."

Squeaky's bar setup will rival anything in the best speakeasies in town. The bar is set in a circle. There are easily six bartenders, all decked out in white shirts and bow ties, with ankle-length white aprons tied at the waist. They're ready to mix any kind of drink you can imagine: drinks with names like Sidecar, Highball, Bee's Knees, and Mary Pickford, just to name a few. Most of the booze has been cut so it takes a few more drinks to get the same effect. After a certain point, if someone complains about a weak drink, they're given an option to either drink without complaining, or be ready for a date with Louie. Most comply with no further fuss.

On the customer side, bar stools full of ready imbibers circle the bar. Behind these are tables full of men decked to the nines and women with ruby red lipstick and marcelled hair, all smoking tailor-made cigarettes and drinking hard liquor. Frankie manages to get to the bar and order a whisky and water. Because of the low ceilings of this lower-level blind pig, the noise level will challenge that of any outdoor sporting event. Nonetheless, within minutes, Louie has returned with a key.

"Go on upstairs to number 3. I don't think you're gonna be disappointed," adds Louie, still deadpan.

Frankie spits in his hands, runs his fingers through his hair, and takes a long drink, finishing it all before he sets it back down on the bar. Taking another moment to light a cigarette, he takes an intense drag, pulling its fumes deep into his lungs. In one motion, he exhales (adding to the smoke that already fills the room), slides off his bar stool, and sets out to meet his paramour.

A creaky, wooden, un-swept stairway with well-worn steps leads to an upper level. The hallway is dim, and the sounds from the bar are muffled so it's like he's entered another world. The only uninterrupted sound is that of his own shoes meeting the uncarpeted floor.

In another moment, he finds himself staring at a large number 3 in the center of the door. When he slips the key into the lock, it turns easy. The door swings to the inside, revealing yet another mood—one of soft light and the scent of roses. What Squeaky often lacks in the personnel who occupy these rooms, he tries to make up through the pleasant ambience.

Frankie is startled. A strangely familiar figure wears a pink satin robe, and holds a cigarette between fingers adorned with red nail polish. "Stella?!"

"Frankie?!"

Stunned, Frankie says, "What the hell are you doing here?" It seems like the only appropriate question to ask. They both stand speechless for an uncomfortably long few seconds.

With an obviously nervous gesture, she butts her cigarette in the ashtray on the night stand. Still struggling for words, her demeanor quickly changes from that of an alluring, demure hooker to that of a child caught with a stolen cookie.

Her name is Stella Mazzara; she's the daughter of Italian immigrant parents. She and Frankie became an item in their mid-teens. Her being Catholic and him Jewish didn't sit well with either family. Without notice, her family had suddenly moved across the river into Canada. Soon after, Frankie joined the army. Neither of them ever said a proper goodbye to their budding relationship.

Neither knows where to take this confrontation next. Stella's eyes dart from Frankie to the wall, and finally settle on a pack of cigarettes. Still showing no signs of settling down from this unsettling encounter, she lights another cigarette, hoping the pause will somehow give her a magical answer to Frankie's question.

"It's a long story, Frankie," she says, still not sure where this is going.

It's been all of seven years since they've seen one another, but it's almost as though it's just been overnight, given the way they're communicating; he's nearly demanding an explanation for her behavior, and she, in turn, struggles to come up with an explanation.

"I got ten bucks wrapped up with you for the next hour, and it's up to me how I want to spend it, so give me a try. I'm a damn good listener." With that said, Frankie slouches down into a chair with arms and ankles crossed, ready to hear her story.

Stella is growing more nervous by the minute. Along with it comes defiance.

"I don't owe you jack shit, Frankie Morgansky. I ain't seen you in six 'r seven years, so don't come in here like ya own me or somethin'. Besides, you didn't come in here like you was just pickin' up a lunch ya just ordered. You ain't Mr. Lily White yerself, ya know." Stella hopes she's mustered all the impudence she needs to bring this inquisition to an end.

"I'm not here to judge you, Stella. Every time I think I've gotten over you, some good memory comes trottin' back into my head. Just seein' you again has woke up stuff I thought had gone away," says Frankie. The sad look on his face reflects the distress in his words.

Still struggling for her own words, Stella takes another long drag on her cigarette, hoping something will come to her. "We was just kids," says Stella, still hoping she can make this conversation go away. "We can't be held responsible for stuff we told each other when we was only sixteen."

Frankie is not hearing much of what Stella is saying. He's still trying to make sense of this whole scenario. "You doin' this for the money?"

Still attempting to hold her ground, Stella barks back, "So what if I am? What the hell's it to ya?"

"I'm not tryin' to press you, Stella, but seein' you again is makin' me want to hear about you." Frankie says this with all the concern he can put together. "Somethin' tells me things ain't gone real good for you. I just want you to know I still think about you, and seein' you again makes me want to see you some more."

Stella still isn't sure where this liaison is going, but her hostility is beginning to fade. "Why d'ya wanna hear about my sorry-ass past?" By answering his question with a question of her own, she hopes to take control and conduct her own interrogation of him. It's a defense mechanism she'd used in their earlier relationship.

"I guess it might sound funny to you, but just seein' you tells me we never really said goodbye. If you remember, your parents couldn't get you away from me fast enough."

Stella is listening. Though she'd wished only a few minutes ago that this reunion had never occurred, she's beginning to remember why she'd cared about Frankie.

"Don't go gettin' all mushy on me, Frankie. I ain't ready fer any a that crap." With both her arms folded in a defiant posture, she adds, "You ready ta take care of the business ya came here for, or ya gonna spend the rest of the hour flappin' yer gums?" she asks.

Frankie rises from his chair, walks across the room, and takes Stella's hands in his. Pulling her to her feet, he takes her face in his hands and presses his lips to hers. Immediately, he feels the tension leave her body. He then releases her face and surrounds her with an embrace.

Stella, in turn, is finding it nearly impossible not to react the same way. They stand in the middle of the room, silently letting their emotions rule the moment.

Without a doubt, Stella has had many encounters with men who've held her close, but those were more one-sided; they held her captive while they fulfilled their own fantasies. This mutual envelopment she's experiencing has been missing in her life. She's having trouble trusting her sudden warm feelings toward this kind of closeness with a man. She can't help but wonder if this is the goodbye they never were allowed to have, or if this is a grand hello after the years of forced separation.

Jerking herself away from Frankie's embrace, Stella says, "What the hell kinda crap are ya tryin' ta pull, big boy?"

It's becoming more obvious to Frankie that his former devotee has lost the innocence she once held. This hostile demeanor wasn't there when they were kids. It's as though some force bigger than both of them has taken control of her and is hell-bent on developing her worst attributes.

"I'm not tryin' ta pull anything, Stella. I'm only thinkin' how much I missed you without really thinkin' that it was this much. I'm sorry if I'm makin' you feel bad. I ain't that way," he says. Whatever lustful desires compelled him into this bordello in the first place have been buried under his genuine concern for the welfare of his past girlfriend.

Stella, in turn, is finding herself constrained by the sudden return of this man she knew as a boy. This unexpected connection is forcing her to once again revisit their years together and recall how even then, despite his bad boy image, she depended on his strength. Maybe for no other reason than a recent habit, she finds herself fighting the tenderness poking its way through this otherwise tough exterior she's taken on. A mistrust of men has surely made its way into her mind. This fact is particularly evident in how she's reacting to Frankie's kindly gestures.

If nothing more, this encounter makes each of them realize there is still a connection between them. Neither is quite sure where to leave things today, but it's clear they both need to absorb what has come to light so far.

"Look, kid. I want to see you again. Can we work it out?" asks Frankie.

Stella's losing her battle to continue looking on him with the same suspicion as she does every other man. She's starting to see Frankie as she remembers him when they were teenagers. For her to say he's not handsome would be a lie. He's grown into the bold individual she recalls he was nurturing as a boy, but on the same note, he still possesses an innocent, almost naïve charm she can't forget.

"What makes you so cock-sure you wanna see me again? You don't know nothin' about me anymore. I ain't that young innocent Catholic girl I used ta be, ya know," she declares.

With a glint in his eye, Frankie says, "Maybe I wanna hear just how damn bad you really are."

Stella spends a moment staring at him. It's as if she's measuring him for trust and what he's capable of taking—how far can she go in revealing the details of her past few years. With a noticeable little sigh and an introspective tone, she says, "I've had some weeds grow up in my life. I don't think you wanna hear about 'em."

Despite the fact that she's no longer the teenage girl Frankie knew six or so years ago, she still manages to reveal a glint of her younger core. He still finds this unnamed stuff mystifying and curiously alluring.

"Well, I'm not so weed-free myself. I got a full-time job whackin' my own creepers without whackin' yours, too," admits Frankie.

"You ain't gonna give up 'til I spill my beans, are ya, Frankie? You always did think you could handle everything. I use ta think you could, too. Now I ain't so sure."

"Tell me when I can see you again, an' you can test me out," says Frankie with the same cock-sure attitude he has about every challenge he meets in his life.

With sadness in her eyes, she opens a small bedside drawer. She removes a small pad and a pencil, scribbles something on the pad, and tears the finished insert off. Handing it to him, she says, "Here's my phone number. Call me."

Folding the small piece of paper with care, he places it in his billfold. "You'll be hearin' from me." Frankie closes the door to room 3. His head is swimming.

Stella is acutely aware of the quiet in the room. She's already experiencing an especially chaotic life, and this chance encounter has left her with more unfinished thoughts than she feels she wants to absorb. At the same time, she has more than a mediocre desire to see him again. It's all very disturbing, and her confusion is mounting. She lights another cigarette in the hopes of hurrying her mind to settle on less complicated issues.

CHAPTER 3
SQUEAKY SCHWARTZ

Making his way back down the stairs to the speakeasy below, Frankie feels the need for a drink. Spotting an empty bar stool, with his mind still reeling from the past hour's ordeal, he orders a whisky and water. His drink has barely touched his lips when an intrusive resonance interrupts his ponderings: the hollow, drum-like sound wood makes just before it breaks.

Every eye, from every barstool, chair, and table, turns toward the ruckus. What only a moment before had been a din of voices is now dead silence, except for a booming male voice breaking the silence. It comes from a suit-and-vest-wearing overweight man with more chins than can quickly be counted: "We're Federal officers. Stay where you are. You're all under arrest!" His fleshy chin sways and wobbles as he shouts orders in every direction.

A horde of men armed with sledgehammers, crowbars, bats, and axes barrels through the knocked-down door which marked the entrance to this polished subterranean hideout just moments before. Another bunch are strong-arming the patrons, rounding them up, and placing them all on a far wall. Women protest with high-pitched screams as these unseemly detractors attempt to herd them into a single waiting area. A few men also attempt to fight their way out of this rumpus, only to find their efforts violently thwarted by uniformed policemen with nightsticks. Many of those who are trying to escape are on the Purples' payroll. A few well placed blows to the head discourage the barroom athletes with snoots full of liquid courage from resisting their fates.

The white-coated bartenders stand aside, making way for a barrage of men, each with a brand new cigar clapped between his teeth. They begin to smash everything in sight with malicious smirks on their faces. They are delighted with their new roles as temperance regulators. The bulk of this horde are trusties from the city jail who are being given an outing along with a reduction on their sentence and a brand-new cigar to perform their "civic duty." Most of these men have themselves been jailed on charges of illegal liquor activity. Some of them have even been frequenters of this very establishment. Nonetheless this group of men take great delight in being legal hooligans while they take out any number of underlying aggressions on Squeaky's furnishings.

This is not exactly the kind of celebration Frankie had in mind a couple hours ago. He finds he's also being herded along with the rest of those caught up in this untimely fracas. Only a few seconds into this melee, one of these slammer cretins butts him with a sledgehammer handle. Considering the general disposition of these jailhouse athletes, he's lucky the man didn't use the other end.

In all the confusion, the men who are trying to funnel Frankie and a few others into captivity are suddenly drawn away to assist another agent who's confronted with another non-compliant detainee. This disruption is enough for those who are quick-witted enough to spot a break when it comes their way. Several of the men in Frankie's group make a break for the door, only to be stopped dead in their tracks because these law enforcers have had the foresight to place men at the entrance.

Finding himself suddenly unattended, Frankie spots a crowbar; it had been cast aside by one of those called to assist in yet another part of the growing melee. With the swift wit of a ferret, Frankie immediately joins in with those who are smashing the room. He takes aim at a pair of barstools, demolishing them. The smashers are in free-for-all mode. They're breaking everything in sight. Seeing a door leading to a back-utility room, Frankie swings his crowbar through the unguarded access, splintering the wood as he pounds his way through. No one seems to be paying attention to his efforts.

Taking advantage of this opportunity, he takes a prompt survey of his situation and quickly reviews the back room's layout. Immediately coming into view is another closed door. He deftly swings the door open, only to be met by a narrow stairway. Taking two steps at a time, Frankie lurches up toward its unknown conclusion. Reaching a landing with another closed door, he hears a commotion on the other side. His breath comes in short, sharp bursts. Slowly, he cracks open the door enough to see Stella being led out of room number 3 by two burly agents. She is cursing them. In an attempt to free herself from the grip of a sweating agent, she manages to slip loose, only to be grabbed around the waist, lifted off her feet, and carried down the stairs, still kicking and screaming.

His first thought is to barge through the door and rescue her from the grasp of these two suited bullies, but he stops himself. Slowly, quietly closing the cracked open door, he waits until he no longer hears them descending the main stairway to the speakeasy. Prudently opening the door once again and hearing no noise, he makes his way through the open door and into room 3. His eyes dart from one side to another, hoping not to see anyone. Not a soul is left.

A hurried exploration of Stella's empty chamber brings to mind a fire escape Frankie recalls seeing outside her window. He pulls the curtains apart to reveal the stoic motionlessness of a steel platform. All that's left to do is to raise the window, slide unobserved onto its surface, and make his way to the ground. It's a perfect plan—until he discovers the window is painted shut.

Sliding back onto the chair he'd only vacated less than twenty minutes ago, he talks aloud to himself. "If you don't like the situation you're in, do somethin' ta change it!"

With that thought quickly settling into an action, he takes his crowbar and smashes the window. With as much caution as a situation like this will permit, he puts one foot on the platform to test its stability. It appears to be solid enough. Careful not to slice himself on the jagged pieces of glass still left in place around the window frame, he slips out through the glass-toothed portal unscathed. Outside, he hears the commanding male voices of yet another barrage of men entering the room. The sound of the breaking glass brought them to investigate its cause.

Frankie is aware his options are limited. He can go up the fire escape ladder, down the fire escape, or back inside to surrender. He instantly dismisses the latter option and chooses to go up. The condition of the ladder isn't one he would have chosen in any other situation. The voices are now becoming clearer, and he sees a head gingerly sticking through the broken glass below him, seemingly satisfied to only look down. Seeing nothing, the head carefully pulls back through the shards, certain the culprit made his way to the ground and got away.

With the immediate danger at bay and with spider-like moves, Frankie is free to scale to the top of the building unnoticed. The ladder is proving to be loose and wobbly, but it still has enough bolts to hold his weight. Thankful he's made it safely and unseen thus far, he's careful not to expose any more of himself than it takes to peer over the roof's rim and view the street below. He can see the federal authorities putting on the best display of law enforcement they can for the gathering public. These neighborhood folks are hungry for anything to disconnect them from a mundane evening. As things wind down, most of the residents watching the confrontation leave; only a few street people stay to watch.

The majority of American citizens are not in compliance with the Prohibition laws. Only twenty percent of the country is in favor of staying dry. The power structure forcing their policies to eliminate alcohol for the good of its citizens cannot imagine that it's their own policies that are creating a lawless community. Somehow these anti-liquor advocates imagined the rest of the country would docilely fall behind the law. Instead, it's become a nation of outlaws.

This community of "drys" has yet to figure out that Prohibition is failing; most citizens just ignore the law. If that were not bad enough, many people—especially the young—find it exciting to defy these laws. An officer of the court was reported to have said, "If the courts acted on every Prohibition infraction, we'd be jammed 'til Jesus comes." The tail wags the dog; the task of enforcing this very unpopular prohibition law is proving to be overwhelming. The amount of money being made every day in the liquor business is irresistible, so many politicians, police agencies, prosecutors, and even judges find it nearly impossible not to take a share. This means many of the courts only go through the motions of prosecuting lawbreakers.

Meanwhile, back on the roof, Frankie keeps an eye on the goings-on down below. He has a good idea which precinct these freshly captured reprobates will be taken to. He intends to lay low until court opens in the morning and the magistrates set bail. Stella's wellbeing has not left his mind for a moment. If he had been sure of a successful outcome, he would have crowbarred those two gorillas who were manhandling her, and he and Stella would be on their way. That kind of guarantee was not available. Talking out loud again, he scolds himself, "Just settle down, Frankie. Morning will come soon enough. Do it right, and everything will work out okay."

Frankie's attempt to sleep on a strange roof is proving to be a challenge. There is no good spot to feel secure. Lying awake what seems to be half the night, he finally drifts off into a restless slumber. When morning finally arrives, Frankie perches with a family of crows sitting on nearly every available high roost and takes one last look around from his own roof roost down to the streets. Nothing below gives the slightest indication of anything involving the previous hours of mayhem. Without the adrenalin surging through his body and motivated on by his pursuers, he's discovering that climbing off the roof is a whole new, frightful experience. Daylight soon exposes the fragility of this corroded ladder. Its rusted bolts are barely held up by a decaying brick wall; they move in and out along with a portion of the rotting mortar that, until now, had held it in place. Frankie goes slowly to safely descend, but feels he can't get to the safety of solid ground fast enough.

Once he's on the ground, Frankie lets out a long sigh of relief. He hurriedly makes a beeline to reach his truck in case someone is still watching the building. With no hesitation, he pulls his starter crank from under the seat, inserts it into the front slot, and gives it a quick turn. *BAAMM!* The engine responds with a loud backfire and rattles the whole frame before it smooths out. Once Frankie is out of the neighborhood and safely on his way, he relaxes.

The courthouse is only a mile away, but the early morning traffic is already a nightmare. Shiny black vehicles dominate the roads, horns honking as each driver pulls in and around traffic, vying for an advantage. Along with his lack of sleep, this inconvenience is thoroughly stretching Frankie's patience. The auto makers are the only people who are happy to see this muddle. After what seems like an unusually long time, he finally reaches the courthouse only to find that this area is also jammed with traffic. Most of the cars here are trying to find parking. Thanks to Henry Ford, Detroit is becoming the Paris of the United States.

The annex to the court is stacked with people. Every waiting bench is filled, many with women with unruly children fighting on the floor, all waiting to bail out a husband, a son, a daughter, all caught up in the city's Prohibition dragnet. Frankie fits in well, given his own disheveled appearance and lack of a bath. The place is as deafening as the previous night's speakeasy. Not to be daunted by the seeming wall of hapless humanity blocking his way, he manages to wiggle through the crowd and into the courtroom. The proceedings are already underway. The judge is busy processing a man who turns out to be the mayor. Also waiting to be processed are the sheriff and the prosecuting attorney. This doesn't surprise him. The only people who are flabbergasted about these officials' behaviors are the naïve "drys" who believe they can successfully legislate people's drinking habits.

    Frankie wonders if he's too late and missed Stella's hearing. At that moment, a half dozen chained women are being ushered into the courtroom. He spots Stella among the them. His spirits quickly lift. He's satisfied he's on track to accomplish his mission. The court sets bond at ten dollars. With that settled, the judge releases the women back into the custody of a uniformed officer of the court. They begin to make their way back to their holding cell, but not before Stella's sad eyes suddenly spot Frankie's anxious look. He's trying not to be too obvious in getting her attention. He's holding up a ten-dollar bill to assure her that she's going to be off the hook soon.

    It's an hour before all the paperwork is finished. Finally, Stella walks through the door a free woman. Just as he had wordlessly signaled back in the courtroom, Frankie is there to meet her. Attempting to appear stoic on the outside, but nonetheless smiling inwardly, she withholds any outward sign of gratitude. Rather, she gives Frankie a bland look of indifference. With a hand on her extended hip, she stands for a moment, wide-eyed. On the one hand, she is truly grateful to be out of jail, but on the other, she's ceding control to a man she hasn't seen in years.

    "Well, I'll be damned if it ain't Frankie Morgansky," says Stella. "What brings you out this early in the morning?"

    Picking up on her attempt at levity, Frankie comes back with, "Oh, I dunno. Somebody told me they just saved a whole batch of bad girls. I come down to have a look an' have 'em save me the best for Saturday night."

"Uh-huh. I'm sure that's a lotta bullshit. You ain't changed a bit, Frankie Morgansky!"

Standing within a foot of Stella and not backing off, Frankie offers her a cigarette. She looks up at him, conscious of how close they are to one another. After lighting her cigarette, he then takes her arm, places it in his, and says, "Where to, Madam?"

As Stella walks into the warm sunshine of a midsummer morning, her attention turns to adjusting her appearance. What had been a carefully coiffed, marcelled hairdo the night before is now an avalanche of dark curls loosely framing her face. Her ruby red lipstick has all but disappeared, leaving her lips the lively natural pink Frankie remembers. She is also very conscious of the pink satin robe she's still wearing because she's getting looks from normal working people who are coming and going on the street. The contrast makes it clear how far removed she is from mainstream women.

Despite their attempt at humor, they understand his purpose in being here. As the awkwardness of this state of affairs sinks in a bit deeper, they realize they are walking together with no real destination in mind. Frankie reaches out with a probing question: "Where can I take you, Stella?"

"Home, Jeeves," she says, exhaling a stream of blue smoke. She's still attempting to apply her sense of fun to an increasingly dour situation.

"I can do that, but now you need ta tell me where you live."

"Over by Belle Isle, on Jefferson."

Just as the two of them are making their way down the outside steps, they're met by a familiar form.

"Where the hell you think yer goin', Stella?" The voice is a familiar one. It's none other than Squeaky Schwartz. At barely five feet, five inches tall, his ever-present cigar is nearly as long as he is tall.

"I'm goin' home, Squeaky. I've had a rough night."

Squeaky's questioning eyes dart from Stella to Frankie. "What the hell's goin' on here? You know damn well I don't go fer havin' my girls fraternize with the customers." Continuing to scrutinize Frankie, he presses in a little tighter on the situation, "I came down here to bail yer ass out an' get you back ta work, an' now I see yer gettin' all cozy with one a yer clients."

Frankie towers over Squeaky by a whole head. Drawing himself up to his full height, Frankie takes a full step, stopping within inches of Squeaky. "Listen hard, Squeaky, lessen you want me ta kick that skinny ass of yours up around your scrawny neck an' kick that pinheaded skull off, you'll watch how you talk ta Stella."

Suddenly Louie Goldman, Squeaky's right hand man, appears. Despite Frankie having had a good rapport with Louie since they were kids, he knows where Louie gets his paycheck. Not even Frankie wants to deal with Louie on a physical level. Seeing where this is all going, Stella steps between the two of them. The last thing in the world she wants to happen is for Squeaky to find a reason to make her life more miserable than it already is.

"Okay, okay you two—stop! Squeaky, just give me a couple hours ta get cleaned up, will ya? I'll be in. Don't worry about it, okay?"

Hearing what Stella has to say, Squeaky pulls the cigar from his mouth. Looking again at the two of them, he spits. It's enough to let Frankie know it will take more than tough words to intimidate him. Putting the cigar back in his mouth between clinched teeth, he slurs, "Ya got 'til four o'clock this afternoon. Then I want yer ass back on the job."

This whole fracas is over in minutes, but it's one of those ordeals that could have gotten real ugly, real fast. Stella abruptly pulls back into defensive mode.

"Frankie, I appreciate what yer tryin' ta do fer me, but you don't understand my life right now. The last thing I need is for Squeaky ta get pissed at me."

Frankie is half listening. His ego wants a piece of Squeaky. "I don't like how he talked ta you, Stella. You deserve better."

"You don't have a clue about me, Frankie. These people own me. I can never pay what I owe them." Her eyes suddenly seem vacant, like two black, lifeless pieces of obsidian.

Stella steps to the curb and throws her arm in the air to hail a cab. As one makes a U-turn, Frankie is taken aback at how quickly circumstances have changed. *What the hell is goin' on?* Feeling very abandoned, Frankie blurts out, "Wait a minute, Stella! Where you goin'?"

Ignoring Frankie's question, she addresses the Cabbie, "13547 E. Jefferson Avenue, please." Then turning back to a stunned Frankie, she adds, "Thanks for all you've done, but things ain't as they seem. I'll get your ten bucks back to you as soon as I can. Thanks again, but I gotta go."

With that, she closes the cab door, leaving Frankie dumbfounded. With only one thought in his mind, he jams his hand deep into his pant pocket and pulls out the slip of paper Stella had given him the night before with her phone number. While it's still fresh in his mind, he uses his fingernail to engrave 13547 E. Jefferson into the paper.

This is not at all the way he'd expected this reunion to end. Perplexed as to what to do next and with a sickening numbness crawling from his feet to his head, he looks once again at his slip of paper, knowing this small engraving is his only connection to Stella. In the next moment, an overwhelming reality of bereavement grips him, turning what had only minutes before been a hopeful reunion into a hopeless sense of loss. His stomach is turning flips with a sensation of hurt and frustration.

CHAPTER 4
A NEW PACT

Prohibition is the very panacea the poverty-ridden Jewish-Russian families around Detroit's lower East Side need. Like many immigrant families, they are at the bottom of the economic ladder. Children raised in these conditions often become delinquent troublemakers. This Hasting Street community of Jews is not an exception. These young boys who banded together were known as the Sugar House Gang. They got into home brewing traffic. With the onset of prohibition, they developed into what became known as the Purple Gang. The very lucrative illegal liquor sales dominated by the Burnstein brothers has catapulted the Purple gang to a level of power that would have not been possible had they merely depended on shaking down the city's merchants for "protection insurance."

Frankie's father, Simon Morgansky, along with his wife and only son, immigrated from Russia in 1910 because of the suppression of Jews in that part of the world. Simon successfully built a fishing business guaranteed by a ready demand for fish by nearly every immigrant arriving in Detroit. The Eastern Market provided a lucrative outlet for his product. A steady flow of "insurance" payments to the Purples enabled him to limit any newcomers from challenging his customer base.

Frankie shares a home with his parents despite the rift between him and his father that occurred in part because Frankie challenged his father's payments to the Purples. The old man is content to pay what Frankie views as an obscene amount of money that's guaranteed to eventually squeeze the profit right out of the business. For there to be any hope of passing a viable business to Frankie, things are going to have to change.

"Frankie, I want you know it break my heart ve ain't gettink long. Ve gotz goot business. You know, I only don't vantz troubles. Ve gotz goot business 'cause ve ain't makin' troublez."

"Ta (dad in Yiddish), you been payin' these *Kadokhes* (worthless persons) too much, too long. We're Jews. It ain't like we're Goyas."

"Son, you gotz learn how stay live. Your ta agree, deez guys all *zun fun a hur* (sons-of-bitches in Yiddish). But zey gotz all da guns. In

Russia, ve learn how stay out vay, zat how ve stay live. Same tink go here. Sztay out vay."

Frankie knows better than to argue with his father now. Simon has never fought in the army, neither in Russia or the United States. His status as a Jew in Russia was that of a foreigner. He still has not applied for citizenship in the United States. He is accustomed to be a passive Jew, and it has always made life easier to go along with those in power.

The two of them have just made up earlier in the day for the differences they had a few days ago. Frankie knows his father, so he decides to leave well enough alone—at least for the present time. The old man is aging and becoming more set in his ways. Simon fully believes he has full command over his son. Instead of creating another strain on his relationship with his father, Frankie works to prepare the day's haul of fish for the market.

Loading up his truck, Frankie begins the hour-long trek to the market. The Purples have managed to gain control of nearly all Detroit's east side, including the Eastern Market. With automobile traffic becoming what it is in Detroit, he tries to make the best time between Harsens Island and metropolitan Detroit. Arriving on schedule, he begins the whole process of paying off the Purples' authorized people in charge of placing the vendors. Silently fuming, he pays what he has to pay, plus a bribe to have the director give him a desirable location.

After spending the day wrangling over the price he's asking for his fish, Frankie finally ends the day with an empty truck. All that comes to mind is how lucrative the booze business is compared to this lousy fish business—and how lately, it's hardly any less risky.

With barely enough cash to live on, he arrives home. They live in a modest bungalow on Hasting Street on Detroit's east side that his father rents. Pulling into the driveway, he wonders where all this is going to end. He can hardly afford to stay with his father's business, considering the way things are going. Looking at his family home, he thinks, *Hell, I can't even afford to build a house like this workin' in the fish business.*

After parking his truck, he makes his way to the back door like he has at least a thousand times before. His father is sitting with Frankie's mother, Aristine, who is applying a large piece of chipped ice from the icebox to his swollen face.

Stopping dead in his tracks, Frankie rushes to his father's side. "Ta! What the hell happened?"

Hardly able to speak through his swollen lips, he forms a slight grin. "You oughtta take you advice. Da Purples comes 'round an' vantz more money. I tell zem I ain't gonna pay no more goddam moneys. Zey hits me viz goddam ball bat. Zey say, 'next time ve breakz you goddam leg, zat don vork, ve break da otter one. Las goddam 'tink ve do break you goddam neck'."

Frankie can feel the rage starting at his ankles and working its way up to his head. By the time it reaches the back of his neck, his father grabs his wrist with all the strength of a seventy-year-old man who has done nothing less than hard manual labor all his life. Pulling Frankie down to where he can speak directly into his ear, he says, "Frankie, don do notink ztupeed! You hear me? I amz you Ta! You listen me!"

Frankie agrees, if only to appease his father. His head is spinning. This does not fit well with his military training; Frankie does not possess his father's tolerance for bullies. He knows this incident needs to be addressed. He's unwilling to sit around and ponder his next move, so Frankie's next stop is to contact Axel Weinberg, a long-time employee. He's sure Axel can fill in the blanks. He finds him in the small cottage down the road from the fishery.

"When your ta stood up to the guy telling him he wasn't going to pay anymore, he sent a guy in with a ball bat. Your ta took an awful beating. They told him he has 'til next week to change his mind."

"Were these the same guys that's been pickin' up my dad's payment for the past year?" asks Frankie. He never approved of his father paying for protection, but these guys never hinted they would take it to the next step.

"No, I never seen these guys before. I think they was Goya. They looked like part of that St. Louis Irish gang callin' themselves Egan's Rats. Somebody was sayin' the Burnsteins was gettin' a couple a tough guys named Fred Burke an' a guy named Gus Winkler to do some strong arm collectin' for 'em. Word around is they're a pair of real schmucks."

Watching Frankie's reaction so far as to what is being said, Axel waits for a second as he contemplates his next move. "I gotta tell you somethin' else, Frankie. Evidently, they figure you was the guy who busted the balls of the Little Jewish Navy a couple nights ago. They said they's gonna take it outta your ol' man's hide 'til they get their money back."

Hesitating only long enough to process as best he can what Axel has been relating, Frankie re-experiences the anger felt after the horrendous show in his parents' kitchen.

"Axel, I don't reckon I can let this slide. These jackasses are getting away with more than I can live with. You up to helpin' me get these sons-a-bitches off our backs?"

Axel Weinberg has been part of the Morgansky fishing crew since it began. He was Frankie's age when he joined the business, and now he's in his thirties. He's proven to be a loyal and able employee, and Frankie has always looked on him as an older brother. Axel helplessly stood by as these gangsters came in and beat his boss nearly to death, so now he's living with the guilt of doing nothing to intervene.

Frankie has always appreciated how Axel has patiently stood by his family over the years while Frankie and his father argued. He's usually proven to have a calming effect on Frankie's impetuous nature. His customary manner is to find a way to get along.

"I don't know what to say, Frankie. I don't see how just the two of us can get that done," says Axel. His usual prudent tone is definitely returning to the forefront.

"I'm not sure, either, but I know I can't live with myself if I let this go unanswered. I see the handwriting is on the wall. These thugs aren't going to quit. They know I don't have a pot ta piss in or a window ta throw it out. To get back at me, they've figured a way ta muscle in on my dad and suck the life out of his business," says Frankie.

Because he can hear the infuriation welling up in Frankie's voice, Axel feels he *really* needs to agree to join him—at least so he can monitor Frankie while he deals with this unsettling new development.

"What d'ya got in mind, kid?" says Axel.

"I think I can come up with a plan. If you're willing to listen, I think we can cut these snakes' heads off before they know what's happened to 'em."

"You know I'll go ta hell and back for your ol' man. Make it good," Axel says hesitantly.

For the next several hours, Frankie lays out a plan. Axel listens intently as Frankie put together a plot that's achievable, but not without risk.

CHAPTER 5
13547 E. JEFFERSON

Waiting is the name of the game. Along with Axel's calming manner and Frankie's old sniper mentality of patience taking root once again, Frankie lays out a plan with enough of Axel's input for them both to feel comfortable with the endgame. The plan involves letting some time pass so the people of interest will let their guard down.

Meanwhile, Frankie's focus has returned to Stella. Taking a moment to study the address that he had engraved with his thumbnail, he carefully retraces it onto a small pad. He lets out a sigh of apprehension and feels a strong compulsion to find a way of reconciling with her. He finally decides he'll take a drive to her address and rethink his strategy if needs be.

Within twenty minutes of leaving his Hasting Street address, Frankie finds himself staring at small house at 13547 E. Jefferson. It could use a coat of paint and a layer of roofing shingles. Nervous perspiration is beginning to make little channels under Frankie's shirt. Parking his truck in front, he makes his way to a closed screen door. Though his urge to drive over here had been strong, he now finds himself anxious to get off the porch. He feels as though he's crossed a line and is now an unwelcome intruder.

He lets out another nervous sigh and raps on the door. No one answers. Something comes over him that he can't call anything but "chicken." He turns to leave, and a small voice from the opposite side of the screen says, "My mommy's not home. I'm not s'posed ta let strangers in."

Frankie turns in time to see a small child disappear back into the darkness of the house. Not sure whether it was a boy or girl, he emboldens himself to try again. "Hey, kid. Come back a minute. I wanna ask ya somethin'."

The same small child reappears along with a cat that presses its nose against the screen as though it hopes Frankie is a benevolent opener of doors. The child is struggling to push a wheelchair with an elderly man occupying its seat. "This is my grandpa. He can't talk 'cause he had a stroke. I can't talk now, 'cause I gotta take care of him." Frankie immediately recognizes the old man as Stella's father, Francis Mazzara, the same guy who'd moved the family to Canada to separate Stella from this "low-class Jewish trash."

"Wait a minute, kid. I wanna ask you a question. When's your momma gonna be home?"

"I can't tell you, mister, 'cause she's sleepin' right now," says the small voice. The screen between them shades out the light so Frankie still can't tell if this is a boy or a girl child he's speaking with. The manner in which the child is answering Frankie's question suggests he or she can't be more than six or seven years old.

"Wait a minute, kid! Are you messin' with me? You just told me your ma wasn't home, and now you're tellin' me she's sleepin'!"

"No, she ain't messin' with ya, Frankie." The voice is coming from somewhere behind the screen, deeper in the house. It's Stella. She's got one hand on her hip as she pushes the child away from the screen. "What the hell are you doin' here?" is the question she asks Frankie. It's obvious from the baggy eyes and crumpled hair that she has indeed been sleeping.

With the ice seemingly broken, Frankie is taking on a more hopeful demeanor. "Oh, I was just driving by. I thought I'd stop and say hello."

"If it's your bail money you're concerned about, I told ya I'd get it as quick as I could," says Stella, with both hands on her hips now.

"To tell you the truth, that's not an issue. It's you I'm concerned with," says Frankie, with a bit more confidence.

"No need ta worry your little head about me. I'm doin' just fine," says Stella. She's still trying to keep the curious child from getting a closer look at this visiting stranger.

Now that things are going in an almost amiable direction, Frankie tries to move things forward. "You gonna invite me in, or you gonna toss me off the property?"

Without a word, Stella manages to unlock the screen without letting the child or cat escape. In doing so, she nearly trips over the wheelchair. Frankie takes advantage of the unlocked screen, regarding it as an invitation to enter.

The house is sparsely decorated. The furnishings are a mishmash of old styles: rickety tables and chairs, a mohair couch, and a rocking armchair. The kitchen sports both an old-time icebox and a modern, white, kerosene-fueled cooking range.

Stella is still attempting to herd her menagerie out of the way. She looks back over her shoulder toward Frankie as she wheels her invalid father into what appears to be his bedroom and says, "Find a place ta sit down. I'll be with ya in a minute."

Frankie's seating choices amount to either the itchy-looking couch or the rocking chair, which is upholstered in a green embossed material. He remembers how one of the matrons at the Old Bishop school had a similar chair and would twist around in it like her ass needed a good scrubbing. For old times' sake, he chooses the green rocker.

Soon Stella joins him. She attempts to blow a dark curl away from her eye. "So ya just happened ta be drivin' through the neighborhood an' thought you'd drop in?" asks Stella, still struggling with the same curl, which insists on drooping over her eye. Her voice has a commanding tone, as though this question is part of an interrogation.

Frankie isn't willing to reveal his obsession with the thought of how he was going to see her again, so he lowballs the question.

"Yeah, that's how I got here. Just takin' a chance you'd be around," says Frankie, attempting to remain nonchalant. Seeing an ashtray sitting on a small end table, he nervously lights a cigarette. *Why's she asking? Maybe she wants me to leave.*

"Well, maybe you came at the right time, 'cause I ran outta cigarettes," Stella says as she reaches for Frankie's pack, which is still laying on the table. Frankie welcomes any exchange with Stella that doesn't involve her dismissing him and is quick to follow up with a light.

Taking a deep drag, she exhales. Looking at him with a kind of defensive curiosity, she says, "Ya wanna cuppa coffee? I don't keep no booze in the house, since I get enough at Squeaky's."

"Coffee's good—yeah, a good cuppa coffee is always good," says Frankie with a nervous smile. He's attempting to be as genteel as he can. As Stella turns to make her way to the kitchen, he's on his feet right behind her. "Can I help with something?"

"You can come keep me company," she says, pointing him to a kitchen chair near a small yellow kitchen table. The table has a red checkered oilcloth covering hanging over the edges. It's the most cheerful furnishing in the whole house.

Stella turns her back to make the coffee, and Frankie can't help but notice her figure. Even as a teenager, she was blessed with curves other girls could only envy. As a mature woman, her alluring qualities have only been enhanced; her angular neck that is set off by her short-cropped dark hair. Her bust line was an early asset, and her long legs angle up to an ample rear.

She takes another nervous drag on her cigarette as she works. "So, what are *you* doin' nowadays?" Stella asks with tinge of sass.

"My ol' man's got me workin' in his fish business—but I got a couple things of my own I'm workin' on," says Frankie. There's a few things he'd like to ask Stella—especially about her need to work at Squeaky's—but he's just biding his time until he feels he's not being too intrusive.

After taking another drag on her cigarette, Stella says, "I s'pose yer wonderin' about my dad?"

"Yeah, as a matter of fact, I am. Looks like he mighta had a stroke."

"Back when he found out I got pregnant, he blew his top. He was threatenin' my boyfriend that he was gonna have the Mafia bump him off, and then he collapsed with a stroke. He's never got no better," says Stella. The unhappiness of her story can't be mistaken.

Giving her answer some thought, Frankie decides not to bring up the fact her father never liked Jews. He was the main reason they moved, and the reason Frankie hadn't seen Stella in some six or seven years or so. In some ways, the old man got what was coming to him.

"I thought you moved to Canada," says Frankie.

"We did, but when my dad got sick, we couldn't find doctors, so my ma moved us back here," says Stella. "Ma works for a doctor, doin' housework and cookin'. The doc helps us out with my dad, too."

A loud, screeching *MEOW* followed by a flurry of fur runs past Frankie. It's the cat. Behind is the child with arms outstretched chasing it. "Stop, Muffin! STOP!" In its effort to escape, it reacts by picking up speed, leaping up on the back of Frankie's chair, and scurrying down behind and under it. The child is suddenly on all fours pulling the trapped feline out by the scruff of its neck.

"Carly, what happened with your Muffin?" calls out an alarmed mother.

"I accidently stepped on her tail," replies the little girl. The tears in her eyes tell the whole story.

Stella holds her daughter on her lap and consoles her with soft, comforting words. Her tender expression hardly makes her look the part of a hardened hooker.

Turning toward Frankie, Stella says, "Carly, Mommy wants you to meet an old friend. This is Mr. Morgansky."

Before the child can return a greeting, Frankie says, "You can just call me Frankie, Carly."

"Hello, Mr. Frankie," replies the little voice. Carly is a pretty little girl with a definite zest for life. So far, the adult tribulations her family is undergoing haven't reached her. As long as she has her cat, life is good.

Soon, things are right with the world. Carly jumps off her mother's lap and scurries away with her cat.

Frankie's thoughts are certainly divided. On one hand, he's looking at a warm, tenderhearted mother who takes care of a handicapped father as well as a young daughter. Next, he's obliged to weigh that image against the tough, mouthy hooker he first ran into a couple days ago, and the hostile attitude Stella has displayed toward him throughout much of his present visit.

There are more matters and uncertainties Frankie would like to probe, but they're going to have to wait. Just as things are beginning to warm up between the two of them, another disruption comes in the back door: Stella's mother, Alina. She stops dead in her tracks as she looks across the room at this unexpected guest.

"Mother, do you remember Frankie Morgansky?"

Alina peers over the top of her glasses long enough to pass judgment. Tilting her head up barely enough to actually look through her lenses, she decides to remain civil— at least for the moment. With a forced smile, Alina makes a quick gesture of recognition. "Hello, Frankie. It's been a while."

Alina is barely into her forties, but she has the appearance of a much older woman. The past few years have not been kind to her, and the strains of life have creased her face almost beyond recognition. If Frankie had met her on the street, he might not have recognized her. She had been a very narrow-minded mother just a few years ago, but now she's actually being somewhat civil.

Frankie gets to his feet and reaches across the small room to shake her hand. "Nice to see you again, Mrs. Mazzara," he says. He remembers the last antagonistic meeting he had with her just a few years ago. Her suspicions concerning how far his rekindled relationship with Stella has already progressed cause her hand to slowly withdraw. Her handshake is awkward, cold, and unwelcoming. Alina excuses herself and retreats to the bedroom to check on Francis. The air in the room seems to have followed her.

"I think maybe it's time I go," says Frankie.

"Yeah, probably so," says Stella, still looking at the closed bedroom door.

"When can I see you again?" Frankie blurts.

The question troubles Stella. She feels torn. Frankie brings an old tension back into her life, but he also brings new possibilities. She hopes he won't ask her to give up too much more of herself.

Stella takes a while to answer. Frankie wants to shout, *Don't think, Stella! Just let me hear your heart.*

"Squeaky ain't able to get us girls back ta work 'til he gets his placed cleaned up. He says it'll be a few more days. So, if ya just happen ta be drivin' by, stop in."

Just this simple invitation is encouraging enough for Frankie. He's satisfied the door is still open. In many, many ways, things have changed for both of them. Their naïve, adolescent days of dating as though their lives together would go on forever are definitely over, but they still feel a lingering sense of ease with each other that they have yet to find with anyone else.

CHAPTER 6
SWEET REVENGE

Still stinging from the Purples' violent intrusion into his father's life and business, Frankie and longtime family friend Axel Weinberg agree to bring their plan to life. Axel has taken his part to heart. It's his job to gather as much information as he can on these new guys, Fred Burke and Gus Winkler. New hit men in town usually carry a lot of rumors about how bad they might be, and what's been rumored about these two has been verified by Axel's research.

The two thugs are indeed former members of St. Louis' Egan's Rats, a group of racketeers known for their ruthlessness. Apparently the Burnstein brothers have hired these two to do some collecting where they figure they're owed something.

In this case, the Burnsteins have learned it was Frankie who ran one of their torpedo boats aground and caused two of their men to drown. Now that they know Frankie Morgansky, a former junior Purple member, is their man, they've contracted these hit men to seek retribution in any way they can. The only stipulation in the contract is that whatever they choose to do can't ever lead back to the Burnstein syndicate.

Fred "Killer" Burke's reputation as a heartless, coldblooded killer precedes him. By anyone's standards, he's unstable, and a mean drunk. There are verifiable accounts of Burke's drinking episodes ending in violence. Once, a man who had passed out at the other end of the bar in a blind pig was snoring, and in a drunken rage, Burke shot the man's nose off from clear across the room.

Gus Winkler isn't much better. He too has a reputation for being one of the most brutal and sought after hit men. He's been known to kidnap a target's loved one in order to draw them out and then murder them both, leaving no witnesses. It's an understatement to say these two men are callous, cold-blooded killers.

Axel has been Simon's right-hand man since he went to work for him years ago. Now he's going beyond the call of duty for Simon's son, Frankie. He's a diminutive man without any outstanding characteristics. Though he didn't go much beyond sixth grade, Axel shows an innate ability to think outside the box and get things done. Because of his more or less nondescript persona, he's also proved to have a knack for sleuthing without drawing attention.

He's managed to learn where both Burke and Winkler live and where they hang out, and he's discovered they both have apartments in Corktown, the Irish neighborhood east of Third Street. They're also frequenters of a blind pig on Third Street. It's a hangout for various paid assassins hired by the Purple Gang or the Italian mobsters. If the price is right, a person could have a contract put on the killer's own mother and he'd fill it.

For this assignment, Axel is hidden in a car across from the Third Street watering hole. He's been on watch for a couple hours waiting for Burke and Winkler to leave. Placing himself at this very spot is part of the plan he and Frankie have worked out. Today is the deadline for Simon to come across with the cash to cover his new "insurance premium" or suffer the consequences.

Axel pulls the last Cigarette from a nearly flattened pack, wads the empty package into a ball, and throws it out his window. It lands on a pile of butts accumulated over the hours he's spent casing the joint. A flick of his lighter ignites his last fag. *I hope these guys show their hand pretty quick, they got me runnin' outta smokes.*

This petty concern is growing into an impatient fretfulness. Over the hours, he's watched countless people come and leave with none being his quarry, but to his relief the pair suddenly appear. Axel feels a flush of excitement overcome him. The time he's spent patiently stalking this duo is coming to a head. He watches as they make their way to their four-door Cord luxury sedan. The driver makes a production of holding the back door open as each takes a seat. He's hopeful this is the beginning of their shake down assignments. He takes a last drag on his fag, flips it out the window, puts the Ford Model T in gear, and begins to bird-dog the sedan.

It isn't long before they reach their first matter of business: a high-class speakeasy. It's run by a German guy named Fritz. Since he's in the middle of Italian, Irish, and Jewish racketeers and there aren't any German gangs to speak of, he's an easy target. Axel watches from down the street as Burke and Winkler come strutting out of the speakeasy carrying a bottle of what is no doubt some of the proprietor's best liquor.

They continue their undertaking and stop at another dozen businesses. Soon enough, they reach the outermost northern regions of Detroit. With no other place to go, they turn off on a northern highway and begin the twenty-mile trek toward Harsens Island and the Morgansky Fishery. Now Axel stops at a payphone and makes the call to Frankie at the Fishery.

Simon is not back to work yet. He soon found his injuries were more extensive than he had first thought. Aristine insisted he stay at home and make a solid recovery. Frankie has promised his father he will pay the money to the thugs without incident. "Frankie, you all ve gots. It ain't worth it ta piss off zees guys. Jus' pay zem zah goddam moneys, okay?"

"Okay, Ta. I promise I'll pay them the 'goddam moneys.'" Frankie intends to keep his promise.

Conveniently, the ringing phone interrupts their conversation. It's Axel. Staring off into the future, Frankie says, "Okay, Axel. Follow the schedule. I'll meet you like we planned."

Frankie makes his way to the fishery with his mind swirling like it always does when he's dealing with obstacles. During the war, at the beginning of a dangerous assignment, he often found he couldn't focus on anything except his mission. He continues to busy himself with thoughtless, mundane tasks around the fishery like mending some nets, but all the while, he's contemplating the problems that are making their way into his life. This is not the paradigm he had imagined he'd find himself drawn into, even a week ago—but it also isn't one he'll readily run from.

After all, all I'm tryin' to do is to make some easy money in the rum-running business. I didn't ask the Purples to try to hijack my load and lose two men because they were stupid. Be that as it may, I still feel responsible for my family. He is more than willing to jump into the fray in order to unravel the monetary noose his unseemly actions have placed around his father's neck.

Having completed all the busy work he's stumbled on, Frankie ends up in the fishery office, poking around at nothing in particular. Within minutes, he hears the distinct sound of a car engine in his parking lot. Peering through the blinds, he sees the expected but unwelcome trouble making its entrance. The big Cord has arrogantly stopped directly in front of the office door. Two strangers in expensive, well-fitted suits make their way through the office door and stand directly in front of Frankie. Frankie places himself behind the desk to give the impression that he's buried in work.

Staring directly at one man and then the other, Frankie opens the desk drawer. Without speaking a word, he takes out a sealed envelope and hands it to the one closest to him. It happens to be Winkler. Winkler takes the cigarette from between his fingers and sandwiches it between his lips. He squints because the smoke is making its way to his eye. Then he snatches the envelope from Frankie's hand and, in one slick motion, rips it open and thumbs through the bills.

"You gettin' smarter, kike boy. You learnin' fast. You mess wi' fire, you's always gonna get burnt," says the insolent Winkler with a little satisfied chuckle. It's obvious he's referring to Frankie learning his lesson from the costly mistake he made in resisting the Purples.

Burke, not to be outdone, adds, "If it was up ta me, I'd a finished yer ol' man off fer givin' me lip. You seem ta be a little smarter and keep yer mouth shut—good thing fer you."

Satisfied they have made their point and as bullies always do, they push the point as far as they can, Winkler adds. "We'll be back next week. Be sure ya stay as smart and have the payment ready, or you gonna end up like yer ol' man."

Frankie continues to remain wordless. Sensing his silence is not wholly a show of compliance, they have a gut feeling all is not going as well as it's appearing, but nonetheless, they opt to let it go and return to their waiting car.

When the big Cord proceeds back to the road, Burke is the first to speak. "Somethin' ain't settin' right wi' me—that kid, he could be trouble."

"I get the same feelin'. Somethin' about him spells trouble," says Winkler.

"He gives me any shit, I'll cut his Jew ass inta little pieces and fed 'em ta the pigs," says Burke broodingly as he looks through the front window like he's looking down the road of time.

Frankie gives them a few minutes' head start before he climbs into his old truck, fires it up, and begins to trail them at a safe distance. He notices that after a few miles, the big Cord suddenly stops for a moment. As can be expected, Axel is right on schedule. He has conveniently set out barriers notifying the big Cord's occupants of a detour. The driver obligingly turns onto a narrow two-track leading into a wooded area.

Not wanting to spook them, Frankie continues to follow at a safe distance. No more than a few hundred yards later, the big Cord stops. The driver is out, and he seems to be checking his tires. Once again, Axel is right on schedule. He's laid enough nails in the road to cause two tires on the Cord to go flat. What's more, he drives toward them from the opposite direction and stops in front of them to ensure they won't go any farther.

Under the guise of giving them a hand, Axel approaches the duo and their driver. By now, Burke and Winkler are both out of the car, kicking dirt, and cursing up a blue storm. Axel is keeping them all bunched together and explaining how they can get some help out here to fix their problem. Meanwhile, at some distance behind, Frankie has stopped short. He has a few items to prepare before, with a bit of luck, he quietly makes his way toward his adversaries by moving unseen through the woods.

Within a few minutes, he can hear their angry prattling along with Axel's calming sympathies. He's attempting to keep them busy until he can get in position. Next, he catches sight of the three men off to his side. Axel is doing an excellent job of keeping them in a group. Seeing and hearing them not more than a stone's throw away gives Frankie enough time to assess the situation. No sooner has he prepared a couple special accessories he's brought to meet this crisis than Burke decides to come tramping into the woods, heading straight toward his position. This is enough to bring him into a near panic until he sees Burke unzip his pants and begin to relieve himself. This is the opportunity he's been waiting for. In a split second, he jumps out in front of Burke.

The expression on Burke's face as this hooded, masked man materializes before him wielding a baseball bat is no less than a look of sheer terror. It's obvious this bully has seldom—if ever—been confronted in such a compromised position and terrifying manner. He stands frozen with shock and holding his penis as the first crack of the bat strikes him in the front of his neck, crashing into his vocal box. All he can do is grab his throat and gasp with a wide-open mouth as the next blow knocks out his front teeth. The blow is so severe that he drops to his knees, only to feel another bone-crushing wallop across his chest break both his clavicles. Frankie continues the beating until the man is all but dead.

Satisfied, he reaches inside Burke's coat to find a shoulder holster holding a .45 caliber automatic. Frankie pulls the pistol out and slowly makes his way around through the foliage until he's behind the Cord. With a .45 in one hand and a ball bat in the other, Frankie makes the same startling appearance before Winkler. Winkler wheels around to find the same terrorizing spectacle his partner faced only minutes before. Holding the .45 inches from Winkler's forehead, Frankie says in a near whisper, "Make one move, and you're a dead man!"

Winkler's pants are suddenly taking on a dark, wet appearance as urine runs down his leg and into a pair of hundred-dollar alligator shoes. He stands frozen while Frankie reaches into his pocket and relieves him of his .45, along with the envelope containing the payoff and a dozen other envelopes with a dozen other payoffs. Stuffing the envelopes into his pocket, Frankie's next step is to toss the guns aside. With one deliberate swing, the bat strikes Winkler so hard across both shins that he falls to the ground, writhing in pain. It's obvious both Winkler's tibias have been shattered. Frankie continues to beat him until he appears to be unconscious. Meanwhile, in a fit of hysteria, the unarmed driver runs off into the woods. Frankie decides to let him go. The man will eventually have to return, tend to his wounded, and to give a report back to those who still imagine Harsens Island is up for grabs.

With this behind them, Frankie and Axel swiftly retreat back to the fishery. Frankie is satisfied he's kept his promise to his father. Turning to Axel, he says, "I told Ta I'd pay them the money. I did that to the letter—he never said anything about not getting it back."

Axel, knowing how Frankie has worked his father over the years and knowing the family dynamics as he does, looks at him through eyes as only someone outside their family can and says, "If yer happy, I'm happy." Now all they can do is get back to business and wait for the fallout.

CHAPTER 7
THE PICNIC

The late summer days are warm on Harsens Island. After a few more weeks of recovery, Simon has returned to work and is suspiciously puzzled about why no one is picking up the weekly "insurance" payments. Little does he know, the Purples are having a difficult time finding young recruits who are willing to go onto Harsens after the tragedies four men have suffered by taking the assignment. Two have drowned, and two others have sustained injuries that will plague them for a lifetime.

Harsens has a reputation among the city-dwelling mobsters as being a wild, remote, and now dangerous place to invade. They are very familiar with big city back streets and alleys, but not with two-track roads, swamps, and woods. In order to fight against an enemy, one must be able to identify the foe. On Harsens, the foe hides behind every tree, in marsh grass, and even in the air. They are clandestine and in complete control of their turf. They rightfully feel completely out of their element.

With things seemingly calm for the moment, Frankie's thoughts turn back toward more amiable undertakings, like rebuilding his relationship with Stella. It's a nice summer Sunday with a nice gentle breeze coming up from the south. Frankie, who just happens to be driving by, stops at 13547 E. Jefferson Avenue. Carly is in the front yard, playing with a doll buggy and her assortment of doll passengers. Stopping at the curb, Frankie calls out, "Hey, kid! Is your mother home?" At that moment, Stella appears at the door.

"You might be a lotta things, Frankie, but a gentleman, you ain't. Is this how you come callin' on a lady? 'Hey kid, is yer mother home'?"

Frankie flushes sheepishly. He knows he's not up to his full role as a suitor. It's just that he feels at home with Stella, and like he doesn't have to put on airs. She, on the other hand, is used to dealing with the brutish sides of men and doesn't want that behavior to have any part in her private life.

After this dressing down, Frankie exits his truck and approaches Stella's screened door. Still peering through the metal weave, she hasn't moved an inch allowing him to make all the advances. Stella has a talent for playing hard to get, and Frankie remembers it well.

Still on the outside looking in through the mesh, Frankie can make out a silhouette he can't get off his mind. "I know better, Stella.

I'm sorry. I shoulda made the effort to get out and come to the door," Frankie sheepishly confesses.

Having stiffened just enough to noticeably relax if things change in her favor, she opens the door and says, "Okay, Frankie Morgansky. I accept your apology." An even more welcoming disposition suddenly takes the place of her previous miffed brashness. "So, what brings ya back to the neighborhood? Still just happenin' ta be drivin' by?" she asks with a cute, knowing little smirk.

Frankie can hear the bit of sarcasm in her voice. It's more than she had as a kid, but things have changed for them both. He's more than willing to explore the root of these changes in this by-gone girlfriend, if she'll let him.

"I came by to ask you out on a date," he declares with a broad smile.

Stella has found his smile to be compelling before. She remembers how she could never stay upset with him for too long; his charming smile would always win over her displeasure.

"Oh, yeah? What kinda date?" is her next question. She tilts her head back, furrowing the space between her eyes just enough to make it appear to be a legitimate concern.

"A regular date, like we used ta do," says Frankie, rather point-blank.

"Yeah? I remember how those 'regular dates' ended—with me on my back," says Stella.

Trying to avoid any unpleasant memories that might sabotage his effort, Frankie chooses not to comment. Instead, he points out his intention as forthrightly as he can. "Since it's such a beautiful day, I came to ask you to come to Harsens Island with me. We can go for a picnic and a boat ride."

The smile on Stella's face says everything; she is overjoyed about this invitation. "I'd love to. Can Carly come, too?"

Frankie hadn't expected this, but he says, "I don't know why not."

"Give us a few minutes to get ready. Come in an' have a seat," says Stella with the teenage-girl kind of excitement Frankie remembers well. She once possessed a rare zest for life that seems to have gone dormant. *I wonder if she'll tell me what made things change.*

Stella's living room is taking on a sense of familiarity for Frankie because it's the second time he's been here in a few days. Her father is also there, still wheelchair bound and sitting in the doorway of his bedroom. He's still a relatively middle-aged man in his forties. Frankie remembers him as a hot-tempered man who ranted in Italian about anything that displeased him. That part of him is the only part that has remained the same. He cannot feed himself or take care of his bathroom needs, and he only moves his lips to swear and curse as he always did. It's as though the stroke left him with Tourette's. He does it in Italian, so it isn't as offensive for those who don't know the language. Now he sits helpless and alone, with a vacant, hopeless look about him. He's mumbling barely audible obscenities. In spite of his hateful attitude toward Jews, Frankie can't help but have a tinge of compassion.

Soon, Stella and Carly emerge. Stella looks absolutely stunning in her white summer frock and broad-brimmed white hat with a pink band around it. Carly is also dressed in a pretty white sundress, and she's carrying a small shovel and pail. Kissing her father on the forehead, Stella says, "Momma will be home soon. I've left her a note. I love you, Daddy." Stella is taken aback at her words for a moment. She hasn't told her father that she loves him in years. Whether it's the idea that Frankie is back in her life, or the weather, or a combination of all of it, it's giving her a sense of better times to come; her heart is open today.

In minutes, they're making their way down the shaded street and on their way to Harsens Island. For many of these Detroiters, friendly-looking, tree-lined streets prove to be misleading. Despite the city's effort to encourage building neighborhoods, the new immigrants find a struggle waiting for them. Even though Detroit is leading the country in wealth as an auto manufacturing hub, many of the new people find the culture, the language, and earlier immigrants are hostile toward them. These circumstances often drive them into poverty.

Because of the conveniences of city life, Stella has not been out of the city since their move to Canada. She is thrilled to have this opportunity, even if it's only for a day. She's also pleased to be sitting next to Frankie, even though she's hesitant to admit it. This is the kind of stuff she's only been able to dream of. She is also particularly pleased that so far, Frankie has overlooked her occupation and is treating her like a lady. Looking at his strong hands on the steering wheel and steady gaze on the road, she can't help but feel a sense of contentment. She's also recapturing some of the lingering emotions that are resurfacing from their erstwhile relationship. She remembers how he would stick up for her when neighborhood toughs would try to intimidate her. Captivated by the moment, she finds herself daring to place her arm through his. She feels the warmth of his skin run through her whole body. It's almost as though on the one hand, she's afraid of being possessed, and on the other hand, she fears being alone. The men she's been involved with at Squeaky's are a sex-obsessed, tension-ridden, money-mad bunch. Stella has always known these are not the kind of men she likes. *Frankie isn't like them. For reasons I can't explain, I feel at ease with him.*

Carly has been lulled to sleep by the hum of the truck engine and rests against her mother side. It's indeed a mystical moment, and at least for this instant, Stella pictures the three of them endlessly going on this way.

After an hour, as if on cue, they arrive at the Algonac Ferry. It's a short, quick ride to the island. Carly is awake again, and truly excited about her first boat ride. By this time, they're getting hungry. They arrive at a small grocery in the island town San Souci. In lieu of a restaurant, they pick up marshmallows, bread, milk, and jars of peanut butter and jelly so they can make sandwiches and roast marshmallows for their picnic.

Given that this is the first time Stella has been out of Detroit since they moved back from Windsor, she can't get over how thick and green the foliage appears. She's actually forgotten what life outside the city looks like. This drive through the woods and marshes has been so inaccessible to her that she had no idea this landscape existed near her.

"It's so healthy and quiet here, Frankie. I understand why you wanted ta bring me here," says Stella. "Why didn't you bring me here when we were kids?"

Frankie is delighted Stella has found so much joy in his choice for their jaunt. He'd initially considered it a gamble to take a city girl this far out of her habitat.

"'Cause I didn't have a car that could get us out here," says Frankie with a chuckle. "Now I get to work out here every day," he adds. "I know this island like I know the back of my hand."

The next stop is the fishery, where Frankie keeps a small sailboat he's had since he was a kid. It's a fifteen-footer, just right to take a jaunt across to a sandy beach on a small, remote island.

Once they get there, Stella is so far out of her element that she's hesitant to get out of the boat. "There ain't any snakes here, is there? I hate snakes!"

"Well, if they're still here by the time this gang has landed, they'll be headin' for another island," says Frankie with yet another chuckle.

Carly, on the other hand has her pail and shovel and is already in the process of building a sand castle. "C'mon, Mommy! Help me," implores this little girl. Her dark hair shines in the sun. "You too, Mr. Frankie. You help too."

Frankie and Carly consolidate their efforts to create a rambling estate of sand castles. When it's finished, it occurs to them that they haven't eaten yet. Stella has used the time to put the peanut butter sandwiches together.

When the castle is complete, Frankie busies himself gathering up driftwood for a bonfire. He takes off his shirt, exposing a chiseled torso. Stella sits on a sandy spot beneath a tree, pulls her dress up above her knees, and digs her bare toes into the warm sand. Frankie works up enough of a sweat to cause the sun to give his body a glistening ruddiness. She can't help but notice how his muscles vary and flow with his movements. He looks so strong and confident as he goes about his task. This is never the case with the men she meets at Squeaky's. They are usually older and much fleshier.

Finishing his bonfire chore, Frankie takes a mock bow before Stella and kisses her hand. "Anything more I can do to serve you, my Queen?"

Embarrassed by his attention, Stella struggles to maintain her cool demeanor. Attempting to downplay her nostalgia, she replies, "Oh, sit yer ass down an' quit bein' so dumb."

Satisfied he's gathered enough wood for a bonfire, Frankie plops down beside her, reclining with his ankles crossed and supporting himself with his elbows. Gazing out across the water, he says, "I never get tired of the scenery out here. It feeds my soul like nothin' else can."

Stella follows his gaze and says, "I see why you love it so much. It's so relaxing."

As they busy themselves with their lunch of peanut butter and jelly sandwiches, they discover how much they both value finding joy in the simple pleasures of life. Jelly is smeared from one side of Carly's face to the other. She delights in splashing in the water. Stella and Frankie finish tidying up. Sipping on a couple bottles of home brew which Frankie chilled in the lake, they settle down to relax.

Frankie is struggling to bring his desire to know all about Stella's life over the years they've been apart under control. He knows being too pushy can destroy the moment, but he also knows they're both experiencing the tension that comes with unanswered questions.

Hoping he can monitor his curiosity, he begins by making small talk. "Do you think your father will get better?"

Stella pauses for a moment. Her expression quickly changes from carefree to one of difficulty. "I don't think so. The doctors say he's got about as much recovery as he'll ever have."

"That's gotta be hard on you and your mom, just to take care of him."

"It sure as hell ain't no walk in the park. He can be very difficult. For the most part, he just sits an' cusses all day. Seems it's his only way of dealin' with his shitty condition. How about your family? They doin' well? I always liked yer ma. She was always good ta me," says Stella.

Frankie is unwilling to get into the details of his family's difficulty with the mob, so he says, "Oh, yeah, they're doin' fine. I haven't told Ma I been seein' you again, or she'd harangue me with questions."

Stella laughs, recalling how inquisitive Aristine can be. "Well, tell her I think about her often. Would you do that for me, Frankie?"

"I will, but it's gonna have ta be when I got at least an hour ta listen to her grillin' me about what you been up to." This seems to be the segue Frankie's been looking for. "Tell me something, if you want to. What did you mean last week when you said that you could never pay what you owe these people, and that they own you?"

Stella's whole countenance suddenly changes; now she seems preoccupied, distant, troubled, and worried. "Frankie, there are some things that nobody but me can fix. I got myself into a goddam mess, and I gotta get myself outta it. Don't bring it up again. It ain't none of yer concern."

Frankie is sure he's made it clear that he wants to be a part of Stella's life, but she's still keeping him at a distance.

Just then, another calamity manifests. Carly screeches to the top of her voice, "Get it away!"

In a split second, Stella is on her feet. "What, Carly? What's wrong, honey?"

"That sewing needle is after me! It wants to sew my eyes shut!" she shrieks.

Frankie anxiously shouts, "What sewing needle are you talking about, Carly?"

She points her finger at a hovering dragonfly.

"Who told you those were sewing needles that want to sew your eyes shut?" asks Frankie. His tone is much quieter now that he realizes there's no real danger.

"Bobby Stevens told me so. He said it happened to his cousin—sewed his eyes right tight. It blinded him forever!" Her panic is real, and she isn't about to be readily consoled.

In a matter of minutes, a nearly idyllic evening has become distressing. Frankie realizes this is a good time to fold up the picnic and head back to Harsens. *What goes up must come down*, he thinks. Stella has transformed from a joyful, innocent soul to a brooding, absorbed, cranky individual. Frankie is frustrated that he has not achieved the level of trust he'd hoped for in his mission to become Stella's confidant once again.

The trip back to Detroit is a lonely one for Frankie; both Stella and Carly have fallen asleep. Once they're back at 13547 E. Jefferson Avenue and everyone is awake, Frankie walks them to the door. Seeing her grandmother, Carly bolts through the door to tell her all about her day.

Frankie and Stella are now alone.

"I'm sorry I ruined your day, Stella. I'm probably rushing things, but it's only because I want so bad to become part of your life," bemoans Frankie.

"You don't have to apologize, Frankie. Overall, it's been a great day. The island is great. I'm just a little touchy about my life right now. I'll get it figured out," Stella says, though she sounds less than confident. With that, she stands on her tiptoes and kisses him. "I'm sorry I can't give you more right now. Maybe later." She turns and enters the house, leaving the door all but closed behind her.

Frankie takes a moment to reflect on how to adjust his emotions before leaving the steps and making his way back to his truck. Frankie can feel his temples begin to tighten. There are so many unresolved strains involved in rekindling this relationship. Frankie can only hope things will begin to resolve themselves soon.

CHAPTER 8
Abe and Eddie

On his way home, Frankie keeps reliving his day with Stella. When he gets there, he immediately notices something he hadn't expected; Axel's sedan is sitting in the yard. It's Saturday evening—one of the few days the fishery isn't open. *That's odd*, thinks Frankie. *I wonder what brings him here.* Entering the house, he's met by his mother, father, and Axel all sitting around the kitchen table. The beleaguered looks on their faces tell him this is not going to be good. His mother's face is tear-streaked.

"What the hell is goin' on? You guys look like someone dragged ya through a knot hole," says Frankie.

His mother takes the lead. "Zey burnt za fishery down," she blurts.

Frankie remains silent as he looks from one face to another, hoping someone will deny his mother's allegation. *I was just out there. It was fine,* is Frankie's silent response. Neither his father nor Axel look up. Axel continues where Aristine left off. "It was right after you left with your friends, Frankie. They came in with cans of gas."

Frankie asks, "Who are the *they* you think done this? Did you get a look at 'em?"

Both his father and Axel look up as if to say, *You have to ask?*

Simon takes the question as facetious. "You go head do zings I tell you not do, now you ask who done zis zing? You bitin' off more zan any uff us can chew, Frankie. Now too late." Simon buries his head in his forearms and sobs. Frankie has never seen his father cry before.

Frankie next peers straight at Axel with a look that says, *How much did you tell my dad?*

Axel remains silent; he doesn't want to meet Frankie's gaze.

Frankie slams his fist on the table hard enough to cause a cup to bounce, turns around, and heads for the door. Axel, recognizing his part in this, follows him out.

Once they're out of earshot, Frankie quickly turns to Axel. "What the hell'd you tell my ol' man?" is all he can think to say.

"I didn't have to tell him much. He already figured out you'd done enough ta screw things up. You know he's been dealin' with one group of mobsters after another for years. He knows they don't screw with ya if ya do as they say. This Purple gang ain't no different—and no, I didn't get a look at 'em. They was too far away," says Axel.

Frankie takes an awkward moment to digest what Axel is saying. He's well aware of why this happened: he outfoxed the boat crew that chased him, and two of them drowned. He's also aware he's the reason why the mob charged his father more in protection money. Now, the mob has retaliated against his crippling the two contract killers by burning his family's only source of income to the ground.

Pacing around the yard and kicking anything in his path, Frankie finally stops and faces Axel with a look of intensity Axel has never seen in him. "Axel, I can't let this go unanswered! These bastards aren't gonna be satisfied until they believe I've been broken, and then they'll put a slug in the middle of my forehead for the hell of it. No matter what I do, I'm a dead man."

Axel finally breaks the silence. "What in name of God do you imagine you can do against these guys? They got all the trump cards, an' we ain't got jack-shit." His frustration is clear.

"I ain't sure yet, but they bleed same as we do. We gotta come up with somethin' that's gonna get their attention."

Axel is listening hard to what Frankie is saying. "Who is this *we* you're talkin' about?"

Realizing he's been presumptuous, Frankie adds, "I know you stuck yer neck out when we beat them mick bastards, but I'm only wondering if yer willin' ta get some information on who the guys that burned my dad's place are. I know they was hired guns, an' the only thing they care about is gettin' paid. That's all I want ya ta do, Axel—

just get the information on these thugs. I guarantee you I won't involve you any further."

The sun is beginning to set. Axel shades his eyes as he tries to digest what Frankie's asking him to do. Lowering the brim on his weather-beaten fedora, Axel makes his pronouncement. "Okay, Frankie. I'll do what I can, but I ain't riskin' my neck again fightin' against these guys."

A couple of days later, Axel stops at the Third Street blind pig. Several high-class cars are parked along the street, which tells him there are probably enough gang affiliates inside for him to begin nosing around. Axel is fairly certain Harsens Island is remote enough for him to remain anonymous and not worry that someone will make the connection between him and the Morgansky family.

Taking full advantage of his ordinary appearance, Axel chooses a secluded table in a dark corner. This will allow him to see what's going on without provoking suspicion. He watches as the men behind the bar bring in wooden boxes with the unquestionable resonance of clanging bottles. He watches as a man at the bar lets a red-haired, sequin-clad lady take his hand and lead him upstairs. At a table not quite across the room, there are two men wearing expensive suits, eating very thick steaks, and drinking the best whiskey the house has to offer. Their raucous behavior sets them apart for Axel to pay a bit closer attention. It seems these two are celebrating a payday of some sort. Throughout the evening, they continue throwing money around as though it were growing on trees.

Axel decides to leave and take a peek at the cars parked around the speakeasy. He has a suspicion he wants to confirm. It's the kind of hunch that could pay off in aces if it pans out. Axel is so ordinary-looking that it would be hard to describe him, so no one takes note of his coming and going.

The automobiles have become his focus. Each of the dozen or so of these vehicles parked up and down the street warrants his attention. His first objective is to allow his nose to lead him. There is nothing to raise his suspicions for the first handful of these expensive steeds, but then Axel catches a whiff of the distinct odor of gasoline. It seems to be coming from a big Buick parked rather haphazardly along the side of the building. Axel peers inside the automobile. Nothing in the front seat or the back seat provides any information to bolster his heightened suspicions.

Nervously looking around, he sees a man and a lady leave the speakeasy and enter the street to make their way to their waiting vehicle. Axel poses as a pedestrian who's just passing through and lackadaisically strolls in the opposite direction. The couple enters a vehicle on the other side of the street, and they are soon lost in the city traffic.

Axel quickly returns to the vehicle of interest. Seeing no one nearby, he carefully turns the handle on the trunk lid. Immediately it releases, and the stench of spilled gasoline overwhelms him. There, sitting in plain sight in the trunk of this expensive Buick, are six empty gas cans. *These look as out of place as a thief in church. Some people might have an extra gas can for emergencies, but not six.*

The next step in this investigation is to watch for the occupant or occupants to come back, so he returns to his own sedan, which is parked discreetly down the street. A half-pack of cigarette butts litters the street beneath his car window before some movement comes from the saloon. Axel quietly puts his car in gear, allowing his headlights to illuminate the two occupants who are entering the big Buick. There is no question that these men were the same two who were celebrating across the room from Axel's post in the blind pig. His next step is to get a read on where they're headed. Staying far enough behind so as not to be noticed while also not losing them in traffic is an art—one he's getting the hang of. Safely watching out for his own wellbeing and not taking needless chances is the way he prefers to do his undercover work.

Evidently, these two men are a long way from giving up on the evening. They go from speakeasy to speakeasy, spending just enough time to have a few drinks. He follows them into Squeaky's renovated blind pig, only to see one of the men go off to a room with Stella. He's hoping he never lets what he's just witnessed come out in Frankie's presence. Interestingly, the man who left with Stella soon returns. It's clear he's agitated. He motions to his partner, and they leave.

It's 4:30 am. The traffic has thinned out enough for Axel to stay at least two blocks back, but close enough to monitor their next move. The two finally call it a night and pull into an east side apartment complex called "The Milaflores." The parking attendant is clearly asleep in the doorway. He's soon awakened by one of these thugs kicking him in the leg so hard it leaves him limping.

Allowing them to get well within the confines of the apartment building, Axel stops under the guise of helping the poor man. "I saw that man kicking you, and I stopped to see if you need some help," says Axel with a sympathetic tone.

"Naw, I'll be okay," says the attendant, "but thanks anyway."

Axel takes advantage of the attendant's undaunted attitude to press him a bit further. "Who were those guys, anyway?"

"Oh, hell, man, they're only Abe Axler and Eddie Fletcher. Purple gangsters—that's who they are." The man says this with a smile on his face, as though it were an honor to be kicked by such a notorious gangster. These names don't ring a bell with Axel. Out on the island, he hears bits and pieces, but he's not well acquainted with the pecking order of gangsters.

After a night of active sleuthing, dawn cracks over the eastern horizon. For Axel to be present for this occasion in downtown Detroit is indeed an anomaly. Axel can't remember the last time he hadn't seen the sun rise from the eastern exposure of his island bedroom. Instead of making his way back to his cabin on Harsens, he opts to go no further than the Morganskys' driveway. The plan is to sleep in his car until he can meet with Frankie later in the morning and bring him up to date on his latest findings.

Aristine is the first to notice Axel's sedan parked in their driveway. Not sure what his can mean, she prefers not to think about it. The last time he visited was to tell them of the disaster at the fishery. Rather than fuss about something she can't do anything about, she opts to spend her time getting breakfast ready.

Simon is the first to rise. He has spent a restless night. Aristine had heard him speaking Russian in his sleep. It's as though he needed to hang onto something familiar. When he arrives at the table, she says nothing and only nods toward the window. Simon rises and makes his way to the window. He stands perplexed, peering out at Axel's sedan parked in the driveway with his stocking feet resting on the open car window. "I hopez ziz ain't more bullsheetz," he mumbles to himself.

By now, he's well aware of what Frankie and Axel did to Burke and Winkler, and he also knows what befell the bootleggers who attempted to hijack Frankie's load of Canadian hooch. Now he's wondering what else these two might have up their sleeves. On the other hand, he can't help but wonder if maybe his son is right. All hell has broken loose, and he's lost all he's worked so many years to achieve. He mumbles something under his breath in Yiddish and sits down to another of Aristine's fine breakfasts of eggs, cream cheese, and a bagel topped with a portion of her own cured lox. This morning, they eat quietly. It's obvious from Simon's silence that he prefers not to talk. Aristine has learned that in these times, it's best to leave him to himself so he work out his worries. He much prefers that to having someone try to cheer him when he feels cheerless.

It isn't long before Frankie has also given in to the early morning sun streaming into his bedroom. Drawn to the window, he looks out to also see Axel's dirty-socked feet poking through his downed car window. Putting that aside, Frankie wonders what he might have learned. When he enters the kitchen, he notices things are much quieter than usual. His mother barely looks up as she places a prepared plate at his place at the table. She looks neither troubled nor perplexed—only quiet.

"Good morning, Momma. Ta," he says, kissing them both.

Simon says nothing. Using his fork, he motions for Frankie to sit. Frankie finds this behavior rather strange, but he doesn't question his father. Instead, he sits and waits. Finally, Simon begins to talk. "Frankie, venz ve comes here from Russia, ve comes for better life. Zings in Russia not goot. Now zings goin' rotten een America. Maybes you right. Maybes ve needs fight now."

Frankie has longed to hear this. Instead of fleeing Michigan as he did Russia, Simon is now willing to stand and fight.

Simon had lost everything in Russia to the upcoming Communist-Bolshevik revolutionaries, and now he is losing everything again, this time to a bunch of lawless bullies in America. Worse, many of these American-Jewish mobsters experienced the same kind of repression in the old country as they were now inflicting on their own fellow Jews. Something in Simon is rising up to resist this tyranny.

Axel is at the door, trying to be as unassuming as possible. "Gut margn, ma'am," says Axel in Yiddish.

"Gut margn, Axel," returns Aristine. "Kumen aun esn" (Come and eat). With hat in hand, Axel gives a slight nod, which he means as a bow to acknowledge Aristine's invitation. Now he looks to Simon and then to Frankie. Unsure what to expect, Axel takes a seat. Aristine sets his breakfast in front of him.

"So, what did you find out?" challenges Frankie.

Axel shoots straight up in his chair, alarmed that Frankie asked such a straightforward question in Simon's presence.

"Maybes I listen for while. Maybes I learn zomzingk," says Simon.

Axel's gaze snaps back in surprise and is met by Frankie's same undaunted, inquisitive demeanor. Still unsure what has precipitated this change in Simon, he shares all he's learned about their most recent nemesis' Abe Axler and Eddie Fletcher. Frankie is listening very intently as Axel goes through what he saw, though he carefully leaves out the part when he saw Stella at work. Finally, he concludes, "Accordin' to what I saw, and the reputation goin' along with these two guys, there'll be trouble for anyone challengin' 'em."

Frankie rises to pour himself another coffee. "I know both these schmucks. They'd do anything ta outdo the other in meanness. They ain't nothin' more than savages dressed in hundred-dollar suits." He takes a sip, deep in thought. Then he says, "We gotta get outta here for a while an' get out on the island. Stayin' here leaves us on their turf. We gotta get them to come to our territory, like we did Burke and Winkler."

Aristine is listening to all this. Her apron suddenly goes to her face, and she begins to weep. "Zeez guys bad likes Lenin communeezt een Russia."

Simon stands to comfort his wife. Putting an assuring arm around her, he places her head against his chest. He remembers doing the same when he came home to announce that they were going to America. "Alts ez oukey, alts ez oukey" (Everything is okay), Simon repeats as he strokes her hair.

For the next several days, the Morganskys pack up their belongings, stuff them onto a borrowed truck, and move to a house they've rented on the island. Leaving the city is harder for Aristine than for any other member of the family. Her friends are here, as is her synagogue.

Their arrival is bittersweet. Simon has a chance to assess what he plans to do to rebuild. He spends much of his time sorting through the charred remains of his fishery, looking for anything worth salvaging. Their boats are no more than hulls burned to the water line. Looking up from his work, Simon spots a sleek looking torpedo boat roaring past his docks. In a moment, it makes a turn and heads directly for the charred remains of a still-standing dock. A chill goes down Simon's back as the craft's motor comes to a close. Its captain ties her to a blackened dock piling. As the person disembarks, Simon can hardly believe his eyes. "It's you, Frankie! Vat de hell goingk on here?" Simon blurts.

"Yeah, it's me, Ta," says a smiling Frankie.

"Vhere een hell you gets zees zing?" asks Simon.

"Remember me tellin' you about those city slickers chasin' me on the river? This here is the boat they cracked up over in Duck Cove. I had a few planks repaired on the hull—hell, it's good as new."

"Vhat een hell ve gonna feesh in boat like dis?" asks Simon, grinning.

"We gonna get us some big fish with this boat," answers Frankie with a wry grin to match his father's.

CHAPTER 9
The Siamese Twins

Frankie's parents have settled into their island house. With the fishery gone, there isn't anything pressing. Frankie's finished with everything that needs his attention. It's a time to take a break and let things settle down. Telling his parents goodbye for the day, he heads for the mainland.

At the Riverside Club, a prime customer of his fathers for fresh fish, he stops to talk with the manager, Floyd Thomas, about the fishery tragedy. He's a rather portly man somewhere in the middle of his career. It's obvious he's devoted to the color maroon: tie, socks, pocket square. "I'm havin' a hell of a time getting good fish since your ol' man's tragedy. I sure miss you. Now I gotta go ta the market run by the Purples. Those thugs been shakin' us down hard for the past few years," he laments, wiping his brow with his maroon handkerchief.

"Yer preachin' to the choir, Floyd. That's why we ain't got a fishery," says Frankie.

"They ain't much different than a bunch a teenage hooligans. They're so damned unpredictable, I never know where I stand with them. They always want more," says Floyd. With a second breath, he continues. "If they go on pressurin' us to pay higher insurance costs, they'll own the club. I'd like to be rid of 'em, but I don't know how. My owners are also at a loss to do anything about it. They've more or less thrown it back in my lap."

Frankie is all ears. Floyd is the kind of fed up that initiates a rebellion. This is the stuff he's listening for in these sufferers. "I know first hand what they're capable of doin'. I'm not quite sure I know how to form a permanent defense against them either, but I know one thing is certain, if we stick together, we got a good chance of making their lives miserable enough to make 'em back off."

After agreeing to meet with Floyd again, Frankie continues his trek to the mainland. His next stop is the ferry, which is run by William Barnes. He's a young entrepreneur who's found a niche business in running the only ferry service between the mainland and the island.

"Sorry to hear of your misfortune, Frankie. Captain Hess told me he ferried you folks with all your household stuff. You've decided to get out of the city and move out here?" asks William.

"We don't have much choice. The mob has put a target on our backs. I figure we can fight them better on a turf where we have the upper hand," admits Frankie.

"I've heard what they did to your father's fishery. They've threatened me, too. They told me if I don't meet their demands for a larger portion of my profits, the same bad things will happen to my business—but then, I heard what you did to those two muggers that beat your father. I wish I had the stones to do something like that." William says this with a true look of despair.

"Well, maybe *you* can't, but maybe *we* can. I'll meet with you again, and we'll talk about it," says Frankie.

While Frankie makes his unremarkable hour-long drive back to the old Detroit neighborhood, his head is full of thoughts. He's definitely heartened by the responses he's been getting from some unlikely sources. Many of these reflections take him back to the battlefields of France. He remembers the ruthlessness of the enemies of freedom.

"I did it there, and I can do it here," he says, affirming his resolve to fight back against these domestic gangsters. He's quite aware of the dynamics involved in dealing with the Purples. After all, he did aspire to become one of them at one time, now he's more involved with distancing himself and his family from their far-reaching tentacles.

Now Frankie realizes he hasn't had any contact with Stella since Sunday, and this is Thursday already. By the time he reaches the mainland, his entire train of thought has switched to Stella. *It seems like all my attempts to woo Stella end in a falling out. I gotta sort through and see where I can do better.* He mentally catalogues his past failings.

Glancing at his watch, Frankie can't believe the hour has sped by, and he's already in front of 13547 E. Jefferson Avenue. Carly is busy in the front yard with her crowd of homemade rag dolls. She even has her cat, Muffin, dressed in doll clothing.

Frankie doesn't make the same mistake twice. This time, he carefully exits his truck and makes his way around several improvised play houses. To give her dolls a proper home, Carly's taken any cast-off materials she can lay her hands on and found another use for them. Old sheets draped over lawn furniture have become apartment units. Wooden crates make great furniture. An old mailbox serves as an oven to bake her bread.

Frankie can't help but smile as he makes his way through this miniature village. "Hello, Carly. How are you today?" It's the only question he's going to risk. Certain that Stella is lurking somewhere, monitoring his stopover, he keeps a wary eye out for her appearance.

"My Mom's been in an accident. She's layin' in bed," declares Carly.

"She's had an accident? An accident!? What kind of accident?" He doesn't wait for Carly to answer. He barges into the living room. There she is, lying on the mohair couch with a blanket pulled up over her head. Rushing past her mother, who is busy with a piece of ice in an attempt to place it on her injuries, he attempts to pull the blanket back. Stella has a death-like grip on it.

"No, no, no! Go away, Frankie," she mumbles from beneath the covering. "I don't want you here right now!"

"Stella, this is no time to be difficult. I'm here to help. Please stop with this nonsense!"

In the end, Frankie manages to pull the blanket away from her face to find a woman who's suffered a horrible devastation. Her eyes are swollen shut with yellow and black skin pulled so tight that it looks like it could split. Her lips are puffed to the point of hardly allowing her to speak. There are traces of blood where the impact to her face caused her teeth to shred the inside of her mouth.

"What, in the name of God happened to you?!" he asks.

"I fell down some steps at the bar," Stella says. Her claim sounds a little too rehearsed. He hardly believes her story, but because he believes her family has no knowledge of her being a prostitute and assumes she's only a bartender at a blind pig, he lets it slide for now. "Squeaky said I can have time off 'til I heal up," she adds. This addendum adds yet another disturbing note to her narrative.

Frankie hangs around for a while, ministering to her when he can. Whenever he looks at her, his brain whirls at nearly peak speed. He cannot let this incident rest. He has to get to the bottom of this horrible misdoing. It's all he can do to hold himself back.

Stella's mother makes another trip to the kitchen to gather up some more shards of broken ice. Frankie can hear her chipping away at a block of rime in the ice box. Taking advantage of Alina's absence, Frankie bends to kiss Stella on the forehead.

"Stella, I don't believe a word you're tellin' me. Believe me when I tell you I intend to get to the bottom of all this," says Frankie. He tenderly strokes her hair away from her forehead with one hand while holding her hand with the other.

Even through her pain and disfigurement, Stella tries to reason with Frankie. In whispered tones, she says, "Don't do nothin' stupid, Frankie. These people have enough power to kill all of us. Just take what I tell you, and don't worry about it. I'm a big girl. I'll handle it."

Alina returns and moves to replace Frankie as her daughter's caretaker, and to remind him that he's not. She's brought a pan full of ice chips. Placing them inside a towel, she applies them to her daughter's wounds.

As much as he would willingly stay right where he is and continue to comfort Stella, Frankie doesn't hesitate to make room for Alina. He's now positioned to face Francis in his bedroom doorway. Staring straight at Frankie, Francis blurts out, "Goddam, shit, hell, damn, bastard, son-of-a-bitch, kike bitch." It's as though Francis would like to be more a part of a solution to his family's struggles instead of a cause, but the stroke has left him frustrated and unable to express his thoughts except as curses.

Frankie takes a moment to have a second thought about Francis. Seeing him sitting helpless with a bib around his neck to catch his drool before it soaks his shirt is unpleasant. As much as he would find it easy to hate this man, instead, a wave of compassion streams over him. He suddenly sees him as a helpless old pit bull trapped in the middle of the road, with traffic racing in both directions.

Frankie decides he's been involved enough for one day. After saying his goodbyes, he returns to the quiet of his truck. There, he takes a moment to reevaluate the situation. *I'm not buyin' this fallin' down the stairs story. I believe I'm gonna make a personal visit ta ol' Squeaky's and see if I can't get to the bottom of this cock-and-bull tale.*

When he arrives at Squeaky's, it's still early in the day. Squeaky lives in an apartment in the building. He stays up all night, so he's probably sleeping now.

"I hope Louie's at the door. I know I can get more out of him than Squeaky," says Frankie under his breath. There's nothing left to do other than to go to the door and find out. A couple of knocks should provide the answer. While he waits, Frankie notices that it seems to be a different door than he remembers. Then he remembers the revenuers kicked it in during the raid, and Squeaky had to have it replaced.

The small peep flap suddenly opens. In spite of its being a different door, Frankie is met by the same blank, lifeless stare of Louie Goldman, who has the same scar running down his face. Recognizing Frankie, he opens the door and lets him in.

"Hey, Louie. How ya doin'? I wanna thank you for the tip you gave me on that Stella broad. She gonna be around t'day"?

With the same blank eyes, Louie takes the question as though someone was asking if he thought it was going to rain. "Nah. She ain't gonna be around for a while."

"No kidding. That's too bad. I was lookin' forward ta havin' a little party with her. What's happened?"

"One a them Purple triggermen beat her up pretty bad," says Louie.

"Really!?"

"Yeah, really. Guy named Abe Axler. He's one a Ray Burnstein's hatchet men."

Frankie immediately recognizes the name as one that Axel mentioned along with a car trunk full of gas cans. Pressing Louie a little more, Frankie asks, "Wasn't there somethin' you coulda done about it?"

"Yeah, he's just a little shit. I coulda beat his ass, but I'd be layin' fulla lead in the morgue right now. There ain't no broad worth gettin' kilt over. Besides, this Abe guy's nuttier 'n a Christmas fruitcake," concludes Louie. It takes him this long to recall seeing Frankie with Stella when he and Squeaky came to post her bond. This causes Louie to attempt a suspicious squint (which is somewhat hampered by the dead nerves in his forehead) and ask, "Why ya askin' about this particular whore? Ya got somethin' goin' with her?"

Knowing how devoted Louie is to Squeaky and not wanting to cause more trouble for Stella, Frankie downplays any special connection to her. "Nah. She's just a good lay." Instead, he focuses on Abe Axler. "Word has it this Abe guy is one mean hombre."

"Mean ain't the word fer it," says Louie, "He and his weaselin' partner, Eddie Fletcher, are sure a pair ya don't wanna have ta draw to. They both crazier 'en shithouse rats. Problem is, ya mess wi' one of 'em, ya gotta deal wi' 'em both—they like Siamese twins."

Frankie makes a mental note of all that Louie's letting slip. If Louie were aware of the history between Stella and Frankie, he would not be so willing to reveal all he knows.

Frankie's background is much the same as Louie's. They're both Russian Jews, children of immigrant parents who fled persecution in Russia. Like all new immigrants, they initially found themselves at the bottom of Detroit's economic ladder.

As teenagers, both Louie and Frankie became products of the Old Bishop vocational school. They were street kids who fought to protect themselves from those that were attempting to take advantage of their freshness. Nonetheless, by virtue of their decisions, each has gone in different directions. For now, Frankie is keeping the names of these two New York additions to the ranks of the Purple Gang's list of muscle-heads at the forefront of his plans.

Satisfied he has the lowdown on Stella's "fall down the stairs," Frankie decides to make one more stop at Stella's before he heads back out to Harsens. What he sees there startles him. An ambulance is parked in front of the house. The street is lined with curious neighbors. Two guys dressed in white uniforms are pushing a gurney out through the front door, followed by a priest. The gurney is completely covered by a sheet. A rush of panic overtakes Frankie. His hands freeze to the steering wheel.

"Stella! No! Please, God, not Stella!" He swallows hard as he cautiously makes his way up the walk, terrified at what he's going to encounter, only to meet Stella's weeping mother. "What happened, Mrs. Mazzara!?" asks Frankie with a clear voice of desperation.

Her face is buried in a handkerchief. All she can be heard to say is, "Oh, Mother of God! Mother of God!" She repeats it over and over. Her grief is preventing her from forming a sentence. Frankie can't wait for Alina to regain enough composure to answer his question. Instead, his eyes dart toward the house. Without a second thought, he bursts through the door and into the living room. The couch Stella had been laying on is vacant. Another wave of panic grips him. Carly suddenly appears before him with tears running down her cheeks. Holding both arms open, she runs toward him. Frankie picks her up, and she throws her arms around his neck, still sobbing inconsolably.

"Carly, tell me what happened!" pleads Frankie.

"My Nonno died!" she sobs.

It takes him a moment to remember that "Nonno" is the Italian name Carly calls her grandfather. At the same moment, Stella appears in the door. She holds a handkerchief to her broken face, and tears force their way through her swollen eyes.

No more has to be said. Though Stella is overcome with grief, she is relieved to have Frankie there—so relieved that she grips hold of Frankie as though he's the only bulwark of strength she's able to hang onto for the moment. With Carly over one shoulder and his arm around Stella, he makes his way to the couch to sit and comfort them as best he can. Whether he had good or bad feelings toward her father is not an important consideration at this moment. He's had both. He thought the man died the way he lived. To expect anything more or less from him would be dishonest. For the next week, he stays over and does what he can to help with all the funeral preparations.

St. Anthony parish is mostly populated by Italian immigrants. Even though most aren't familiar with all parish members, there's a sense of oneness when a member is suffering through a death and needs consolation. Many more turned out for the funeral to convey their feelings of sympathy for the Alina and Stella than visited the family during Francis' illness.

For the funeral, Stella wears a very dark veil to conceal her injuries. Being a Jew, Frankie has never been in a Christian church in his life, but he feels compelled to be with Stella through her sadness. He finds it perplexing that the priest can bring back Jesus and fit Him in a cup of wine or a chunk of bread and actually eat Him. Nonetheless, he maintains a reverent demeanor in deference to Stella and the other Catholics.

Frankie has not been home all week. Rather than leave, he wears a suit that belonged to Francis to the funeral. The day after the funeral, Frankie prepares to spirit Stella off to Harsens for the day. He uses the excuse that she needs a change of scenery. She agrees to accompany him. After all the emotional interaction her father's death has produced between the two of them, this kind of outing sounds like it could be the ticket to bring about a closer union between them. What Frankie truly hopes is that he's gained enough of Stella's trust to bring up issues he feels need to be aired if they are to ever have a sincere relationship.

When they arrive on the island, their first stop is at his parents' cottage. Aristine is thrilled to see Stella. "Oh my, you becomes grown up lady already." She begins by giving Stella the biggest hug she can get away with. She then continues by sympathizing over the loss of her father, and then she asks Stella about her tragic "fall down the steps."

Hoping to stop her before she overwhelms Stella, Frankie says, "Mamma, I'm going to take Stella around and show her the sights. We'll be back in time for dinner."

"Vell, you makes sure you comes back zupper. Mamma fix borsht."

Thanking her for her kindness, Stella turns to Frankie, who is already standing at the door and ready to escape from his mother's elated pleasure in seeing the two of them together again; a nice Jewish girl might be better, but Aristine has always liked Stella.

Finally, on their way, Frankie has a quiet little cove that overlooks the boat traffic on the river in mind. It's quiet and secluded, and it's only a fifteen-minute drive away.

When they turn off the main road and onto a two-track, the overhanging branches of huge river trees give the entrance a tunnel-like appearance. The trees part as they enter an opening along the shore line. It's covered in soft green grasses on which they can sit or stretch out in the warmth of the sun. She can't dispute the peacefulness radiating from this place; it's almost mystical. Frankie's couldn't have chosen a better spot. To further enhance its splendor, the offshore breeze means there'll be no mosquitoes.

"This is beautiful," Stella says as she pushes her windswept hair off her face. Much of her swelling has gone down, leaving her with mostly yellow pockets from broken blood vessels beneath her skin. Continuing to look out across the water in a self-conscious attempt to avoid a deliberate faceoff with Frankie, she says, "I want to thank you from the bottom of my heart for what you did for my family. Especially when I remember what my father used to put you through." The words are definitely an effort to ask forgiveness for her parents' attitude toward him.

Frankie is moved by her kind words. Placing his hand beneath her chin, he gently turns her face toward him until their eyes meet, and then very softly kisses her bruised lips. Her eyes begin to dampen with tears. "Frankie, I don't deserve you."

"That's not for you to decide," says Frankie, drawing her closer.

"You don't understand, Frankie; my life has taken a course that's out of my control—and out of yours, for sure."

"Don't be so sure. Sometimes things take a turn nobody sees comin'," says Frankie with an air of assurance.

Stella, is caught up in her own thoughts and hears little of Frankie's words. "They own me, Frankie!" Her eyes drop for a moment as she gathers her thoughts. "Squeaky agreed a few years ago to pay for all my dad's medical expenses and now his funeral in exchange for me whorin' for him. It'll be a cold day in hell 'fore he lets me outta that agreement."

The water makes tiny lapping noises against the shoreline as Frankie mulls over what Stella has just told him. "If you let me get involved, I think Squeaky will come to his senses and make a deal. He sure as hell didn't do anything to protect you from that twisted son-of-a-bitch Axler."

Her head whips around like someone's just given her a left hook to the jaw. "How'd you know about that?!"

"Let's put it this way: nothin' stays hidden in this town for long," says Frankie with an added air of certainty. "Even though I'm Jewish too, I know these Purple Gang Jews are sons of the devil. They've been workin' my family over for years. They burned our fishery to the ground because we resisted them. It's time we begin to protect what's ours and to fight for our own lives and dignity."

She looks at him as though he's just declared war on the all the powers in hell. "Are you crazy in the head, Frankie Morgansky? I've seen what these people are capable of doin', and it ain't pretty."

"They bleed just like everybody else, Stella. 'Sides, like your priest was sayin', we all got us a guardian angel lookin' out for our sorry asses."

Looking at his stoic demeanor and listening to his words, Stella can tell he's determined. She's speechless, but not thoughtless. *It's gonna take more 'n one angel for yer sorry ass, Frankie Morgansky.*

Now Frankie says, "I want you, your mom, and Carly to move out here to the island."

Stella looks at him as though he's just asked her to move to Mars. "What'd you just say?" she asks as though she hasn't heard him.

Frankie continues without missing a beat. "It'll be a lot safer than staying in the city. These city slickin' mobsters know they can rule the asphalt jungle, but they have no idea what's waiting for them on Harsens Island," he declares.

This is the kind of open discussion Frankie has been waiting to have with Stella. He has her attention now, and he's not holding back.

"The only good reason your family had for stayin' in the city was to be near medical help for your father. That's no longer a part of the equation. I know you and your mother can find good work in any number of hotels here," declares Frankie, "and Carly can start school where she won't be bullied by neighborhood thugs."

It's obvious he feels this plan offers a sense of safety. There are hundreds if not thousands of coves that offer a person who knows the area numerous places to make a successful escape. Frankie knows places that are so remote, the only way to reach them is by water. He has no fear of the Purple Gang on Harsens. His hope is that before his strategy to defeat this adversary has come to a head, he'll have recruited enough local support to put his plan into action. In the meantime, he's hoping to get all the people he loves safely out of the city before he puts his plan into motion.

Frankie would like nothing more than to have Stella make her decision along with her next heartbeat.

"Frankie, I have no idea what you're askin'. Everything you do is so fast—who has time to think?" Stella has no idea what will happen if she agrees or disagrees to be part of Frankie's venture. For Stella, nearly everything she sees, hears, even experiences is a gamble. Her life has been so full of chaos that it's been easy for unscrupulous men to take advantage of her. On the one hand, she places more trust in Frankie than anyone else, but he's still just one more man who wants to take control of her life. She's promised herself that if she ever got out from under Squeaky, she won't have another man run her life, and that includes Frankie. On the other hand, she finds it refreshing that Frankie is talking to her as an adult rather than a "dumb broad."

Frankie remembers her from the old days, when she was much more impressionable. Now he feels she's being overly cautious.

Stella isn't sure about this big plot Frankie is cooking up. She listens with one ear, but is careful not to get caught up in Frankie's conjectures and make a hasty decision. She remains skeptical. "Sometimes I just want to punch you, especially when you come up with this pie-in-the-sky stuff," she tells him.

Looking at the lack of understanding in her eyes, he realizes they are not on the same page. Frankie is suddenly lost for words. "I been hopin' I could have a partner in you, Stella. We could work together. What do you think the flaws in my plan are?" he asks.

Stella hears the dismay in Frankie's voice. She pauses for a moment to pick her words carefully. "Because these guys think I'm just a dumb whore, they talk their guff in front of me. They're vicious, Frankie, and most of 'em do what they do 'cause they get a sick enjoyment outta watchin' some poor slob feel pain."

"You're right, Stella, but the only reason they're emboldened enough ta make somebody's life miserable is 'cause they're makin' all the rules. Once they get out here on Harsens, the rules change, and they're not in their favor."

"What makes you think you can get these guys to come out here and play your games?" asks Stella.

Frankie answers, "Because they're dumb enough ta do it." He's serious.

Figuring he's finished with all the stuff he's wanted to talk to Stella about, they decide to return to the house and share a meal with Simon and Aristine. Given ample time for Aristine to grill Stella about anything and everything, the day is soon running short. Frankie is finally able to pull Stella loose from his mother's grip and return her to the city. The ride back is restful; Stella cuddles close to Frankie. He stops at 13547 Jefferson Avenue—hopefully for the last time. After he walks Stella to her door, Frankie lifts her chin so she'll look at him. "Promise you'll discuss a move to the island with your mother." He then kisses her and holds her for a moment before releasing her to answer Carly's call.

"Mommy! Mommy, you're home!"

Stella doesn't release Frankie's hand. Instead she leads him into the house. Carly leaps at her mother.

"Why didn't I get to go? I wanted to go really bad momma!" Carly says. Her legs are locked around her mother's waist and her hands fastened behind her mother's neck as she looks her in the eye.

"Next time, sweetheart. You can go next time," assures Stella.

They spend the evening drinking coffee with Alina and discussing the Harsens Island move and the reasons why it's a good idea. After Frankie's compassionate character became apparent to Alina during her husband's ordeal, she has developed a new sense of trust in him that she never had before. Speaking of other things, as a mother, Alina has always suspected her daughter's role as bartender went beyond that simple calling. Now, with Francis gone, Alina can envision a more promising future that involves leaving the city. Harsens sounds as though it might have better opportunities in store for both Stella and Carly, as well as herself.

By the time all this discussion is finished, it's too late to return to the island this evening. Fittingly, Stella asks Frankie to stay the night. Alina and Carly have both retired. After he slings an afghan covering across the back of the couch, Frankie is prepared to spend the rest of the night on the mohair sofa. Instead, Stella takes him by the hand once again, this time leading him to her bedroom.

CHAPTER 10
The Citizens' Committee

They wake to a damp, misty morning full of fog. For both Stella and Frankie, this is truly a night to remember. It's the end of an old, adolescent chapter they shared and the beginning of a new, challenging experience. Frankie realizes he must have an overall plan Stella can understand if he's going to win her over.

"I've approached several business owners on the island who are very disgruntled because the Purples have invaded their lives and are always demanding more of their livelihoods. They're all left with threats of violence and destruction if they renege on their payments."

Frankie hopes that by working together and setting aside mistrust, these people with similar experiences can find a common solution to their dilemmas.

Stella has had hands on experience with these brutal mobsters. Not wanting to sound pessimistic, Stella asks, "And just how do you think you can fix that? I mean, there are lives at stake here."

"I believe that, like in any good business plan, when it becomes too expensive to continue doing business the old way, these guys will have to abandon the Harsens Island venture. Right now, it's easy pickin's; they've divided and conquered, and they're just pickin' us off one by one," says Frankie. He rips a piece of toast in half to demonstrate.

This conversation can't be timelier. There's a knock at the door. Peering out the window, Stella spots an all too familiar maroon-colored Buick sedan. Squeaky stands before her in the rain, bright and grinning. He has his ever-present cigar clamped off to the side of his thin-lipped mouth, and Louie towers over him, holding an umbrella. Stella freezes for a second.

"Well, ya gonna ask me in, or ya gonna make me a porch ornament?" barks Squeaky.

Stella stammers, "Yeah, sure. Come on in."

Squeaky steps inside, leaving Louie to go wait in the car.

Stella knows this visit is bad news. Squeaky doesn't make these trips to broaden his horizons. He has something very specific in mind, and it's sure to make her life miserable.

"Ya know, kid, I been very patient with your injuries and taken care of yer ol' man's funeral expenses, and I'm beginnin' ta get the feelin' yer takin' advantage of my generosity by not showin' up at the club and fulfillin' yer obligations."

Just then, Frankie enters the room. Squeaky's jaw slackens enough to force him to catch his cigar before it hits the floor. This is the last person he hoped to see.

Frankie stares Squeaky down and moves in a little closer.

"What kind of misery ya carryin' with ya this morning, Squeaky?" asks Frankie. His intimidating demeanor is still in full force.

"What business I got goin' here ain't any concern of yours, unless you wanna make it yours. That could be expensive, so maybe you oughtta back out while yer still able," says Squeaky.

"Gimme a try, Squeaky. Let's see what kinda screwin' yer tryin' ta pass on. I wanna hear if yer brain's as shriveled up as yer dick."

Squeaky knows he can't pull any shenanigans with Frankie like he does with Stella, and he's beginning to have second thoughts on how he's going to regain the upper hand in this negotiation. His second thoughts center around who his cousins are and how he fits into the whole Purple Gang scenario. With this reality in his corner, he regains enough of his confidence to put his mouth back in gear.

"Yer startin' ta breed a scab on the end of yer nose, kid. You might wanna think twice about who yer messin' with. You might find yer diggin' yer own grave. In the meantime, I expect Stella's ass back ta work tonight. So, if yer lookin' fer trouble, ya come ta the right place. Ya get what I'm sayin'?" says Squeaky, jamming his cigar back in the corner of his mouth as he heads toward the door.

Not willing to let Squeaky have the last word, Frankie chooses to extend this ongoing pissing contest. "You tryin' ta make me believe a top-shelf girl like Stella ain't more than paid her own way?"

Squeaky stops dead in his tracks, swings his scrawny body around to face Frankie, pulls the cigar from between his tobacco-stained teeth, and snarls, "You still don't get it, kid. I call the shots 'round here, not you!" With that, Squeaky leaves.

Squeaky paid little attention to who in Stella's family might have had to overhear his reproaches. Carly has been exposed to many of Squeaky's tirades, and today is not an exception. Holding her cat close, she looks up at her mother and asks, "Mommy, why don't you know any nice people anymore?"

Alina bursts out of her bedroom. "If we could move today, it wouldn't be soon enough."

The vote to move to the island has suddenly become an overwhelming, unanimous yes.

Frankie couldn't be happier. Within the hour, he arranges to have a moving truck pack up their meager possessions and gives its operators orders to get it to the island as quickly as possible. Another phone call secures a small inexpensive cottage near where the fishery once stood. The truck is packed by midafternoon.

They have mixed feelings about saying goodbye to 13547 E. Jefferson Avenue. It's the only home Carly has ever known. She's taking a moment to say goodbye to all the little nooks and crannies she was able to escape to for an adventure. "Goodbye, tree. Goodbye, porch. Goodbye, bedroom," she says as she touches each of them.

Soon, they're on their way. The family has never been able to afford a car, so they all pack into Frankie's truck, with Carly clutching her cat in the truck bed and the three adults squeezed into the little cab. Getting out of Detroit traffic is almost impossible. Cars and trucks are everywhere, and the drivers show little respect for others. It seems each has his own agenda and regards all other drivers as a hindrance. Eventually, they reach the country road that leads to the island.

It's not long before they see a plume of smoke ahead. When they reach it, the see their moving van is charred and smoldering by the side of the road. It's been firebombed.

This has Squeaky's signature all over it.

Alina tears up. She has lost so much, and now this. A lifetime of mementoes has been destroyed in minutes, here on a strange road. It's another death she's must deal with.

Stella stares at the rubble. Her thoughts are *this is exactly what I had expected.* Being around the underworld, she has listened to and seen the cruel course these individuals have taken on as a normal way of life. She is nearly immune to anything these people could inflict on her short of death—even death would be too late to shake her.

"Momma, do you think Gertrude and Molly went to heaven?" Carly asks. It takes Stella a moment to remember these are her favorite dolls' names.

Seeing the hurt in her daughter's eyes, Stella forgets her own losses. "Yes, sweetheart. I think so."

Hugging her cat, Carly says, "See, Muffin? I told you so."

Frankie's face remains expressionless. In the war, this was the kind of cowardly torment the enemy forces would inflict on their own people for aiding and abetting a wounded American soldier. This cruelty only serves to strengthen his resolve to destroy as many of these enemies as he can.

Frankie gathers this little family into a huddle so he can put his arms around them all. "We'll get through this. I promise. We *will* be the winners before this is all done." These words are not easily understood by a family that's just lost all their belongings.

The family has no choice but to suck it up and continue on their course. They have lived with risk in the city and are well acquainted with it, but they're beginning to realize freedom always comes with a price.

When he reaches the Algonac ferry launch, Frankie gets the word out about what happened. The people on this island may have differing reasons for being here, but there is a sense of community here, regardless of the residents' individual agendas. Much of it centers around a cottage industry of moving illegal Canadian liquor into the United States across the lakes and rivers. This industry has its risks from the border police without the added fear provoked by the Purple Gang. It's common practice for these Purples to hijack loads of liquor from unsuspecting rumrunners, sink their boats, and shoot anyone who tries to resist. The whole community hates the Purple Gang because they shake down every business for protection money and inflict sadistic punishments on anyone who resists.

By the time they reach the cottage, pieces of furniture—beds, tables, and chairs—are already beginning to stack up on the lawn. Stella and her mother can hardly believe this outpouring of care and concern from people they have never met. They spend the rest of the day sorting through the furniture.

The cottage is larger than the rental they left behind in Detroit. Alina makes her way from room to room, marveling at the airiness of each one and finally settling on a room where she can see the water. Carly and Stella decide on a room that will accommodate themselves as well as a cat. This leaves a small living room, a kitchen, and a bathroom with a tub.

Once they're settled in, Frankie attends to the other things on his mind. His plan to begin a resistance movement against the Purples is ready to be put into action. The people on Harsens used to hang on to the slim hope that the Purples would be satisfied with sharing a portion of the liquor business. That hope has dried up and transformed into loathing. These mobsters are proving to be heartless mongrels; they want it all. The Harsens population is beginning to see their circumstances in a new light. Frankie is a brilliant organizer, and he knows he has the skills he'll need to rally these folks into a militia. There's risk involved for sure, but risk has always been the price of freedom.

Because he knows the Purples pay off informers, Frankie begins by only revealing his plan to Axel. "There're practical problems that we gotta meet head on. We need a trusted team to bring this plan into action. We need people who are more than merely fed up with the Purples—they also gotta have the guts ta resist their bullyin'. In particular, we're gonna need members who can be trusted to keep their damn mouths shut and keep others identities a sworn secret."

To launch their campaign, they start by taking William Barnes, the ferry boat owner, out for lunch. Barnes is singularly outspoken against the Purples, since they have consistently threatened his boats with the possibility of an unexplained gasoline explosion if he should decide he can manage without their "insurance" plan.

Frankie is nervously playing with his spoon as he begins to unveil his designs against the most feared, vicious, and hated mob in town. (The Purple Gang got its name when a shop owner said, "They're not like other kids. They're purple—the color of rotten meat.")

"I believe we can continue to pay our so-called insurance while secretly making war on these guys. If we do it right, they'll never know where or who or what's hitting them. The only clue they'll have is that it has something to do with Harsens Island. It has ta start with you, William. I need you to keep track of when these guys are coming onto the island, and let me know. The Purples use the island as their personal party grounds. We need their money, so we have to separate the partiers from the collectors, but I need a call from you to alert me to check out any of these goons comin' over here for any reason. We need to keep a wary eye on all of 'em."

William has been listening hard to every word Frankie says. Now he breaks into the conversation with a view of his own. "One thing is for damn certain: there isn't one law enforcement in the city or on this island that isn't in the back pocket of these thugs. None of them can be trusted. If we're gonna survive, we're gonna have to take things into our own hands."

This is the kind of affirmation Frankie is looking for. Vigilante groups often get things wrong, but when law enforcement becomes so corrupt it no longer has the trust of the people, citizen groups break out. These groups are usually unsympathetic toward corruption within the legal system. The result is that law enforcement officials are often eager to straighten up their act and get a handle on the dishonesty that exposes them.

Everyone Frankie and Axel talk with for the rest of the day that is fed up with the way they're treated by the gangs. What started out as paid protection against harassment from other gangs has become extorted protection against the insurers themselves.

Frankie wants to feel each candidate out to see what level of commitment they're willing to make, and often relies on each of them to give him another trusted postulant to interview. He's interested in getting a cross section of solutions to see how far each can move them in putting an end to the weekly shakedowns.

Rhetoric flows from guys like Bob Machala, who wants to "Tommy Gun every damn one of 'em sons-ah-bitches." Others are peaceniks, like Ralph Van Nord who says, "We just need to understand one another." Frankie is suspicious of the type of cooperation he'd get from each of these types. He's looking more for team players who prove to be creative, can read a situation quickly enough to not overreact and still stay alive, and are not opposed to deadly force where deadly force will protect the community and themselves.

As is usually the case, Axel is typically the one who shines the light of common sense on a particular temperament as one that might be useful or might pose risks. "The important thing, as I'm seein' it, is to have enough trust that we can comfortably stay open among our inner group, but keep decisions under wraps to the rest of 'em 'til they need ta know."

Ferry owner William Barnes, general manager at the Old Club Jerry Ferris, and manager of the Riverside Hotel Floyd Thomas become members of Frankie's inner circle. Their decisions typically won't be scrutinized. This basically means they aren't required to do much other than act on situations that require immediate action. This inner core are the men who need to be kept informed so they have all available information about the dealings between gangsters and the resistance membership. All information is kept confidential. The important thing is that the broader membership agrees to never divulge the names of other members.

The implementation of all this goes much more quickly and smoothly than Frankie first imagined. Within a day, he has already gotten word from William that their old friend Squeaky and his driver/bodyguard Louie are on the island and asking questions about the whereabouts of a Stella Mazzara and a guy named Frankie Morgansky. Frankie's instructions are to give just enough information so as to not make oneself a suspect, but also not enough to further endanger the Purples' targets. In other words, keep the exchange low key.

Frankie has decided to make his move on a remote stretch of road he knows these two will have to travel before they get to the Old Club. This is a favorite haunt of Squeaky's. He never misses an opportunity to get a fresh perch dinner before he does any other business on the island. What he doesn't know is how drastically his life is about to change.

Now that he's gleaned the information he needs from William, Frankie makes a phone call to Jerry Ferris, the Old Club's manager and a member of the resistance inner circle. Frankie informs him that Squeaky and his bodyguard have arrived on the island. Squeaky's habit is to head for the Old Club first and then get down to business. In this instance, his goal is to find his targets: Frankie and Stella.

Today, Frankie also has business. He has his own plan for Squeaky and his goon driver. Jerry is getting a big laugh out of what could prove to be the most dangerous conspiracy he's ever been involved in.

The fix is in. Squeaky's whereabouts are being monitored by Axel at his usual safe distance. The description of Squeaky's maroon-colored sedan is enough to set him and Louie apart from the general population and make them a target. Much to Frankie's delight, a few more citizens also contact him to inform him of the movements of these inauspicious intruders.

Frankie is in place when he spots the maroon sedan making its way down the road. He's chosen a tree covered rising with just the right amount of covering not to be seen. It's providing him the appropriate opportunity he's looking forward to. BANG! One shot rings out from this clump of box elder trees at a distance of two hundred yards.

Frankie has successfully placed a round from his 1903 .30-06 Springfield sniper rifle into the sedan's front tire. It's the same reliable rifle he used during the war. The big car careens off the road and into a water filled ditch tipping on its side, nearly upside down. The vehicle immediately begins to fill with muddy ditch water. It's difficult to tell what is transpiring inside, but most assuredly the two occupants are scrambling for some sure footing to make their way out of this unforeseen water maze.

Frustration meets them at their every effort as they continue to thrash around like flies on a hot griddle, stepping on each other, whacking each other with flailing arms in their attempt to save themselves. This only serves to further disorient them. Panicked, wet, and coughing up every kind of plankton the ditch water has to offer, Squeaky and Louie finally make their way to the high ground back on the road.

The big maroon sedan lays more upside down than on its side, all the while spewing out small water geysers as each little air cavity is slowly being replaced with a greenish-brown liquid.

For Frankie things couldn't be more perfect, everything's going as planned. Axel is on the scene in a matter of a minute of them extricating themselves.

"Howdy. You two look like you could use some help. What happened to ya?" asks Axel appearing to be the sympathetic hick here only to help a neighbor in need.

These two hapless bedraggled swamp rats look upon him as the savior they hoped would be available to deliver them from what is nearly perceived as a fate worse than death. For Axel, despite the danger these two are posing, he can't quite get over how tailored suits, and well-polished shoes look so much better covered in swamp muck.

Louie is the first to speak. "I don't know what happened. I heard an explosion, the next thing I knew we were upside down in this goddam ditch."

Squeaky is gagging so harshly, he's unable to speak.

Knowing he's in complete control and using his most empathetic voice, Axel asks, "Can I give you boys a lift somewhere?"

"Hell yes. We're on our way to the Old Club," answers Louie. Without waiting for a second invitation, they both open a rear door and with a sigh of near exhaustion deposit themselves soaked to the bone on the seat.

"We're only a half-mile from the Old Club. You boys are lucky I just happened by. Normally I don't go this way, but t'day I got a couple guys I'm s'posed ta meet." says Axel, keeping an air of neighborly consideration as well as a bit of satisfaction of a parody well done.

Once in the car, they become broodingly non-talkative. The first thing they become aware of is their .45s are gone. In the struggle to get out of the water filled sedan, their pistols dropped from their holsters. They're presently not retrievable. They are definitely out of their element and both feel a very strange and uncomfortable sense of vulnerability. Still attempting to go over the circumstances that brought them to this juncture, but since it all happened so quickly, they can't get a handle on it. All they care about now is to get to civilization, and to get out of their wet clothing.

In a couple minutes, Axel is dropping off his new custodies at the lobby door of the Old Club. He has successfully completed his leg of this mission.

Briefly made aware of the circumstances, manager Jerry Ferris meets this slogging crew in the lobby. His sympathies and heartfelt concern for these two reprobates couldn't be sincerer as they deem they have found a confidant willing to share their calamity. They both have a need to continue to relive their story with anyone willing to listen. As they go through detail after detail, it's as though they had gone through hell and had stopped to take pictures—all in the hopes a light of understanding will come on. After recognizing their fright over the odd incident, and sympathizing with their attempt to recall the circumstances that led to it, Ferris gives them a word of assurance, "Mr. Schwartz, when your ready, I can arrange to have a car take you to the mainland if you prefer."

Squeaky's thoughts are swirling around inside his head, banging off the sides of his skull. Despite this set back, he isn't anywhere near ready to give up on his mission of retribution. "Right now, all we need is a room, a bath and our cloths laundered—and a couple Havana Dark cigars." Pausing for a moment, he adds, "Lemme give that ride offer some thought."

Assuring Squeaky he'll see to their clothing, Ferris adds, "If there is anything you need, please feel free to call me personally."

Once in their rooms, Squeaky makes a call to his Detroit establishment ordering a bartender to bring a car the next day, and an extra .45 in his desk drawer. "Clarence, I'll meet you at Algonac on the island side of the river around noon tomorrow," Squeaky commands.

Cloaked in a huge hooded robe provided by the hotel, Squeaky appears at Louie's room. With the cowling pulled over his head and a cigar sticking out of his face, he gives the appearance of an oversized, cigar smoking rat poking its head out of a hole. "Louie, I gotta call inta Clarence ta come meet me at Algonac tomorrow at noon. I'm gonna have him drive me back down the island an' meet you here. Meanwhile, I wan' you ta stay here with the car. See if you can figure out what the hell's goin' on." Switching thoughts, Squeaky adds, "We gotta get that shit done with that punk Frankie. He's gotta learn he don't go taken what ain't his ta take an' get away with it."

It's wake-up time in the morning, Squeaky hears a knock at his door. It's a waiter bringing a food cart with a cloche covering a breakfast of eggs benedict, and coffee along with his ever present cleaned and blocked fedora, pinstriped suit, shirt, tie, socks, under clothing, shoes all spit shined, and a box of cigars—all compliments of the house.

At least these guys know who the hell they're dealin' with. This thought gives Squeaky a boost to begin his day.

Another knock at the door. This time it's the concierge. He has a message that the hotel's car is available with a driver at Squeaky's disposal—all compliments of the house. On different occasions, Squeaky has watched concierges fawn all over his cousin, Ray Burnstein, but then Ray is a Purple Gang big shot, but this is the first time he's merited this kind of treatment himself. He's rather relishes basking in it.

Taking advantage of the offer, Squeaky informs the concierge to have the car ready within the hour to drive him to the ferry landing. This gives him ample time to stroll around the lobby with the intention of demonstrating his importance to the other guests. Soon the car arrives. It's a hotel provided limousine with a uniformed driver. Squeaky makes all the pretenses of being an important guest by waiting until he's paged to slowly and purposely—with his ever-present Havana cigar, his fedora cocked off to one side, and with both hands shallowly placed in his suit coat pockets—swaggers his way to the waiting vehicle.

The limo makes a satisfactory, ostentatious exit from the Old Club, turning toward the north. Squeaky feels a vindication for all the times he has been shoved aside as a minor Purple Gang associate. At last he's getting the recognition he feels he's deserved. Settling himself in for the half-hour ride to meet Clarence, there suddenly appears a truck in front of the limo and in the next moment there is sedan closing in behind. The truck slows to a stop all the while preventing the limo from passing.

A complete sense of a vulnerability that Squeaky had endured the day before with his ditch experience has roared back. It's once again looming over his person in an ominous, menacing fashion. He feels conspicuously naked without his .45, and especially without Louie.

His driver has exited the limo. Squeaky is expecting him to be speaking with the other drivers enquiring why they are blocking the road, when suddenly, without warning, his back door is jerked open. Squeaky stares helplessly at a group of hooded men yanking him out and mercilessly throwing him to the ground. A gag is jammed in his mouth, a hood is placed over his head, his hands are bound with wire behind him. He's next pulled to his feet, and dragged to the waiting truck. Without a moment's hesitation, he's thrown unto the bed of the truck and covered under a heavy canvas tarp. His first awareness is the distinct odor of fish. He struggles to prevent it from overwhelming him. With the gag in his mouth and a worry of regurgitating his breakfast, Squeaky is left with either settling down or risk choking to death.

    The present jaunt Squeaky's suffering is hardly the luxury limo jaunt he had been reveling in only minutes before. He's quickly made aware of every bump and turn in the road. It's all he can do to position his bound body in such a way to prevent the rough ride from knocking him unconscious. His unprotected head is definitely taking the brunt of the lack of good springs in this transport.

    What seems like a never-ending ride to hell comes to a halt as abruptly as it began. Next, he feels himself dragged into what he senses is some kind of shelter. His captors do this all wordlessly.

    His next awareness is becoming subjected to his clothing being stripped from his body. The eyeless hood covering his head is the last piece of cloth left on his otherwise naked frame. It, too, is removed. As his eyes adjust to the light, he becomes aware of a damp, musty smell. His last view before the cabin door closes is the backside of a hooded man as he steps outside. The only sound is the resonance of a vehicle as it makes it's driven away from the cabin.

    Squeaky is left bound to a wooden kitchen chair. *My fate is sealed! I'm a dead man!* He has no clue where he is, who his captors are, or what's going on, but he senses it's not going to end well for him. His only distraction in this twelve-by-twelve-foot, cell-like cabin is a large spider weaving a web across an open window. He can hear the occasional loud creak from some tortured board overhead as it struggles to prevent the whole structure from collapsing. He's increasingly preoccupied by an excruciating pinch on his bare behind from a slight crack in the wooden seat. There doesn't seem to be a way he can adequately position himself to avoid a nip. At this moment, there no place, including hell, where he wouldn't prefer to be.

Meantime, back at the Old Club, Louie is provided similar amenities, all under the guise of aiding him in getting their sedan repaired. As tough a guy as Louie is, when he finds himself surrounded by a secretive crew of hooded, shotgun-carrying men who butt him with their hard wooden gun stocks, he has second thoughts about taking them on. All it takes for these men to bring him to his knees is the slightest impression that he might be noncompliant. Like most bullies, when the shoe is on the other foot, they turn into wimpy victims. Louie has established his defenselessness immediately. As soon as his hands are bound, he, too, is hooded and thrown into the back of a sedan. After he's driven to another outpost, he's stripped naked and left gagged and bound to a wooden chair, same as his boss.

They sit all afternoon with no indication that this nightmare is ever going to end. They don't know why they're being tormented. They're both picked up by the same silent hooded men with only their eyes visible through cut holes in the cloth. Squeaky and Louie are hooded again, but as before, their hoods contain no eyeholes. Still naked and bound, they're driven to another outpost.

The sound of water gives them an indication of their whereabouts. The men handling them are silent and competent, although neither Squeaky nor Louie are able to discern this by sight. Their bare feet hurt as they're mercilessly led across what feels like sharpened rocks. Both let out cries of pain. They quickly recognize the sounds of each other's voices. "Is that you, Squeaky?" asks Louie through his gag and from the darkness of his hooded world. As soon as his words fall out of his mouth, he's on his knees. He's been hit again by one of these shotgun-carrying vigilantes. He understands that he's not going to be allowed to speak.

Overwhelming fear grips both men. They know the only men who endure this kind of treatment are on their way to be executed.

Because neither of them can see, they can only guess what awaits them. Both flail their arms out in front hoping they are able to prevent a major fall. At one point they are both pushed, stumble, and ultimately collapse onto a waiting platform below them. Left there for only a moment, they feel a sensation of something wrapping around their ankles and being cinched. The next sensation is one of movement. It suddenly occurs to each of them that they're on a boat. Without the slightest idea why they're here or even where they are, they feel themselves being hoisted into the air by their ankles. Both their hoods slip off, and for the first time, they realize how totally and completely powerless they are as they're left to swing upside down by a rope slipped over a yard arm.

    Neither of these gangsters have ever had to endure this kind of drawn out, day-long torment. Typically, *they* are the tormentors. It's become a trial in physical as well as mental endurance. These so-called tough guys are falling apart. They're both are whimpering undetectable utterings and shaking uncontrollably.

    One of the hooded captors gives a slight nod to another hooded man holding a rope connected to a block-and-tackle rigging that supports the two reprobates above the water. The man allows the rope to slowly slide through his hands. These two see what's in store for them and begin to holler through their gags as if fighting could make all this stop. The rope-tender lets the line slide until Squeaky and Louie both have their sweat-soaked heads submerged. They are suddenly aware of the cold silence of the water surrounding their skulls. Meanwhile, their bound bodies flail wildly in the limited range of motion they still have left. Another nod from their captor brings them back to the surface. Their gags have washed out of their mouths. Their eyes look buggy as a result of the force they must use to clear the water out of their lungs.

    Another nod is followed by another dunking. This time they're left beneath the water until their bodies begin to go limp—it's been nearly a full minute. Reality has a way of presenting itself in paradox; calm sun glistening water on the top side with a raging tempest of survival under its surface. After the signal to bring them up things have notably changed. This time it's become obvious these two toughs have been broken. Neither are fighting to win over their situation any longer, they're both chocking, gagging, and sobbing like baby girls begging for mercy.

    They're brought back on board, dumped in a heap, naked as j-birds, left alone to attempt to sort themselves out as best they can. All this is overseen by their captors without a word spoken and with their faces still remaining mysteriously hooded. The next step of this rather unique nightmare is to refit the slipped off hoods back over the heads of these near drowned rats. This serves to raise their level of panic once again, leaving them to wonder if anything worse could still be looming. Remaining helplessly bound and re-gagged, they're thrown onto the truck bed and recovered with the same heavy, fish odor canvas. What they don't realize is they are being driven, still bound and naked, back to the ferry. Once there, they're deposited into the rear seat of their own mud-filled, disabled sedan towed by a wrecker.

    Squeaky and Louie can hear the chatter of men and women's voices, but cannot see them. They know full well they're in a public setting and naked. They can feel the cooler air coming off the water enwrapping them without judgment. With all that's happened to them, nakedness is the least of their worries. After being unsympathetically warned if they ever choose to return, their island trials are guaranteed not to have such a merciful ending.

    William has joyfully canceled their ferry tariff and is readily sending them on their way back to the mainland to be dealt with as someone else sees fit. The last sighting of these two humiliated, naked men sitting in the back seat of a muck-encrusted, maroon-colored touring car hooked to a tow truck, with their hands bound behind their backs and bags over their heads, is on the ferry carrying them from Harsens Island to the mainland. People are willing to stare, but no one comes the rescue. What's going to become of them from here on is anyone's guess. Frankie and the rest of his team, happy to be done with the ordeal, congratulate each other on a fine performance.

CHAPTER 11
A New Sheriff in Town

The humiliating treatment of these two Purple Gang members is not to go unnoticed. Within an hour of the wrecker dumping Squeaky and Louie in Algonac, a car is seen arriving to transport the two unfortunate wretches back to the safety of the city. It appears when the local law enforcement was made aware of who they were dealing with, they alerted certain people in the city, and a rescue undertaking was initiated.

The Burnstein Brothers in typical fashion don't personally wish to handle any of these difficulties. They prefer as many layers as they can create between themselves and any impropriety. But ignoring situations like what is happening over and over on Harsens Island is not an option. They are suffering humiliations they never would tolerate in the city. To save face, they know something has to be done.

Ray Burnstein takes the initiative. He begins by bringing everyone who's failed on a Harsens Island assignment into a meeting. It begins with the lone survivor back earlier in the summer who ran aground while chasing a bootlegger in what has been loosely described as an "eighteen-foot duck boat." If it were merely an isolated incident, it could easily be dismissed as an anomaly, but when aligned with the other recent incidents, in Ray Burnstein's words, "Something ain't addin' up."

Gus Winkler and Fred Burke are still hospitalized with an indefinite release timetable. Winkler voice has barely healed beyond a whisper from the ball bat crushing his larynx. He still requires several more surgeries. Burke isn't faring any better. His shins are also going to require a much longer period to mend before he'll no longer need a wheelchair. The most recent episode involving Burnstein's cousin, Squeaky and his secondary, Louie Goldman are just as disturbing.

When all of these events are placed side by side, it indicates a mastermind behind all this. "Shit like this crap don't just happen ta fall outta the goddam sky," says Burnstein. "It's gotta have a source. What we need ta do is get to the goddam snake's head an' cut the son of a bitch off."

Burnstein's patience has come to a halt. The only pair that had success on Harsens has been Abe Axler and Eddie Fletcher when they burned the Morgansky fishery. Burnstein had ordered it along with the other failed assignments. What had promised to be nothing more than a minor problem with a suspected young irritant named Frankie Morgansky has turned into an even more problematic matter because of his men's failure to bring him to task.

He orders a meeting with Axler and Fletcher, it's to convene with him at his headquarters in the Book Cadillac Hotel in downtown Detroit. Axler and Fletcher are imports from out east and have a reputation for being ruthless when given an assignment.

Axler has already served a sentence for burglary. He's barely over five foot six and weighs no more than 140 pounds. Nonetheless, he carries a New York tough guy image that no one is willing to challenge more than once. He'll wrap an arm around your neck and sink a shiv between your ribs, twisting the blade until he's sure the threat has been canceled out.

Fletcher has a background as a boxer in New York City, that is until he discovers mobsters are willing to pay a lot more for his pugilist skills outside of the ring than inside. Becoming an enforcer for hire soon enough finds himself and Axler joining forces in an unholy alliance. Both these men are experienced in convincing slow, hesitant, reluctant payers to cough up their insurance payment.

Burnstein, a chronic "Schvitzer" (Yiddish for "a guy who sweats"), plans the meeting in the hotels Turkish steam bath. His idea is to make sure people he doesn't know really well (also some of those he knows much better, but doesn't trust) aren't wearing a wire as informers. Moreover, it's nearly impossible for the police to bug the place because of all the moisture. Furthermore, no one is able to conceal a weapon when they're naked. For Burnstein, it's the safest place to hold small conferences. They're on his turf, with his armed bodyguards ready to eliminate any threat at a moment's notice. He holds all the cards.

Three men sitting naked in a ten by ten-foot steam room reaching temperatures of 150 degrees doesn't seem as though it will be a comfortable place to conduct business. The advantage is, these meetings get to the objective rather quickly without a lot of side talk. Burnstein wastes no time in getting straight to the point.

"I don't know what the hell is going on out there on Harsens Island, but I sure as hell gotta beef with 'em. These guys can't be much more than a bunch of rubes tryin ta run their own rackets. They gotta be reeled in and I'm told you guys are the ones ta do it. I got five grand for each of ya if you can get the job done." With one hand, Burnstein throws a packet containing money to each of them. With the other hand, he tosses another bucket of water onto the hot stones. The steam jettisoning off the rocks causes the membranes inside everyone's nostrils to feel the slight prickle of almost boiling water.

Axler and Fletcher sit holding their payoff with sweat pouring out of every pore in their bodies as they listen to the infuriation this Purple Gang legend holds toward those who fail him. Once someone has been summoned by Ray Burnstein to do a job, a refusal is viewed as an insult that brings their dependability into question, and their fate into even greater question.

Axler, who does most of the thinking, says, "Mr. Burnstein, if you'll give us a few weeks, I'm damn sure your problem can be solved."

Another bucket of water brings the temperature near the hubs of hell. Pointing to the packets containing their fee, Burnstein pronounces, "Good. Then we got a deal. Half now, and half when the job is completed."

With the temperature well over 170 degrees Fahrenheit, Axler and Fletcher are pleased they have this settled. Believing this meeting is now convened and they will get out of this near hell-like misery, they are met at the door by an attendant carrying a bundle oak leaves. Motioning Axler and Fletcher back in with the word, "Plaetza?" (a message). He then begins to soak the leaves in a soapy solution. Taking his time, he begins to rub each of them down with the soapy combination starting with Burnstein. The attendant finally makes his way to each of these neophytes, it's a welcome relief from the intensity of the "Schvitz." Within fifteen minutes they are satisfactorily dismissed as novice "Schvitzers." Exiting the steam room, they are aware of how much they each smell like a wet tea bag.

Despite their seeming camaraderie with a Purple Gang legend, they both know it will only continue if they are effective.

****

Meanwhile, back on Harsens Island, Frankie has been busy. Word has gotten around. The island natives are bragging up the shake down success his resistance group has had on the "silk suits" from the mainland. These victories have ostensibly placed him as a target, but has also encouraged a growing number of independent rumrunners and bootleggers to seek mutually beneficial bonds with this new syndicate.

It's been common practice for "The Jewish Navy" (a moniker placed on Purple Gang torpedo boat affiliates) to hijack the load of Canadian liquor from these independent, rogue "runners" in the Detroit River, Lake St. Clair or the St. Clair River. They overtake the smaller crafts at gun point and steal their shipment. If there is no resistance, the victim is often allowed to live. Anything less, they're killed and their boat is scuttled.

Frankie has set his mind to a plan to discourage the Purple Gang from running roughshod on the Harsens Islanders. In reviewing how he intends to bring this to fruition, he has chiefly set his eye on other war veterans on the island, especially those that experienced combat, in particular those that are familiar with rifles and large caliber machine guns. There are a number of these young men, much like himself who have had special training useful in the Great War, and can once again put it to use against the tyranny of these domestic terrorists.

These men are an outdoor breed that are war hardened survivors, much different than the "tough guys" from the cities asphalt jungles. They are self-sufficient, and possess a particular type of independence. They work well together providing there is a healthy regard for their individuality and it serves an immediate purpose.

These veterans are Harsens Island natives, who much like Frankie's family have made their living as fishermen, and on occasion, as poachers, and now as independent rumrunners. They've grown up with firearms. Many have set these hunting and fishing skills aside only after discovering the lucrative returns flowing from the booze industry.

Frankie has set apart this group of young men with hunting and military training for special assignments. They all possess a knack for boat handling, and small arms usage, especially the Springfield army-issue .30-06 and the long-range .50-caliber rifles. The idea that a good defense is a better offense is an agreed mindset among this group of would-be vigilantes.

The time has come to co-ordinate all these details into a workable plan. The scheme is to lure the Jewish Navy into a confrontation. To accomplish this is going to require patience and communications. The military training these men have undergone is giving them an edge the city slickers can only fantasize they hold.

The mob is intensifying their menacing tactics toward local bootleggers and rumrunners in direct proportion to the demands the markets are producing. The bigger the demand for hooch, the higher the profits, and the higher the profits, the greater the efforts to land a top position in controlling this lucrative market. All this results in added brutality. It seems there is no law enforcement willing to involve themselves with restricting any of this activity. They are often on the payroll of one rumrunner or another, expected to turn a blind eye. Or if this isn't the case, another notion seems to be "They're all a bunch of outlaws, let 'em kill each other off."

The weather is cooling. It's mid-September already. The trees along the shoreline are beginning to display a change in seasons. It's a Thursday, and because it's the middle of the week, the recreational traffic on the lake and rivers is nonexistent, which means the chances of the citizenry getting in the way of flying bullets involving the illegal liquor wars is at a low. It's a perfect day to implement Frankie's long-awaited stratagem. Frankie's plan is to place himself as bait. The idea is to use his ordinary eighteen-foot duck boat with a small outboard motor. He'll conspicuously make his way from a point on the Michigan side of the St. Clair river across to the Canadian side and pick up a load of booze from a designated Canadian exporter.

It's in this area that the Jewish Navy are heavy with spotters to inform them of renegade rumrunners attempting to make an easy buck. The wind is coming out of the northeast making it more difficult to buck the choppy seas. Frankie is sure he's being watched. No one gets a pass in this territory. It's all staked out by various Purple Gangsters. Their typical method is to wait as inconspicuously as possible on the American side until you have your load then hit you on the Canadian side where the US Coast Guard has no jurisdiction. Their boats are always top of the line and faster than anything law enforcement has. In this instance, as in all others, once it's determined to be secure on the American side at a preselected site, a car will be waiting to pick up the contraband and get it to a Purple Gang warehouse inconspicuously named "The Art Novelty Co." From here it will be labeled and prepared for distribution all across the country.

The Purples have become so efficient at this feat that they are now supplying 80% of the illegal liquor sold in the United States, even Al Capone has deemed them as his official alcohol agent. The Purples have become the wealthiest and most feared mob in the country.

Their magnitude doesn't daunt Frankie as he is prepared to take them on one at a time, and all taking place under his terms. As soon as he has passed into Canadian waters, he heads for the cove designated for his rendezvous with his Canadian liquor connection. The deal is quickly made. With the money exchanged and the boat quickly loaded, he's on his way. As if on cue, a torpedo boat suddenly appears and slowly makes its way toward Frankie. Without a single letter on the boat, it has Purple Gang written all over it. It's a top of the line speedboat with an inboard motor. What isn't apparent to these pursuers is the torpedo boat that is dogging them. At first it is taken to be one of their own. The gaps between the boats are no more than a hundred feet apart, close enough to make it apparent that each has an interest in the other. It's apparent to both parties these vessels are not recreational.

Something the way this boat is behaving is making it very suspicious to the Purples. In a very menacing display of dominance, the Jewish Navy has suddenly postured two men on deck posing with Thompson machine guns. One man has his pointing at Frankie, the other at this supposed intruder.

This unknown intruder happens to be a select pair of veterans chosen by Frankie because of their individual skills. One of these young men in particular is adamant to seek reprisal against these hijackers. His name is Jake Freebold. Jake lost his boat along with its cargo of ten gallons of Canadian whiskey to the Jewish Navy. They hijacked his whiskey and sunk his boat with him still on it. The only reason he's still alive is the heist was interrupted by the US Coast Guard. It allowed the hijackers an immediate escape while the Coast Guard spent their time pulling him out of the water.

Jake's specialty is souped-up boat engines. He's reputed to enable a factory engine to squeeze out a few more horse power than they're designed to produce. Frankie has turned over the torpedo boat he recovered from his incident with the Jewish Navy to Jake with the imperative to "make this the fastest son-of-a-bitch on the lake." Within the week and with a pleasurable smile Jake is demonstrating to Frankie the modifications he has built into an already deluxe motor making it even faster. This modified motor is capable of doing fifty knots. Frankie couldn't be more pleased. Things are beginning to fall in place with each new recruit working in his own arena.

Another of these veterans is Ezra Church. His specialty is handling the .50-caliber rifle or machine gun. Since the black market is rife with a surplus of these weapons from the Great War and their ammunition, Frankie has had little trouble in finding a seller. Ezra's task is to discreetly fit the .50-caliber under the bow covering of the torpedo boat so it can be hidden from view. It has required he cut a narrow port hole between the ribbings of the bow that can be open or closed enabling them to control water wanting to make its way inside. This allows the shooter to see his target and allows room for the barrel to swivel. The last detail is to reinforce the deck under the tripod supporting the .50-caliber weapon.

Without a moments worth of intimidation, Ezra has unlatched the port door in the bow and released a volley of .50-caliber rounds in the direction of these pursuers purposely missing them. The response of the pursuers is a mixture of "fight or flight." The men with the Tommy guns return fire. It's obvious they have little experience with these weapons, as their recoil sends most if not all of the rounds flying off overhead. At the same time, the person running their boat opens the throttle all the way, causing the craft to lurch out of the water. The idea seems to be to escape what obviously is superior firepower.

With Jake in command, he follows suit. The souped-up motor roars alive sending a plum of water ten feet high out behind him. The men in charge of the oppositional boat's Tommy guns continue their feckless outward show of intimidation by sending round after round into the air. They are beginning to realize the game has changed—and not in their favor. Within a minute, Jake has overtaken them. It's enough to permit Ezra to discharge another volley, this time intended to do some serious damage.

The adversarial boat is abruptly torn to shreds as huge pieces of splintered planking explode through the air. In less than thirty seconds, there is nothing left of this boat but pieces of driftwood giving themselves over to the mercy of the current. What's left of the bodies of its three occupants soon joins the floating debris as it independently drifts off with the flow.

Meanwhile, Frankie is taking all this in at a distance. The carnage is apparent. Frankie's face remains stoic, but it's the kind of stoic satisfaction that stems from a belief these racketeers can be intimidated and beaten.

It's noticeably interfered with Purple Gang "insurance" collections on the island enough that they aren't attempting to collect while all this change is taking place. It's apparent there's a new sheriff in town. How long he can last is another question.

CHAPTER 12
Don't Mess with the Sideburns

Thanks to Jerry Ferris, Stella and Alina have both found waitress work at the Old Club. Out of the kindness of Aristine's heart, she looks after Carly when either of them have schedules that conflict. Aristine couldn't be happier. She has longed for a grandchild, since Frankie hasn't met her need, she is willing to play this role out with Carly having her refer to her as "Bubbie" (grandmother in Yiddish). Aristine can't be more indulgent; she fills Carly with babka (a sweet yeast cake) at every opportunity. When Frankie and Stella ask why she continues to do this in spite of their protestations, Aristine declares, "'Cause I vant her to like me!"

On Frankie's behest, Axel has been keeping his ear to the ground so to speak in the local mob hangouts. It took several days before a fisherman from the mainland came across bloated body parts in Lake St. Clair. It took another few days for anyone to identify the body and a few more days before anyone came forward to claim the body. The other two took several more days before their parts began to wash ashore on the Canadian side. The word is of disbelief. No one can fit all the pieces together since there were no witnesses. Law enforcement merely dismisses the incident as "rumrunners murdering rumrunners."

To Burnstein, it's another Harsens Island incident he'd like more than anything to have behind him. There are certain objects a man can will, like placing men like Axler and Fletcher on the details of the skirmish, but not being able to will the outcome has him in a pickle. This is a puzzle he and his brothers have never experienced before. The Irish and Italian, and Jewish mobs all play on the same urban turf. The Purples cannot be beat here. This Harsens Island incidents are different. They're like the Indian wars when the Indians would hide behind trees and sneak-attack their nemeses before they could counterattack. So far, the score is the Harsens Islanders, four, and the Purples, zero.

The Burnsteins have given Axler and Fletcher a stern, no-nonsense, straight forward directive to get to the bottom of this Harsens fiasco and end it once and for all. For the time being they're spending most of their time sitting in the local hangouts drinking bootlegged whiskey, talking about it.

"Burnsteins expecting an execution and an end to this Harsens bullshit," says Fletcher, "So what's next—other than our ass if we don't get it done?" The Harsens rubes are calling all the shots. Axler and Fletcher are well aware they need to come up with an inventive and innovative strategy.

Axler takes a long draw on his cigarette, holding it long enough to butt it. Then he lets out a plume of smoke intermingled and the words, "Too damn many loose ends. We need more information."

"What say we get a mole on the island—maybe as a guest in a hotel. He can hang around the drinkin' joints and get some feedback?" suggests Fletcher.

Axler pauses for a moment. "You might be onto somethin', Eddie. What ya got in mind?"

"I'm thinkin' we give the job ta one a the "Juniors." They're always lookin for somethin' that'll move 'em up."

"Who ya got in mind?" asks Axler.

"You remember that young guy who come along with Burnsteins accountant, Pierre Woodard—I think it was his nephew or cousin or somethin'. Didn't he call him Lyman?"

"Yeah, come ta think of it, I do remember that kid. Kinda clean cut, wasn't he?"

"More than that. He asked me for a job. When I asked him what he thought he was good at, he said anything I ask him ta do. So what d'ya think, Abe?"

"It sure as hell is worth a try. We gotta get somethin' goin'," says Axler, "So you handle it. Right now, I need a shave and a haircut."

The two separate with Fletcher on the hunt for the "Purple JV," Lyman Woodard, and Axler heads for Joe Elliot's barbershop.

Joe has been Axler's barber since he arrived in Detroit a few years back. He has always met Axler's rigorous standards as to what a haircut should look like. Joe can make a pair of scissors and a razor sing. Today, Axler expects nothing different, but instead he's met by a total stranger standing behind Joe's chair. It's a much younger guy who looks to be no more than about seventeen or eighteen.

"Where the hell is Joe?" asks Axler with a more than disgruntled tone. It's obvious he doesn't need another upset disrupting his day. After all, he came to the barbershop to relax with a shave and a haircut, not to be met by some kid wearing a barber smock looking like he just got out of grade school.

"Joe took the day off. My name is John Borman. I'm Joe's apprentice. Can I help you?"

Axler's face drops as he's faced with a decision he hadn't expected. "Can ya cut hair and give a shave?"

"Yes, sir, I can do that," answers the fresh-faced kid.

"Good. I'll give ya a crack. Jus' follow Joe's pattern an' don't screw my sideburns up," barks Axler. "Ya got that, kid? Don't mess my sideburns up!"

"Okay, sir. I'll do my absolute best," says John with an air of professional confidence.

If Axler didn't look forward to the peace and quiet he enjoyed when Joe took care of him, he would turn down young John's offer. Instead, he reluctantly slips himself into the barber chair. In a rather ostentatious manner, John steps behind the chair and lifts the hair cloth from its hook. Reaching around front of this less than enthusiastic client, he whips the covering in the air, creating a snapping noise, and then patiently lets it drift down around Axler's torso. If this were meant to impress this less than impressionable client, it isn't coming close. Axler has more years on the earth than this young man has given professional haircuts, let alone shaves. Now, if anything, this young apprentice is going to have to live up to the image he's attempting to create.

John's intention is to start first with the shave hoping to calm his client. Tilting Axler back in the chair he carefully begins with a neck and temple massage. Axler's response is encouraging. His tenseness is being replaced with a sudden calmness. Completing this little extra service, he takes a heated towel—careful it's not too hot—and applies it to Axler's face. There's an immediate heavy sigh coming from Axler sounding as though someone had let the air out of a tire. John's confidence is increasing directly proportional to this ominous client's ability to relax. The only sound in the shop is the slap of the razor stroking the strop.

Confident he's making headway with Axler, John continues with the shave. His blade is sharp and his hand is steady. His self-assurance is growing with every smooth stroke of his razor. Finally, finished with the shave, he gives this near snoozing client one more steam cloth to remove remnants of lather. All that's left is to apply a touch of Bay Rum to Axler's face. Raising him from his recline position to a sitting position, John prepares for the haircut faze of this spa treatment. Putting both hands to his face, Axler can't help but be impressed. "You got some skills kid, this is as smooth as a baby's ass." He welcomes the next phase of the treatment if it's as proficient as the last.

Axler feels relaxed for the first time in days. His thoughts are centered on the attention he's receiving. He has to admit this kid is appearing to be as good as Joe. The near muted clicking of the scissors and the delicate touch of the comb puts Axler in a near trance. He can't remember when he has felt this far removed from stress.

At last the experience comes to an end. The haircut is finished. John hands the mirror to Axler for his final approval. Axler sits motionless, but another change is occurring. A red blush is beginning to work its way from his neck to the top of his head. In a single motion, he has thrown the hand mirror across the room, he's to his feet ripping the hair cloth off, tossing it to the floor. In what can't be described as anything other than a rage, he shouts, "You son-of-a-bitch, you messed my goddam sideburns up! I told you don't mess my goddam sideburns up! In another motion, Axler has unholstered his .38 caliber pistol and fired a shot into the barber's leg. The kid goes down to the floor like a pole-axed steer. He writhes in pain as his former client puts on his hat and jacket and storms out the door, muttering to himself, "The son-of-a-bitchin' kid can't cut hair worth a shit."

Meantime Fletcher has made some headway in finding Lyman Woodard. What he has discovered about this JV Purple is that he's an entertainer. "This Kid plays the goddam piano, can you believe it—the goddam piano! I'm thinkin' we can get him in that Old Club joint out on Harsens. What d'you think?" says an enthusiastic Fletcher.

"I dunno. Can we trust 'im?" asks Axler.

"His uncle says he'd do a good job at somethin' like that. I dunno, we ain't got much choice, Burnstein ain't gonna wait forever," says Fletcher. There is no doubt both of them are aware at how unschooled they are to meet this crisis. Nonetheless, they're going to give it their best effort. They're locked in and they know it. Now they need to come up with something they know will impress Burnstein and the same time deal with the Harsens Island curse.

"How we gonna get that kid ta get a job out there, I don't trust anybody near that place right now," continues Axler with the same negative vein of thought.

"I think we send the kid out there alone. Them people ain't gonna know he's one of ours lessen he spill the beans. Let him hit the different clubs on the island. I gotta say, the kid ain't a bad piano player. One of 'em gonna be impressed enough ta take 'im on," declares Fletcher with an air of hopeful assurance.

Not willing to put this move off any longer, they collude as to how to get the kid onto the island without suspicion.

Axler's mind is going a mile a minute with a thought he's come up with. "Eddie, you remember that place up north we went to ta lay low for a while that had them wild ass, backwoods chicks that hung around the club?"

"You talkin' about Graceland up in Lupton?" answers Fletcher.

"Yeah, that's the name I was tryin' ta think of. What say we get him a resume sayin' he played up there signed by that one-armed Mike guy who owns the place.

"You're talkin' about Mike Gelfand. All it's gonna take is a phone call ta get that done. Now I think we're gettin' someplace. I know damn well those hicks over on Harsens don't know nothin' about Lupton," assures Fletcher.

Within a few days, they've managed to get a call to Lupton to assure one-armed-Mike's cooperation. Lyman's bankrolled sufficiently to hang around Harsens long enough to either get a job or to gather all the information he can on who's organizing the resistance.

Lyman's a savvy guy for his age. He's a good-looking guy and has a rare sophistication. He's been playing music around clubs since he was twelve. Now he's eighteen. Not knowing how to read music, he learned to play by ear. Not only can he play any song he's ever listened to, but he also has composed songs of his own.

His uncle Pierre has been his idol since he was a young boy. He still finds himself fascinated by his uncle's connections to all these legendary gangsters. Fully willing to become part of this gangster caste, he's anxious to get going with his first important underground assignment. Supplied with a much less ostentatious automobile than he'd hoped for, he's ready to get started. Piling into his 1917 Model T, Lyman begins his mission to get the highly sought-after evidence his bosses, Axler and Fletcher, are bankrolling him to find.

CHAPTER 13
The Trojan Horse

Axel has been diligent in his covert role as an extra pair of ears. "Burnstein ain't happy with the ass-kickin' his syndicates been takin' at the hands of a bunch of hicks and has hired a couple strong-arms named Abe Axler and Eddie Fletcher ta straighten us out," reports Axel, "I doubt they'll show up down here personally, but we don't know who they got on the payroll willin' ta get loose-tongued for a few extra bucks."

Axel's even managed to get his hands on a police mug shot of each of them. These have been reproduced and handed out to various people involved with the resistance group. With the knowledge that some of Harsens residents have been compromised by Purple money, they are careful about how publically they're known.

Frankie's time is more and more taken up with this new obsession to rid the island of what one observer had taken notice of in this gang. "There's a shopkeeper over on Hastings that says these guy ain't like other people, but tainted off color, rotten, purple like the color of bad meat." It seems this description has taken root and is widely repeated.

Because his family is personally suffering the wrath of these profane members of the human community, Frankie is becoming determined to rid his world of any trace of their influence.

"This guy Axler has a special spot in my gun sights. He's the guy who give Stella that beatin'. Unfortunately, she's been more involved with these thugs on a personal level than the rest of us," expresses Frankie to Axel with a regretful, almost apologetic tone.

Not wanting to spend any more time discussing Stella and her profession with Frankie, Axel slips away to cover some more of his sleuthing.

As is his habit, Frankie stops by the Old Club to meet with Ferris, keeping him up to date with the latest developments, especially this new development involving these out-of-towners, Axler and Fletcher. Even though Stella is often busy with her waitress and bartender duties, it's also an excuse to have a moment with her. Knowing that it remains a sore spot to bring her past into her present, Frankie carefully chooses his words. "Stella, we got word that Axler and Fletcher are leading the Burnstein charge to settle his problems with Harsens Island."

With a quiet stare, Stella says, "I wish you wouldn't bring Axler up in my presence," declares Stella in a voice matching her stare. She's staring at nothing in particular. It doesn't *have* to be anything in particular to have a film running through her head to relive the incident all over again. She remembers how she insisted he wear a skin before intercourse, and he insisted he only goes barefoot. When she decided to hold her ground, he began to beat her with closed fists as he raped her, all the while spitting on her and, with continuous blows, berating her as an uppity whore who needed to be brought down.

Frankie can see the hurt in her face. He is aware of the deep care and concern he has for this woman as he witnesses the hurt in her eyes. *If only there was something I could do to make her whole again, so we can put this behind us.* He feels a haunting sense of failure for not protecting her from this segment of her life, as though he had a role in it happening. Her eyes begin to well up as it brings back not only the physical hurt, but the damage the rape did to her personhood. Frankie is sharing her hurt, and it rekindles his own hatred for this man.

"I'm sorry, Stella, the only reason I'm bringing this up is I want you to be attentive to a possible link between things that may be unusual here and the possibility Axler might be behind it. I can't say with assurance what they have planned, and I'm not sure they do either. But word has it they might be sending a mole to infiltrate our resistance movement," says Frankie.

Stella can sense the concern he has for her safety. He's by far the most trusting male she has ever known. "Believe me, Frankie, if any a those creeps show up here, I'll kill 'em!" cries Stella in a near panic.

"No! No! Don't do anything stupid like that, Stella. So far, we've managed to stay ahead of these mugs 'cause we've kept our heads on straight." Taking both her hands and placing them between his, he adds, "If you see or hear anything unusual, promise you'll get a hold of me right away?"

Stella feels the strength of his hands around hers; they feel stable and reliable. "I promise," she says. Lifting her eyes to meet his, she gives him a peck on the lips. "I gotta get back ta work."

****

Things on Harsens continue to move along without interruption. It seems the Purples are not willing to risk any more defeats at the hands of a bunch of Reubens (hicks) until they figure out a way to win. Frankie is taking advantage of the lull by having his group move as much liquor as they can without the constant interruption from the Jewish Navy. He's managed to gain the confidence of many of the other club owners on the island other than just the Old Club, names such as, Grande Point Hotel, Star Island House, Sans Souci, Riverside Hotel, and many others, supplying them all with the liquor they need to stay busy. This pause is also giving his crew a supply of money they need to maintain a living. There's a sense of a higher purpose in belonging to a group of like-minded people willing to band together and use their skills for a greater cause.

Even the big-city high-roller duck hunters are beginning to return. A share of Frankie's crew are guides, and some have been doing this since they were kids. They know these swamps like their homes because their job is to ensure the duck hunters a good supply of birds. The money's good, and it keeps both parties in touch with their primordial roots. Even for the few days out of the year these men are able to retreat, they find common ground in exchanging hunting stories—most turn into nearly believable lies if repeated often enough, especially if they're told to top the last guy's yarn. They all yearn for a new adventure that promises to advance a new and unique tale that might someday become a legend to linger on long after they're long gone. This becomes a secret wish. But then, this is all part of the lure to Harsens flats for many of this kind. They return year after year until one year they don't show up, it just happens that way, their stories are quickly forgotten, then there's another one to fill the vacancy, and more stories replace those that were hoped to become legends.

    It's a busy time for every business on the island. Barnes' ferry is working overtime with little time to reference each client. All of the clubs on the island depend on tourists from the surrounding areas of the mainland, like Detroit, Pontiac, Dearborn, St. Clair Shores, etc. They come in many varieties of garb, but none come like the gangsters. They always have a wise guy attitude, dress in expensive suits, drive fancy automobiles, and usually got a fancy lookin' hooker on their arm for the evening. Nonetheless William is doing the best he can to keep an eye open for any unusual looking "duck hunters." The kind that slip through the cracks are the unassuming types like single, clean cut young men with hardly enough beard to notice.

    Lyman Woodard is one of these. He can easily pass himself as a college student on a week-end sabbatical. He has lightly loaded his older Model T with a small suitcase and the clothes on his back. In all honesty, this is hardly the kind of gangster Barnes is going to be unhesitatingly cautious to be on the lookout for.

    Lyman is taking his role as seriously as he knows how. He doesn't fit the mold of a hard-core gangster, but at his young age, he is captivated by the notoriety these men receive—especially from the press. For reasons only the young can explain there is a side of this gangster life that has been romanticized. At this point, he is stimulated by the anticipated excitement and action.

He remains guarded. He's been made aware of the citizens underground resistance movement on the island and that the reason he's being placed here is to infiltrate as best he can its foundation. Axler is giving him his last marching instructions before he sends him off with the incentive, "You do a good job and I'll guarantee you Mr. Burnstein 'ell find a place for a guy like you. Anything you see or hear, I expect you to get back to us with the information. I wanna hear from you every day. Ya got that, kid?"

"Yes sir, Mr. Axler, you can depend on me. I'll get 'er done," says Lyman with all the bravado an eighteen-year-old wannabe wise guy can muster.

The ferry trip from Algonac to Harsens Island is a ten-minute, uneventful ride. The ferryboat makes a landing at a designated dock on the island. In another minute or two, the ramp is clear, the deck hand motions his Model T onto the short road at the docks entrance. Here he is met by a road allowing him to go right or left. After studying his options, for no other reason than to make a choice, he turns left. Since he has no idea where he's going but ends up in the island village, San Souci. Finding a restaurant, he stops for lunch.

This is Lyman's first experience on the island. He's spent most of his working career in night clubs that cultivate a night life. Stopping in this local restaurant for a noon lunch is like eating in another world for him. These folks are day time people, they emanate a type of energy and self-assurance an up-tight city dweller is never comfortable with. He's beginning to understand the frustration a city person would have with the locals. These people are typically much more transparent and unguarded. They have a much more laid-back lifestyle with a whole different set of survivor skills than city dwellers. Friendliness seems to be an effortless first response given off by these neighbors from an hour away.

After lunch, Lyman turns south making his way down the island. He can't help but be taken by its primitiveness. The roads are all dirt; many are only a two track with channels of water emerging on each side. Muskrats are frequently seen sunning themselves along the roads waiting until a car is only a few feet from striking them before they scurry back to the safety of the water filled ditches. There are residences varying from fishing shacks to elegant homes. Some of these seem to be marooned on small tracts of land surrounded by water with no obvious egress.

It's late in the afternoon when Lyman arrives at the Old Club. It's at the end of the road, with no choice other than to turn around. He's tired, ready for a room. But as tired as he is, he can't get over the elegance of this place. It strikes him in a way he's never experienced. Not that he isn't accustomed to poverty and elegance, it's that in the cities it's relegated to individual districts, each with its own culture. Out here, it's like finding a crown jewel in the middle of a swamp. With all its windows, green lawns, fresh paint, and uniformed staff, it's palatial compared with most of the small fishing cottages and boat houses scattered along the way.

He's just in time to see a familiar vessel. It makes him smile. It's the Tashmoo—the only familiar object he's seen since he arrived. In an odd way, it kind of welcomes and connects him with the mainland. This is the mother ship of the White Star Line, which is fully capable of carrying several thousand passengers at a time. He's seen this ship loading passengers on the Detroit side, but he had no idea this was its destination.

He might be sophisticated and worldly on his own turf, but this is beginning to look like he has dropped into a world he has never before known existed. His mind is going a mile a minute. Somehow he *must* find the key to opening its door for himself. No longer a kid, but not an adult, he must set in motion the adult slice of his mentality. If he's to get anywhere with this assignment, he must prove he can enter alternative worlds on an equal footing.

After checking in at the desk, Lyman is shown to his room. It's pleasant enough, with a bed, a desk, a dresser with a mirror, and a wash basin with a pitcher of water. After refreshing himself, he decides to explore his temporary home away from home. Making his way to the lobby he passes Stella in the lobby. Until now, there has been no reason for her to pay any attention to him. She's recently been promoted to consigner, dealing with specific requests from hotel guests. It's an important role in that it's her job to make the guest she's dealing with feel much more important than anyone in their hometown would ever tolerate. She's wearing a fitted suit rather than a waitress uniform and carries herself in a more cultured way. This Harsens Island experience is forcing its way on both of these newcomers in such a way that they actually exchange a greeting with one another—something they would never do on the streets of Detroit.

"Welcome to the Old Club. I hope your stay with us is enjoyable, sir. If there's anything we can do for you to make your stay with us more agreeable, please let me know," says Stella with a warm smile that's coming easier now.

Lyman pauses for a moment. This woman looks slightly familiar to him, he just can't put his finger on where or how. "You might be able to help me," says Lyman. "I'm an entertainer. I play piano, and I'm looking for a gig. I'm curious—who handles your bookings?"

Suddenly Stella realizes this is the young man who occasionally played piano at Squeaky's during the dinner hour. She's not ready to remind him of their past affiliation, so she quickly passes him off to the program director.

This is the first link to Stella's past that's crossed her path since she came to the island. It's a reminder that *yesterdays* do not part company easily. They have a way of weaseling their way back to the forefront. She isn't certain he recognized her, nonetheless, this recap is enough to give her pause.

Seeing Jerry Ferris across the lobby busy with the desk, she has to decide quick if this chancing needs to have another look. *As long as he's here, I may as well run it by him.*

"Jerry, can I have a word with you?" she asks in a near whisper.

Jerry is a no-nonsense manager. Barely thirty, he's been employed by the owners because of his ability to get the best out of his employees and his passion to advance the reputation of the Old Club. He's a company man through and through. It's not unusual for him to go from table to table in the dining room, making acquaintance with guests as though they were all his personal friends.

"Sure, Stella, I got a minute. What d'ya need?" His smile is genuine and inviting.

In the time it took her to cross the room, this chance encounter with Lyman has grown into concern. She carefully measures her words.

"This business about keeping an eye open for things that are odd brings me over here. I'm not sure this is a problem or maybe I just think it could be." Nodding her head toward Lyman having a word with the program director, she continues, "You see that kid over there, talking with Joe? He used ta play piano at that Purple joint I worked in. I know his uncle is a big shot of some kind with the Burnsteins, and he got him the job. I don't have a clue what he's doin' way out here, but it just feels kinda fishy ta me ta see him show up."

In an attempt not to be overly curious, Jerry casts a quick glance at Joe and the kid. "Well, let me check this out for myself." Turning to leave, Jerry gives Stella a gentle pat on the arm, saying, "Good eye, kid. Ya did the right thing." Without a lot of to-do, Jerry casually makes his way across the lobby toward the program director and Lyman.

"Hey Joe, what ya got goin'?" asks Jerry while engaging Lyman with his finest smile.

"This kid here's name is Lyman Woodard. He says he's a piano player. Says he worked at that big club up in Lupton. He's got a reference sayin' he's a reliable guy, and don't drink much. I ain't heard him play yet, but we're headed toward the piano right now."

"Well, let's hear what ya got, kid," says Jerry, shaking Lyman's hand as he graciously directs him toward the baby grand across the lobby.

Lyman can't be more thrilled. This is all going much smoother than he had expected. Walking across the room to this great piano puts him in his element. With the deftness of one who has made this trip many times, he adjusts the bench and enters a world not shared by those who only listen to music. He makes music happen. With his long, illustrious fingers, he caresses the keys as one would a fine sculpture. With his eyes closed and lips pursed, his deft fingers begin to create a pleasant melody. The tune "Cuban Moon" begins to waft through the lobby. It occasions the guests to stop for a moment as they realize this is not a phonograph rendition, but a live performance. With each blend of the notes, his body, soul, and the music he's creating have become as one. He sways to its rhythm. Utter amazement sweeps across the room. The arrangement soon ends, and the lobby guests break into spontaneous applause.

Jerry and Joe both look at one another. Both have sat through an electrifying recital with unexpected chills making their way up and down their spines. It's obvious this kid has a talent. As young a man as he appears to be, both agree that when he began to play, the child disappeared and a much more mature soul emerged. With what appears to be an agreeable nod from Jerry, Joe turns to Lyman and says, "Ya just got yerself a job, kid."

After the information Stella laid out, Jerry is also cognizant this kid could be a Trojan horse making his way into the resistance movement. He's also of the opinion that one should keep his friends close, and his enemies closer, so he thinks it's still a good idea to keep the young man in house, where he can be monitored.

Seeing Stella again, Jerry commends her once more for her astuteness and confesses he hired the young man without knowing what else he might be up to. He also asks her to continue to keep an eye on him and feel free to report any unusual behavior.

Stella promises to do just that with the resolve of one who knows the vicious nature of this evil consortium firsthand.

CHAPTER 14
The Wasp and the Spider

Lyman is proving to be a big hit. There doesn't seem to be a request he can't satisfy. His tips are already exceeding his pay. Joe has him opening for the headliner this Saturday night. What is striking Stella as odd, is when she offered to find him an inexpensive fishing cottage, he turned her offer down insisting he preferred to stay at the hotel for now. "Geez-o-Pete's, kid, you know your hotel room is eatin' up all your bucks. Why don't you let me get you somethin' close by that's cheap?"

Lyman appears to be annoyed at her insistence. "No thanks. I'm fine where I am. I prefer the swank atmosphere to some shack in the woods. Everything I need is right here—phone, food, drink, hot water—what more could a man ask for?"

Stella wastes no time in reporting this eccentricity to Jerry. With some simple math, Jerry quickly calculates the kid should be going in the hole, but seems to have an outside reserve to meet his obligation. "Thanks, Stella. You're right—this sure as hell ain't addin' up for a kid his age to be throwin' money around like he's doin'. Keep on keepin' an eye on him. I'm with ya on this one. I think somethin' is rotten in Denmark."

Lyman wastes no time making acquaintances of the hotel staff. On the surface, he is making favorable impressions with this set. After all, he's witty, amiable, and certainly talented. But to Stella, who has certainly been with enough men to discern when there's dishonesty, she is not taken in by his charming ways. To her, he seems to be cleverly disguising himself as a responsible adult. She also is not so sure that he is not deceptive in acting as though he doesn't know her.

Though Lyman's room is one of the lower cost accommodations, it proves to be convenient. It's placed with a rear view over the service door. This allows him to monitor those who are coming and going that are not guests. One in particular he's noticed is a man that has visited several times. He's also noticed the same man speaking privately with Stella and Jerry.

Pulling one of the busboys aside, discreetly nodding toward a conference occurring between Jerry, Stella, and this man, Lyman asks, "Who is that guy talking with Stella and Jerry?"

Taking a glance at the trio, the busboy says, "That there is Frankie Morgansky, he's only the guy who's kickin' the ass of them city slickin' gangsters tryin' ta take over our island."

This information sends chills down Lyman's spine. After all this is the very stuff he's been hired to pay attention to. Still trying to remain discreet, Lyman takes another look at the three deep in conversation. What he doesn't realize is the conversation is centering around him. Stella is the one speaking at the moment. "I see him in the lobby phone booth every day. So far I haven't been able to hear his conversations."

Contemplating what Stella has just revealed, Frankie notices a possible solution to that dilemma, saying, "Stella, take notice the two phone booths are connected. The next time you see him in one, go to the other and check if you can hear enough through the wall to get a handle on who he's talkin' with, and better yet, about what."

It's the middle of the week at the Old Club. The guest list is sparse: a few duck hunters, plus Lyman. Aristine has brought Carly to visit her mother during her break. Carly takes advantage of the visit to investigate anything that catches her interest. At the moment, she's drawn to the piano. Lyman is rehearsing a new piece of music he's writing. The melody gets Carly's attention as she demonstrates in typical six-year-old fashion, her penchant to dance to any tune that has a beat.

Lyman, being the typical entertainer, responds by picking up the tempo. Carly's dance movements are much more sophisticated than those of a typical little girl her age.

Stella looks on with a suspicious eye. Not wanting to draw any premature animosity toward this possible nemesis, she holds her tongue letting the incident play itself to a conclusion.

Carly is out of breath and pleased she could flaunt her stuff. With the kind of smile only a six-year-old can give, she looks to her musical director for his approval.

"You're pretty darn good, kid. How'd you learn how ta dance like that?"

"My ma taught me," says Carly, proudly pointing back at her mother. Stella would rather not have her daughter befriend Lyman, a potential enemy. Nonetheless, she makes herself give a little wave and an equally forced smile.

Like a typical six-year-old, Carly concludes this chapter of her day and moves on to something else. Lyman's gaze hangs on Stella for an uncomfortable moment. He's nervously blinking, and his smile is quickly replaced by a serious face. He quickly looks away. *He's remembered where he knows me from* Stella thinks as she takes in this unseemly change. She decides the best thing to do is continue to take her time and let things play out—after all, so far, Harsens Island is holding all the cards. This gives her a sense of security she never experienced in Detroit.

Less than an hour later, Stella has returned to her duties when she notices Lyman quietly slipping into one of the phone booths. While she considers her next move, she waits for his attention to focus on the number he's dialing. In a carefully timed move, she slips into the adjoining booth. She can clearly hear the clicking of the rotary dial as it registers the number being called. *What if he's just calling his mother?*

"Hello, Mr. Axler. This is Lyman Woodard."

Stella's hands begin to sweat; she feels like a spy, or like an intruder who's about to be found out, but she finds the resolve to hold her ground. She can only hear one side of the conversation.

"Yes, sir. I have been doing that. Yes, sir. I believe I do have something you might find interesting. You remember that workin' girl Stella that Squeaky put up? Well, she and her kid are here on the island. Matter a fact, she works here at the club. What's more, she's all tied up with that guy Frankie Morgansky I was tellin' you about. Ya know, the guy givin' you all the trouble?"

Stella can hardly believe her ears. This is chilling—hardly a comforting state of affairs. It's all she can do to keep from bolting out of the booth and running. Even so, she manages to hold her ground and allow the conversation to run its course. She keeps her back to the folding door and hunches into the corner of the booth with the phone to her ear. She hopes Lyman pays no attention to her booth as he hurries away.

After a few minutes, Stella cautiously peers through the windows. Seeing no sign of Lyman, she stealthily exits the phone booth. Certain she can prove this piano player is much more than merely a young musician looking for work, she seeks out Jerry. He's all ears as she lays out all she overheard.

"This is the stuff we need to be aware of," says Jerry. "I'm convinced these guys aren't gonna give up this easy. In the meantime, we'll keep an extra eye open for your protection, Stella."

She can't wish this problem away. The part that troubles her the most is her concern for Carly. *How do I protect my daughter from these thugs?* Sitting and contemplating all of this new development, her gaze turns toward a window. There, a wasp is attacking a spider. The weight of the two grasping on to one another causes the web to break, releasing them onto the brick patio below. Locked in mortal combat, the two roll around as they try to inject their venom into one another. Five minutes of this unresolved conflict finally produces a winner; the wasp flies off with the spider's head tucked in its jaws.

Stella pauses for a moment, her head bowed. Knowing what she was like as a girl, and what she has lived through these past few years, she can't help but wonder where she would fit into this kind of combat. Then she realizes she's already in it; now that her naiveté has been replaced with a certain cynicism, all she can do is try to become the wasp.

CHAPTER 15
Navy vs. Air Force

    Frankie's returned after another successful rum run from Canada. With the Purples taking a sabbatical, the cottage industry rumrunners are making their own deals unmolested.

    Having received a telephone call from Stella, and made aware they have been compromised by this infiltrator the Purples have planted in the Old Club, Frankie stands in the doorway of Stella's small cottage. His hands are firmly planted on his hips as he considers how he's going to address this latest development. Wordlessly, she answers the door and immediately turns away, leaving him standing with no bidding to come in, continue standing, or leave. It's undeniably certain she has something bothering her. Not being a mind reader, Frankie invites himself in. Not ready to second-guess what Stella has on her mind, he sits down in the closest chair willing to wait out her silence.

    She has lit a cigarette, nervously flicking a nonexistent ash. Frankie follows suit, both sit silently in opposite sides of the room blowing smoke into a wordless space. Carly's cat is the only one welcoming him with her meow and dragging her body across his pant leg. Another couple of minutes pass by while he plays with the cat.

    Finally, Stella reacts. Her voice has a ring like cold metal. "Frankie, I know you've had some bad dealin's with these guys. So far, you've always been on the winnin' side. I've also had my share of goin's-on with this breed. I know 'em. They're heartless pigs. They stop at nothin' to make someone suffer. So far, I've lived through what I know they can do—I don't know if they'll let me live next time," she exclaims. Then with a purposeful pause and a much weaker bearing, she adds, "I worry about Carly."

    Patiently listening to Stella's concerns, Frankie waits until he believes she's finished. "Stella, believe me when I tell you there ain't ever gonna be a next time as long as I'm suckin' air."

    "Maybe that's what's worryin' me. I know of at least a dozen guys they've murdered for less than what you're doin'. I still owe 'em a debt. They don't forget that stuff. If somethin' happens to you, I don't know where Carly and I would go to get away from 'em," says Stella. Her worry is clearly coming through.

He can feel her anxiety rising with her fears leading her thoughts. Rising, he crosses the room and takes her in his arms, saying, "Trust me when I say I love you and will go to any length to assure yours and Carly's safety."

Stella doesn't doubt Frankie's resolve—but then, she is not as easily won over on how successful his future can be. After all, she has only hours earlier heard Lyman ushering her circumstances into a conversation with her personal nemesis, Abe Axler.

"Believe me Stella, these silk suits have no idea how dangerous Harsens can get for them. One of the reasons they have planted that Woodard kid, is because they have no other options. All we have ta do is keep a good watch on him like we been doin'. This territory is as strange as the moon ta these guys. They'll keep showin' up like a bad penny hopin' they can find an ace ta play. What they don't know is we are holdin' all the cards." Looking Stella straight in the eye, he continues as though he' just had an epiphany, "I ain't askin' you to risk anything more than you was back at Squeaky's, I'm just askin' you to see things for a minute, the way I see 'em."

Still wordless, Stella prolongs, shrinking deeper into her worries. She's looking at everything around the room but Frankie. It's obvious there is a lot more angst produced in this conversation than she is comfortable with. Finally looking his way, she says, "All I can say is I'll try my damnedest, but I ain't promisin' any more than that."

From time to time, Frankie's face can take on the assured look of one who has had many victories; It's a look of a mature wisdom. "That's all I'm askin' of you, Stella," he says with an expression both significant and clear.

In all this uneasiness, there remains a ray of sun shine, it's a happy sound coming from the back yard. Since Lyman's encouragement, Carly's been practicing her dance moves; presently moving to and fro to a song only she hears in her pretty little bell tower. Gazing hard at her playful daughter's trusting innocence, Stella wipes a little tear that's struggling to squeeze out through the corner of her eyes, she lets out a little laugh that could just as easily be a cry. Her emotions are running rampant. Seeing the innocent exuberance in her daughter through the window, she reaches out blindly for Frankie drawing him close. His arm passing about her waist. Stella hangs on to Frankie; She frightfully hangs on as one who still has unresolved issues that haven't been shared, at the same time not willing to bring them to the surface at this point. There is no caress on her part, rather it's an embrace of one becoming fearful of tumbling helplessly over a cliff without a net.

Stella's tough image is beginning to crack. She's been attempting to balance her life with work and being a mother to Carly. Her fears of losing what she is just beginning to hold dear are hanging over her head. It's as though her youth is being stripped from her, day by day. Looking for a diversion, she busies herself with making coffee.

Frankie sits back, lights another cigarette, and offers Stella a drag, which she readily takes. He's not quite able to read her. Frankie watches her worry. "You just gotta stay cool, Stella, and keep an eye on our little piano player. He can't do anything," Frankie proclaims.

Stella begins to pour them each a cup of coffee. Finally breaking her silence, she exclaims, "It ain't just me keeping my eye on him. That's easy. It's his eye on me that's givin' me heartburn."

Trying to be as sympathetic to her concerns as he can, but still with an eye on the crisis from the mainland crawling in on them, Frankie comments back, "I don't blame you for your frettin', Stella, but we gotta deal with the hand we're dealt. But, so do they. So far, we're doin' okay. We got 'em on the ropes. Now all we gotta do is make sure we keep 'em there."

Stella stares out of the window, past her daughter, and out into the emptiness of the lake. Her old environment at Squeaky's was miserable, but the misery had a degree of familiar predictability about it. "I sure hope yer right, Frankie. If there ain't nothin' else I've learned in this life, it's hope can be a cruel thing," she says, tucking her head deep into his shoulder.

Frankie contemplates the full brunt of his responsibility to avoid bringing the wrath of these thugs down on not just himself, but also on everyone he holds dear. He remains silent for the moment. It's tearing him up to have to see his family's business destroyed, his father beaten near to death, and now his girlfriend falling apart over the pressure of dealing with all this unrest. *I just want to get a gun and blow their damn heads off* is his first thought. He's well aware of how many he's already sent to hell as a sniper, and it wouldn't bother him to send this bunch to join them, but there's something that has gotten much deeper into his character. Remembering his sniper training in 'remaining patient', Frankie catches himself. With a deep breath and an exhale, he lets his second thoughts begin to move toward the forefront *If we stay calm, keep our resolve, I know we can win this war—we just gotta stay smart.* Rising from this confrontation with Stella more slowly, he says his goodbyes for the moment. It's time, once again, to face their ragged reality as it comes at them.

With this befuddling new Purple threat forcing its way into their lives, Frankie decides it's best to meet personally with all his compatriots. He needs to update them in their adversary's change in tactics. Hardly able to trust everyone completely, he nonetheless calls for a meeting for the next day. Because of his fear of nosy ears, his plan is to convene as casual as possible on one of Barnes' private ferry boats making a trip downriver.

His inner group consists of Axel Weinberg; Jerry Ferris from the Old Club; William Barnes, who owns the ferry service; Mark Kingsbury, who manages the Riverside Hotel; Harry Knapp from the Grand Point Hotel; and Bob Jansen from the Star Island House. This group has all suffered enough at the hands of the Purples to have long ago turned the corner in desiring to rid themselves of this stifling plague at any cost. Come hell or high water, today they have all committed themselves to solve the problems they altogether share in their misfortune of having to deal with the Burnstein brothers.

It's a beautiful fall day. The river is calm. Frankie has gotten an early start. *It's a shame to have to waste a day like this waging war against the likes of these men.* Frankie makes his way north to the ferry landing. As he gazes out in the distance, his eye catches the steamer Tashmoo steaming its way to its destination. It's already loaded with tourists hoping to enjoy these last few days of fall. The flats are also occupied by flocks of Canadian geese and wild Mallards, which are all honking at once, as if to notify hunters that they're preparing themselves for the fall sacrifice.

With this committee of "resistance brothers" converging all at once, they remain as discreet as possible and attempt to look like a random group of recreationalists preparing for some informal destination downriver. They position their cars on board as casually as ever. In an attempt to prevent some hired captain with a possible allegiance to another entity from overhearing their discussions, Barnes has personally assumed the position of skipper.

With no special revelation, Barnes guides the boat out of its slip as though it's nothing more than an unhurried excursion downriver. Once they have rounded a bend, which takes them south, he anchors the ferry and joins the group that's already gathered across the deck. This assembly of men from different walks of life has joined together and is prepared to hammer out a plan of action to stave off the Detroit interlopers.

Bob Jansen is the first to throw his hat in the ring on this latest development. "I ain't never shot anybody in my life, but after what they put us through at Star Island, I could put a gun in each hand and empty 'em both in their heartless carcasses." He pauses for a moment, hoping to gain approval from his compatriots. He adds, "When we decided we couldn't continue to pay the insurance they demanded, they took one of our innocent employees, splayed him open like a hog, and hung him from our flag pole. They're worse than animals."

Mark Kingsbury has his own horror stories to recount. "They kidnapped my daughter and held her hostage, and they put her on the phone as one of them was violating her. They told me I had no one other to blame than myself for being so selfish in taking my family out from under their protection. They then continued demanding payment, and threatened that things would get worse. We had no other choice but to pay. My wife still blames me for our daughter's trauma."

Several others continued in the same vein, recounting similar atrocities that only an evil horde could initiate. All this was done in the name of some underworld business paradigm designed to bring their greedy, unstable ends to completion.

Listening to account after account of malevolence on the part of these criminals, Frankie has no doubt as to his crew's commitment to right all the wrongs, but he knows they all need to be on the same page. To do this, they need to continue to seek well thought out plans that will lay out solid methods to counter any attempt on the Purples' part to imagine they have come anywhere near winning this war. The discussion continues late into the afternoon.

Frankie listens to each, letting them individually air their grievances. His patience only serves to further the group's resolve to push these intruders off their island. He knows many of these ordinary men are reaching far above their individual courage to even dare to imagine this can be accomplished. If this meeting does nothing more than set their souls on fire with their desire to remain free to lead their lives without the threat of a group of racketeering bullies from the city determining their livelihoods, he will consider it a good start.

Frankie ultimately finds he needs to give the group some direction. Careful not to allow a blind battle madness to overtake his crew, he starts with, "What we're sayin' here are big words, but they ain't worth a tinker's dam 'less we can back 'em up. We know they've planted a mole in that piano playin' kid over at the Old Club." Pointing toward Jerry, he continues, "Jerry's got that one nailed down pretty good, but their next move is anybody's guess. This war's just beginnin'. Bein' diligent and ready ta move when we need to is gonna go a long way in stayin' on top a these mongrels."

Mark Kingsbury is the most fragile of the group of all the men in this meeting. It's without a doubt because of his own harrowing firsthand experiences in his personal struggle with the Purples to get his daughter back unharmed. As if anything more needed to be added to that point, he decides to bring his concerns to the floor. "I ain't a gun fighter like you Frankie, I just ain't made for it. I know a lot of you guys, 'cause of your huntin' skills, an' how ya all been in the military, are all first-rate gun handlers, but I ain't never even shot a gun, much less kilt a man."

Frankie's thoughts are whirling around wildly. It remains plain Frankie is the acknowledged leader with all eyes focused on him awaiting a response. His desire is to have a good cohesive group of men that are not only trustworthy, but also with some back bone.

He listens to Mark's concerns with understanding, and then says, "I ain't ever gonna ask a man ta do something' he ain't comfortable doin', Mark. But there's a lot of other stuff you can be doin', like keepin' a damn good eye and ear open for what you see that ain't fittin' in good with the island. Besides, you did a damn good job drivin' that naked bunch to the ferry." They all get a good laugh out of that scenario, and it's enough to place Mark at ease.

What prevails among this group of diverse individuals is a longing to rid their island of the type of beasts the Purples are sending to do their dirty work. It's a first rate "common cause." Within this resistance group, some are like Mark wanting to protect their family, others are just sick and tired of the intimidation and the shakedowns.

What they're battling against are fighting men of the most brutal descriptions. These men enjoy killing—the more ruthlessly, the better. They've become hardened to whatever killing requires, and they're always finding new methods to demonstrate their professional proficiency. The more callous, cruel, pitiless behavior they display in dealing with their victims, the more in demand they become. They're beyond socially and morally dysfunctional.

In Frankie's corner, matters are running in a satisfactory direction. This gives him hope he can see more of the successes this group effort has been able to achieve to date. Frankie's natural ability to manage these volunteers is proving to be an advantage. He's pleased they've arrived at a mutual consensus and wishes to leave them in an upbeat mode, so he shakes their hands while he says, "Before we all go our separate ways, I want to commend you men on how well you've all worked together. It's truly a piece of good fortune to have us all on the same team."

Satisfied that they indeed are a strong team, and considering this a rare blessing, the group returns to the mainland. Soon they're getting back on the roads that lead to their individual homes. Each feels a renewed assurance that they have the other's back. If they continue to work together, they can win this confrontation.

****

Back in Detroit, in contrast, the Purples are having problems. The term "There is no honor among thieves" holds a special place in the Purples' organization. Many of the "Juniors" are feeling their being played and not being brought into the gang's front lines as expeditiously as they seek. They tend to get pushy and mouthy about their unlikable status quo. Consequently, many of these underdogs find themselves losing favor among those in power, being shoved aside for a more useful contender. This, in turn, is causing a few of these Juniors to believe the only way they can move forward is to seek a level of competition with the mainstream racketeers on their own.

This rebellion is not going unnoticed.

Some are working to break into the numbers game, some in prostitution, and those that are gaining the quickest attention of their much more powerful counterparts are gaining ground in selling liquor. This is a narrow tightrope walk. If these underlings don't find themselves in position to provide a service essential to the good of the syndicate at large, they will quickly be viewed as competitors and eliminated.

Detroit is unique; it's different than Chicago and New York. There is so much money available here that it's unbelievable there's anyone left in the public sector that is not receiving a payoff. It's reported that the illegal liquor business is generating 250 million dollars a year in revenues. This amount of money is second only to General Motors. With so many in law enforcement on the take, there is a huge void in the prosecution of rumrunners and bootleggers. In turn, when disputes arise among this group, it's usually deadly, and there is very little interference from law enforcement.

This brings into scrutiny the Little Jewish Navy. It's bankrolled by a group of these juniors who have managed to carve out a little chunk of the liquor business for themselves. In spite of this group being outsiders, they're tolerated by the Burnsteins because they have agreed to exclusively supply the mainline Purples with liquor. In other words, they have found a niche that the Purples consider essential.

They're bankrolled up by men with monikers like "One-Armed Gelfin and Moe Dalitz." They in turn have employed a group of juniors who have made themselves valuable by their ruthlessness. With money that could only come from the vast profits in rum-running, this group has outfitted themselves with high-powered speedboats that are unevenly matched against the average cottage industry rumrunner. Nor have law enforcement, whose budgets hardly cover their wages, been able to rid the waters of this invader. They have been running rough shod over some of Frankie's "resistance" supporters by waiting until they are on their way back with a load of Canadian liquor, and hijack their cargo. When this action is repeated many times a week, it only adds to the bottom line of the mob.

Albie Lieberman is one of these unfortunates. He has a small boat, but he's been able to supply a couple of small speakeasies in Algonac. Despite the fact that the Purples control some twenty thousand speakeasies in Detroit, they are of the mind they can't permit anyone to get a foothold in what they consider is theirs alone to profit. Daily exhibitions of this navy, first in their hijacking a load of liquor from one of these small-time guys, then, pillaging and plundering anything else of value they might have on board has become the signature this faction of the syndicate wishes to leave with its victims. Those that show the slightest resistance find themselves fish food.

Albie, along with a few other bush-league Harsens Island rumrunners, have contacted Frankie about their plight in the hopes they can get some support. The problem is, the Little Jewish Navy might only have half a dozen of these boats in this area, but they have no recognizable order as to who and where they are going to hit. In the meantime, there are most likely several hundred little guys up and down the St. Clair and Detroit rivers. Everything from small duck boats to canoes crosses the short span to Canada and risks being attacked in the hopes of making a few bucks.

Frankie listens to what each of them has to voice, then challenges each of them by saying, "Since you're coming to our resistance group for help, you realize we're all in this together, I need you to have some skin in the game too, so what I expect you to do is to spend some time locating the harbors these culprits are hiding their boats. When you pull that off, come back with the information and we'll talk some more."

Albie, along with his group of protestors, are at first put off by Frankie's abrupt stipulation to become part of the solution to their ongoing problem with the Purples. But, the longer they spend with Frankie, the more he is able to convince them of the value of working together. In the end, a kindlier spirit comes over them, and they leave convinced Frankie's way is feasible. They have reached an agreement to make this effort, not only for their own benefit, but also for their neighbors who are suffering the same difficulties.

They begin their surveillance by hanging around the drinking clubs on the Michigan side of the river. This is the most logical place to begin since alcohol has a way of making lips a lot looser than a restaurant garden salad. It takes a few days, but as predicted they run into a loose-tongued junior who can't stop bragging how fast these boats are able to travel, and his role in their operation. Part of becoming a hardcore gangster is the ability to drink heavy and let people know in various drunken ways that you're not someone who is easily dismissed.

Albie plays right into this guy's self-importance by giving him the impression that he's impressed by his rank within the Purples. This, in turn, frees the tongue of this stooge, who identifies himself as Bob. With the ego of one who wishes to show his standing, he invites these newly made drinking pals to take a look at these vessels.

Finishing his drink, and with a sense of prominence, he loads them up in his own sedan, beginning his trek to this little-known cove. "It ain't that far from here. I'm here ta tell ya these boats are slicker 'n shit runnin' through a tin horn. There ain't nothin' can touch 'em. They grind these Harsens Island rubes (hicks) inta little pieces and spits 'em out," he says with a knowing little chuckle. In showing off his importance, he naively reveals the location of the cove in which the boats are harbored. It's in a little-known, sparsely populated area. The only road in and out is more of a trail than a road. Unless one knew of this cove, it would be easier to overlook it than to discover it. To further add to its seclusion, the channel leading to the dock is canopied under a double line of Weeping Willow limbs spreading from one side of the channel to the other. It's one of thousands of hidden coves up and down the river.

With this information, Albie can't wait to get back with Frankie. Hardly able to hold back the excitement he has for their success, he's nearly coming apart. "I can't believe how this shitfaced dumbass showed us these boats! He even bragged how he's a spotter watchin' for boats goin' and comin' from Canada. These guys must think they're invincible, ta be that open."

Contemplating on Albie's account of his reconnaissance activities, Frankie lowers his head in thought. Raising his head back up, he congratulates Albie for work well down. A wry little grin begins to spread across his face. He might have another surprise for this group of city slickers. Shaking Albie's hand, continuing his approval on his efforts, Frankie confidently adds "They might think they're untouchable, but I think we can put a wrench in their cog. Keep me posted if you learn anything more."

For the present, Frankie has all the information he needs to take this mission to the next level. He's familiar with the cove these boats are harbored and decides to make a personal inspection. It's a well concealed lair with a twisted channel concealing it with over hanging trees. To accomplish this exploit, he drives to the other side of the island with the intention of contacting his friend Dave Schindler.

Dave is a fellow veteran of the Great War and a pilot with an Areomarine 40 flying boat. He's outwitted the Navy by managing to buy as salvage one of their boat/aircraft that served as a training plane during the Great War. Using every Army-Navy surplus depot across the country, he's also managed to hunt down the spare parts he needs. This endeavor has allowed him to reconstruct this prototype nearly back into the original version. The only change he's made is to have augmented the fuselage a bit to meet his own needs. He did this by retrofitting a portion of it as a cargo area capable of carrying twenty-five cases of liquor. This craft is capable of doing seventy knots in the air—nothing comes close to competing with him. With this air advantage, it's no wonder rum-running has provided him with a successful land office business. The last time the Purples attempted to use airplanes, they all crashed. This was a fifty-thousand-dollar lesson they're not ready to test again anytime soon.

Frankie has made his way to the middle channel where Dave keeps his plane out of sight in a boathouse. They haven't seen much of one another since they returned home on the same ship from the war.

"Well, I'll be hanged if it ain't Mrs. Morgansky's little boy, Frankie!" declares Dave with his biggest good-hearted smile. "I been hearin' rumors 'bout you, ya ol' dog. Hell Frankie, yer damn near a legend here on Harsens nowadays."

"Good ta see you too. Been hearin' how there ain't nothin on the water or in the air 'at can run ya down," replies Frankie just as good naturedly.

"That don't mean they don't try. Them damnable Purples with their speedboats, and Tommy guns give me a headache, but so far I been able ta get in the air and outta range of any fatal shots."

Taking off his cap and smoothing out his hair, Frankie signals he's got something in mind. "How'd you like ta get rid a that headache for a while with a change in a line of attack?" asks Frankie in a little more serious voice.

The question stops Dave for a moment. He looks puzzled.

Seeing Dave's bewilderment, Frankie opts to keep talking, "The straight of it is, this harassment from these damnable Purples is what's bringin' me over here ta see you."

Dave's head shoots up like he's just received an upper-cut. "Keep talkin', I'm all ears," is all Dave has to say. He's making it clear the aggravation caused by these derelict Jewish Navy boats plagues him to distraction, realizing, "One lucky shot from one of those "Chicago typewriters" is all it will take to put me out of commission."

Confident he's gained Dave's attention, Frankie continues, "I got some good information on the cove where they hide their speedboats. I need ta check it out. The way I got it figured is, ta do it without suspicion is from the air. That's where you come in. I figure we can fly over that area an' get an eyeball on their set up."

Seeing he's more than caught Dave's interest, and with even a more serious voice, he adds, "After we get that out of the way, I got a plan I wanna share with ya that's certain ta be an expensive lesson that will definitely get their attention."

Dave listens with a bent ear. He's been plagued as much as anyone by these sea-faring hustlers ever since his entrance into the rum-running business.

"I ain't willin' ta wait, Frankie. If I'm gonna get involved, I wanna know from the get-go what I'm gettin' into," says Dave. His face indicates a kind of savage resolve.

Realizing he might be losing Dave's support, Frankie quickly attempts to think of a good way of presenting his idea, "There ain't no doubt these guys are stronger than us out in the open. But when it comes to guerilla tactics, we beat 'em every time. There ain't no way we're gonna end this with one terrible headlong attack, but I know ways we can make a thousand small cuts on 'em, in the end it'll be just as fatal on 'em as a knife in the heart."

Listening to himself, Frankie pauses in an attempt to present his scheme in a more scholarly manner, instead, he just blurts out, "I figure we can bomb the dirty bastard's navy from the air before they know what hit 'em!"

Dave looks straight at Frankie with a blank stare. With no good way to scrutinize Dave's indifferent reaction, it catches Frankie off guard placing him somewhere between despair and delight. Frankie has no idea from Dave's near expressionless face how he's taking to this scheme. Suddenly, Dave's countenance goes from vacant to an explosive laugh. It's quickly becoming apparent this proposal has certainly gone beyond Dave's indifference.

In that moment, Dave makes his response clear-cut. Slapping Frankie on the back, he shouts, "Now this is damned exciting! Count me in, man! I ain't had a good sortie since the war ended. This is just what I need! I don't know why I never thought of doin' that myself."

Frankie is inwardly electrified with Dave's enthusiasm. Entering into a fracas with the Purples is no minor decision. Trying to maintain a cool decorum over this major accomplishment, Frankie opts to hold his tongue and let Dave make the next move.

He immediately finds himself being enthusiastically motioned forward. Dave leads Frankie inside his boathouse. The boat/airplane hangar is on its own private river channel. It's an expensive, state-of-the-art building that significantly reflects his success as a rumrunner. It's a fieldstone structure built with several levels allowing his prized Areomarine 40 to set on hydraulic rails raising it out of the water. The enclosed boathouse also keeps prying eyes from viewing more of his business than needs be.

Walking him up a small flight of stairs where they are met by a wing on the plane, Dave takes a moment to draw Frankie's attention to several patches. Far from being conciliatory, he points to them and says, "This is what I was tellin' you about bein' lucky. This was caused by a stray .45 cartridge from one of their goddam Tommy guns."

Frankie sees a kind of bullet damage he hasn't witnessed since he was in the war. "You're damn lucky it wasn't yer head," says Frankie with the concern of one who shares the same uneasiness.

Readily dismissing any thoughts like this comment that has never materialized, Dave prefers to live in the moment—so far, the present moment lacks any thing to fear. With a bravado of a military pilot, he continues to wave him forward. In the back of this structure they are met by a set of double doors. Standing in front of these closures with a carved lions head in high relief on each of them, Dave reaches into his pocket producing a set of keys, ceremoniously unlocks them, and with a confident flair, he swings them opened. Frankie isn't totally surprised to see them lead into a tunnel system that runs to the main house, complete with storage areas along the way where cases of liquor can be stowed. This storage accommodation also allows Dave to play the fluctuations of the liquor market by buying low and selling high.

Off to the side of this entrance is another set of steps. These lead up to a third level over the boathouse. This proves to be a pavilion that's used to entertain friends and enjoy the spectacular view of river events such as the sailboat races, and other water activities. Dave has a series of telescopes and binoculars that allow him and his guests to become more of a part of these actions—that's not to minimize their use in aiding him in a heads up on the lake activity provided by the Little Jewish Navy.

Dave's excitement can hardly be contained as he next leads Frankie into his elaborate home and furnishing—all thanks to prohibition.

"I never could have had the life I'm enjoying now if it hadn't been for that 'brilliant' Volstead Act. But what come with it is these punks in their goddam silk-suits and Tommy-guns," says Dave with a bit of sharpness in his words. There's a little dramatic pause before he continues. "I'm with you a hundred percent, Frankie. Since I'm only a one man show, I ain't been able ta come up with anything more than a goddam resentment toward these mongrels. I've heard a lot about what you been doin', Frankie, an' been half-tempted ta join up with ya."

Frankie is more than delighted to discover Dave's enthusiasm to become a part of the island's resistance. "Well, yer here now an' I'm here now, so let's getter done. I know this part is somethin' we can finish," says an elated Frankie.

After going over Frankie's plan, they decide the best time for their surprise attack is, *at the crack of dawn when these bimbos are, more than likely, sleepin' one off.*

In the meantime, Frankie obliges one more component of this operation that needs attention. "What we need ta do next is ta put together a supply of what the Russkies call Molotov cocktails." They spend the next hour filling empty liquor bottles with gasoline and stuffing a rag fuse in the opening of each one. They are careful to store them in a container that can be safely placed in the cockpit.

The time has finally come to act. Agreeing to put off more of this action until morning, they part. Frankie makes his way to Axel's cottage alerting him to what he and Dave have set up for the next day. Listening thoughtfully, Axel crushes out the butt of his cigarette in an ash tray. Reaching into his shirt pocket, he produces a half-filled pack of Murad's. After shaking another one out of the pack, he lights it. With a look somewhere between quizzical and worried, he says, "I hope you ain't openin' a hornet's nest. It's one thing ta be defendin' ourselves, an' another ta be goin' after 'em."

For a moment, Axel's words strike a new chord. Frankie has gotten so obsessed with his quest to be rid of these adversaries that he hadn't noticed the shift he's made from defense to offense. The only thought he can come up with to respond to Axel's perception is, "Well, you know the best defense is a strong offense." He hopes this axiom will be true in his case.

Taking a deep drag on his Murad, Axel says, "I hope you ain't bitin' off more 'n you can chew, Frankie."

Frankie has always had the highest regard for Axel's input, and this is no exception, but Frankie is also consumed with his desire to rid the island of this plague of mobsters.

"Your point is well taken, Axel. Right now, the only thing that keeps breath in my body is that I can rid Harsens of these parasites. I still feel this maneuver will prove to be an expensive loss for those guys providin' the Purples with this navy. They'll have to think twice about the possibility of the same fate happenin' again when they're considerin' on replacin' 'em."

"Believe me Frankie, them Purples can afford ta buy as many of them boats as they can build," echoes Axel.

"And we can wreck 'em just as fast," comes back Frankie followed by an unwound silence.

Recognizing Frankie's stoic gaze as one of an iron resolve, Axel voices, "You know I'm with ya all the way, Frankie, I jus' want ya ta think about what I'm sayin'."

Frankie mind is in a whirl. This dilemma is definitely causing him to juggle around Axel's concern with the fact that his resistance membership is growing, and many of these like Dave are bringing resources *to* bear he never knew existed. *A good night's sleep is what I need. I'll think this over tomorrow* is his final resolution for the day. With that settled, he hits the pillow satisfied he's on a fruitful course. The night is shortened with his alarm clock waking him in time to make good his commitment to meet Dave at dawn.

Meeting Dave is merely the beginning of a process of thought that must go beyond the moment. They have dangerous work to do, a hesitation in attention can only be considered as a digression in completing their mission. Both of these men are relying on a common practice of combat training that has become a part of them. This class of wide-range training results in a mindset of anticipating the other's move without extensive conversation. This schooling has always proven to have an advantage over those without comprehensive combat preparation.

Dave begins the process by lowering his flying boat from its elaborate rail system above the water back down into the boathouse's still waters below. It's a wonderful machine with its powerful hundred horsepower engine mounted behind the open cockpit. It's a bi-winged bird with side-by-side seating and a contoured, boat-like hull for a nose. The view is perfect from this position with the accompaniment of two side by side curved windshields protecting the pilot and passenger.

Dave has maneuvered it out of its berth and is arranging all his gauges to allow a takeoff. Before he puts this flying machine in the air, he demands the same serious routine from himself in appraising its every aspect as would a surgeon before an appendectomy. After Dave completes a careful study of the multiple gauges, they reveal they're in sync and prepared to have him put this rig in the air.

Without warning, Dave moves the throttle to a wide-open position, causing the sea plane to skim across the water at a speed not undergone by most land or sea dwellers. Frankie feels a pull on his body that he's never experienced before in his life. It's as though some parts of nature are fighting for his possession; one part of his body is being driven forward, while another part is fighting to stay put. With a roar that only a machine of this type can produce, its nose lifts off the water's surface, pulling its two passengers and the tail section into the air as though they've all suddenly become weightless.

A sense of wonder overtakes Frankie. He's suddenly viewing his beloved Harsens Island from a perspective he could only have imagined. The higher they go, the more prominent the rising eastern sun becomes; it's as though they have hooked it with an invisible cable and are dragging it higher into the sky. Everything is brilliant. The blues are bluer, the sections of marshes around the island all flaunt their distinctness by displaying their own color variations with hues of green to brown. The waters are also exhibiting their ability to refract the sun in an array of colors, depths, and currents with varying undulations of waves and ripples. This picture has Frankie mesmerized. It would all be nothing more than a pleasurable jaunt in the sky if it weren't for the urgency of their mission.

Frankie has given Dave the location of their target. Dave is all business in finding the site as he banks the plane and begins to follow the river.

"We need to pay attention to land marks," shouts Dave in an attempt to make himself heard above the roar of the engine.

Frankie finds this perspective strange as he struggles to rewire his thinking. This is all brand new to him, after all, he's never been in an airplane in his life. Seeing what he believes to be land mark below, he signals Dave to fly in that direction. It's soon apparent they have flown past their objective, but in a corrective move, Dave banks the plane and repositions it. They're high enough to remain above suspicion should anyone notice a plane in the sky this early in the day. Suddenly, there below them, veiled by the trees, sit a half-dozen speed boats, all in a row, all tied to a single dock. There doesn't appear to be any human activity—no cars in the parking area. All in all, the whole scene appears just the way Albie described it.

Absolutely sure they've pinpointed their target, Dave heads back downriver to their starting point. They need to return to pick up the Molotov Cocktails as well as to plan out the details of their strategy. To say this is going to be a dangerous undertaking is to understate the entire operation. Flying a plane has its own challenges without adding a box of gasoline-filled bottles to its cargo.

With the sure realization time is of the essence, they quickly agree on a tactic. The next step is to safely load the gasoline bombs into a space where they won't spill. Dave has supplied an empty, metal ammunition box with a lid. The hope is this will isolate all the bombs except the one being prepared. It's agreed the only practical place for easy access to these is at Frankie's feet. A box of kitchen matches and a windless place to light them are going to become a contest to get the wicks lit and not blow the plane to smithereens in the process.

With nothing more than resolve, a reasonable amount of tenacity and skill to get the job done, they embark on their quest. Dave has planned out a strategy for Frankie to follow. It involves a series of hand signals since speaking over the noise of the motor is unreasonable. All of the bomb drops have to be synchronized with the height and speed the plane will be traveling over the targets so they won't fall short or over shoot the target.

Mindful of each of their tasks, the target comes in sight. A bank of clouds has rolled in bringing the sky's ceiling down allowing Dave to fly in several different directions without a blazing sun blinding their efforts. Their intensity increases. Dave makes a pass to assess the current situation. By all indications, it continues to remain free of human activity. Banking the plane to return, he drops down to within treetop level of their target. On a signal, crouching in his cockpit area, Frankie strikes the kitchen match, which quickly ignites the rag fuse. In a single fluid motion, he lobs the bomb overboard. Its blaze sends a trail of yellow flame as it drops short of the target.

"Oh shit, I missed it," says Frankie, unheard over the rumble of the engine.

Undaunted, Dave pulls back on the stick, returning the plane to a position to make another run. This time, he waits another second before signaling Frankie. Frankie's heart is racing with anticipation. With the same calm dexterity, he used to pull the trigger on his sniper rifle, he strikes the match. The bomb is lit and over the side, dropping the fifty feet to its hopeful mark. All that is seen but not heard is the yellow ball of fire as it hits the boats.

"BINGO!" shouts Frankie.

All that can be seen of Dave is the satisfied smile breaking out across his face. Revenge has its sweet spots, and needs to be celebrated quickly, as it can be short lived. All warriors know this and waste no time in celebrating victories. With their timing more or less perfected, they manage to dump the rest of their bomb concoctions ensuring these boats will never float again. This leg of the operation has taken no more than twenty minutes, hopefully unseen. Returning to Dave's boat/plane hangar, Dave breaks out a bottle of his "Real

McCoy" and lavishly pours each a glass as they sit above in the pavilion satisfied to watch a distant patch of smoke against the sky.

CHAPTER 16
A Righteous Date

Passing by Jerry Ferris's office window at the Old Club, Stella finds him making an effort to get her attention. He's behind his desk, talking on the phone and gesturing for her to come in. She cautiously cracks open his door, giving him a questioning gaze. He's still engrossed with the phone call while he's beckoning her to sit.

With a hand on his hip, he asks the mystery party on the other end of the call, "Who else is aware of these details?" Of course, only Jerry is privy to the answer.

"Okay. That's fine as long as you keep me in the loop," declares Jerry, with a mark of purpose manifesting in his voice.

Stella gingerly steps into the room and cautiously takes a seat across from Jerry's desk. Without complaining, she waits for him to get to the point of this sit-down. After a few more exchanges with this mystery person, Jerry faces Stella, hands her the telephone across his desk, and says, "It's Frankie. He'd like to speak with you."

With an even more questioning gaze, Stella puts the phone to her ear. "Hello," she says. There is a tinge of caution in her speech as she absentmindedly twists the cord around her finger several times.

"Hello, Stella. I hope this call didn't startle you." It's unmistakably Frankie's voice.

"Well, it's not your usual way of gettin' a hold of me, now is it?"

"No, it ain't, but circumstances have changed again, and I need to make you aware of them."

Spending the next few minutes to catch Stella up on the success he and Dave had in destroying the Jewish Navy, he concludes with an indispensable question. "Can you keep an extra watchful eye on our pigeon, Lyman? Chances are, he'll be gettin' a call from Axler. I know damn well this ain't gonna set good with these goons, so if you can get any information as to what they might be up to, it will go a long way."

Stella is listening to every word Frankie is saying. She is attempting to process the consequences of this new episode. She runs her hand across her cheek. The lingering soreness reminds her why she has this haunting fear of a repeat attack. On the other hand, she knows these people won't stop until they achieve their goal. *It's tiring me to have to think about this stuff.* Her previous hope of moving to the island for a quiet, stress-free life for herself and Carly has all but evaporated. This latest development is quickly putting any idea of a beautiful ending to bed. The stress in her voice tells it all.

"Frankie, I don't know how much longer I can live with this worrying how and when these bullies are going to torment our lives and you keep throwin' gas on the fire by doin' shit that I know they ain't gonna sit still for," says Stella.

After the exhilaration of giving the mob still another failure, Frankie is taken aback by Stella's seeming negativity. "Stella why are you so negative? We've beat their ass at every turn."

"Because I know first-hand how ruthless these guys are gonna be now that we've established ourselves as the baby pit bull nippin' at their heels. They'll stop at nothing to take you out. There'll be so goddam many guys tryin' ta collect on the contract put on your head, they'll be killin' each other ta just get a crack at ya. I've seen 'em do it a hunnerd times!" exclaims Stella. She is truly distraught. Her hand is shaking the phone against her ear as she tries to pay attention to Frankie's reply.

"Stella, we didn't win the war in Europe by hidin' our heads in the sand, an' I ain't gonna start now. These thugs ain't no different than them German muggers. We can defeat 'em if we stick together and don't lose our willpower."

Stella is finding it hard to live in this spot. Adapting and overcoming have not been things in which she's had formal schooling; she's not spent one day in military training the likes of Frankie.

"Frankie, lessen you get done with all this, you gonna be the death of us all," she laments.

Clearly hearing the distress in Stella's voice, Frankie's hoping to paint a clearer picture. Carefully picking his words in an attempt not to mirror her angst, he says, "I know how you feel Stella, but none of us are gonna be free of these cockroaches unless we fight back. They'll suck the life outta all of Harsens just like they're tryin'. We gotta stay together and not let these bastards grind us down. We can win if we stick together—just like we learned in Europe—freedom ain't cheap."

Even though she is speaking to Frankie over the phone and isn't face to face, Stella can't miss the commitment and perseverance in Frankie's voice. It gives her hope despite her fears. He's always been there to pick up the pieces. *This is why I love you, Frankie*, she thinks, surprising herself.

With a deep sigh of resignation, Stella says, "Okay, big boy. You win again. I hope you ain't dreamin'. I'll do my part, but don't get the idea I'm some kinda wonder woman, 'cause I ain't. I jus' don't see that star as bright as you do."

"That's all I ask, Stella. You just do the part of keepin' an eye an' ear open with this rat. It's better to deal with a devil we know than one we don't," says a reconciled Frankie. "Just like you, Stella, I wish this wasn't happenin', but it is. Life goes in its own direction. How we react is up ta us, so we gotta play the hand we're dealt as best we can."

Stella hands the phone back to Jerry. He can't help but see the worry in Stella's face. It compels him enough to comment, "Don't worry so much, Stella. I agree with you that Frankie sees this whole bout with these damnable Purples through different eyes, but you must remember it wasn't that long ago that he was fightin' in a war we won."

Stella hears what Jerry is saying. Nonetheless, she can't help but remain in worry mode. *All I want is my dumb little life to be normal.* She has no more words to say. Alone with her thoughts, she turns and walks out of the office, closing the door behind her.

Without thought, Stella finds herself wandering outside. Everything is normal. The fall air is pure and crisp. The lawns are still a deep green although the leaves are beginning to take on falls paintbrush of reds and yellows. Her gaze drifts out across the bay toward the mainland. From here, it's hard to imagine there could be an evil lurking to defile this beautiful place.

With this menacing possibility lingering in her thoughts, her restlessness suddenly comes to a halt. She spots a familiar form making his way across the lawns. It's Lyman. It seems he's been talking over the gate at the club's entrance to an unidentified man. It's obvious he has finished a conversation with what appears to be a stranger. The man outside the gate hastily returns to his car and leaves. Whatever this conversation might have consisted of, it's left Lyman on a dead heat to get inside the club.

Watching Lyman's behavior returns her to the real world. All her senses are suddenly intensified. She is suddenly jerked onto another course of action. Without hesitation, careful not to give her hand away, and without a second thought, she is on him like hound.

Unaware of Stella, Lymie ducks into one of the two phone booths. Stella waits until he closes his door before she also abruptly follows suit in the adjoining compartment. The clang of his coin and the clicking noise of the dial tell her he is making a call.

"Hello, Mr. Fletcher. This is Lyman Woodard. My I speak with Mr. Axler?"

Long pause.

"Hello Mr. Axler, this is Lyman. Uh, I'm fine. Thank you, sir."

Another slight pause. It's obvious there is unheard conversation coming from the other end of the line.

"I believe I have some pertinent information."

Pause.

"It has to do with the destruction of your boats, sir."

Pause.

"I'm pretty sure the information is good, it came from an island constable—you know, the guy you told me was on the payroll."

Pause.

"He told me he had information linking Frankie Morgansky and a guy named Dave Schindler, who owns a plane. Evidently they flew in there and dropped Molotov cocktails."

Pause.

"You're welcome, sir."

Pause.

"No, sir, there isn't anything I need at the moment."

Pause.

"No, sir. I won't hesitate to let you know if anything else comes to the surface."

Pause.

"Goodbye, sir."

The next thing Stella hears is the click of the hand unit hitting the hanger and the neighboring booth door opening. With her own door closed, her back turned, phone to her ear pretending to be talking, she crouches into the corner, hoping to be ignored by this stool-pigeon passing by. He is on his usual full court press to somewhere and pays no attention.

Waiting until she feels he's left, Stella cautiously places her coin in the slot and dials a number that has become quite familiar.

In a low, nearly inaudible voice, Stella says, "Hello, Frankie—got bad news. That fink Lyman just told Axler you was behind that boat burnin'."

There is an expected hesitation on Frankie's part as he digests this information.

"Well, ain't that just the bees' knees. So our little stoolie is doin' his job. Well, done Stella. Then on another note Frankie continues in another whole direction. "What say we get together tomorrow? I miss you."

She can't think of a reason to say no. Her heart nearly skips a beat as she says, "I was hopin' you'd find some time. I was thinkin' you forgot about us."

"No, sweetheart. It's lonesome bein' out here without you."

Even though Stella is on the other end of the phone line, she shoots a glare that Frankie can hear in her voice. "All I feel is agony. Yer off doin' this combat stuff. All I do is gaze at where your footsteps are takin' us and wonder if we're ever gonna have a life worth livin'."

Frankie fires back. "If I gotta brace up for you kickin up a fuss at everything I'm sayin' an' tryin' ta do for us an' everybody else on this island, I'm gonna bust!" His voice has definitely taken on a different tone from the complying Frankie she's accustomed to, to that of a war worn battler. "I feel like all you're doin' is kickin' me in the head."

This is the first time since their reunion that Frankie has spoken harshly with Stella. After a moment of near shock, she collects her wits. "I don't mean ta do that, Frankie. It's just I been hopin' I'd have more of you. Like you said, it's a lonesome town out here alone."

Frankie takes a moment to process where this argument might be heading. Wanting to cut it off at the pass, he declares, "I think we're both worn out and aren't very nice, we probably said all we need to say for a while."

The conversation halts; both of them see where this is leading. *Get a hold of yourself* is the thought running through both their minds.

Frankie is next to speak. "I wish I could be there for you like you want. I'm sure I can at some point, but right now, we have no chance of that happenin'. We need to get these predators off our island. These people have a way of consuming everything they touch—the powerful always do."

"I hear your words, Frankie, but I'm still afraid. I wish I had your strength."

"You do, Stella. You just don't know it."

****

It's morning. Frankie is up early. His goal is to make sure he can keep all the promises he made to Stella. Aristine is ready with a hearty breakfast of lox and bagels. She watches him slurp his coffee and makes sure he leaves nothing on his plate.

"You lookin' scrawny, Frankie. You need keep strength up. Your body needs food. Eat!" says his mother, tapping a knife on his plate.

Frankie suddenly feels an unsolicited appreciation for his mother in her acceptance of Stella despite her knowledge of Stella's sordid past. "I wanna thank you for all you've done to help Stella. She's havin' a rough time right now, and you helpin' out with Carly is deeply appreciated."

Aristine continues to stand above Frankie with her fresh apron wrapped around her matronly torso, her hands on her hips and still sporting the bagel knife, she says, "Eef I vait for you bring me grandchild, I vait unteel hell freeze. Carly fillin' za bill."

Not wanting to become embroiled in this conversation, and knowing how hard it will be to remove himself from his mother's scrutiny, Frankie glances at his watch. "You're right!" he says, readily admitting his disappointing ways, kissing her on her forehead, he says "Gotta go, Mutie. I'll bring Carly back, if it's okay."

"No need ask. She and I make cakes," says Aristine.

Stella has made arrangements to take the day off. She is up early to prepare for what she hopes will be some time alone with Frankie. As promised, he arrives on time. All dressed and ready to go, Carly is there to meet him. Leaping into his arms, she gives him a big hug and says, "Hello, Mr. Frankie. You come to pick my mom up?"

"You betcha, Carly. We got a date. You know what a date is?" asks Frankie, grinning from ear to ear.

"That's where you and mom kiss and hug all day," says Carly rolling her eyes.

"Well, not all day—just part of the day," says Frankie amazed at her budding precociousness. "Let me ask you—would you rather hang out with your mom and me, watchin' us kiss and hug all day, or go to Bubbie's and bake cakes?"

"Bubbie's!" she exclaims, jumping up and down.

Stella steps into the room just in time to encounter all the commotion. "I thought you wanted to go with Frankie and me," says Stella. Carly already spends much of her time between her and Frankie's mothers while she's working. Stella's disappointment is apparent. She had been hoping she could divide her day off between both Carly and Frankie.

With her lower lip sticking out and her eyes welling with tears, Carly sobs, "Mr. Frankie says I can go to Bubbie's and bake cakes."

Frankie intervenes, "Bubbie is looking forward to her coming. She doesn't mind her around. They seemed to have hit it off pretty good."

Looking the two up and down and seeing she's been outvoted, Stella gives a reluctant shrug. Throwing a sweater around her shoulders, she says, "Okay, okay. Let's go before the day's gone."

Stepping outside, Stella looks up at the cloudy sky. She wonders if it means rain and considers how damned organized Frankie is. In one sense, she sees this as an attractive attribute, but it conflicts with her own haphazard lifestyle. These are the things that make her grumpy. Still determined to make this a good day, Stella manages a smirk.

Frankie brings up the rear. He can't help but notice Stella's beauty. Her black and white patterned dress shows off her slender form and olive skin tone, and a soft white sweater draws attention to her ample breasts. As she walks on ahead, her configuration is like a hot ray of sunlight against the morning clouds. To Frankie, she could not be more beautiful. He can't imagine ever tiring of being with her.

They soon reach the Morgansky cottage, where they visit with Aristine for a few minutes. Aristine is a sweet woman who has always been there for Stella and deserves a visit. Nonetheless, Stella is anxiously looking toward her time alone with Frankie.

At last, Frankie slaps his hands on the table and gets to his feet. "Well, Mutie, have a great time with Carly. We're gonna get on the road now."

As they make their way to the truck, Frankie says, "What say we take a ride over to Denzel Merz's place? I wanna show you somethin'."

"Who in hell is Denzel—what'd you say his name is?" replies Stella.

"Denzel Merz. He's one of my new business partners," answers Frankie.

It's obvious this is not the alone time she had in mind for the two of them. In a less than conciliatory voice, Stella declares, "I s'pose so, if it ain't gonna take all day." She'd like to say more, but is managing to hold her tongue.

In his usual single-minded way, Frankie wheels his truck back onto the road and heads for the east channel. It's only been a fifteen-minute drive when he pulls off the road onto a two-track side road. It leads through a marshy area with channels of water on each side of the way and ends at a small cottage with a boathouse on the shoreline. A Ford sedan is parked in the driveway. In a moment, a door cracks opens in the boat house. What is unmistakably a rifle barrel pokes through it. Soon a hand, then an arm, and then the full body of a short, wide-eyed man with a huge, drooping mustache appears. Seeing who it is, he lowers the rifle.

"Why the hell didn't ya honk, comin' in here? You'd like ta scare the pants off me. Fer all I knew, you was one a them Purples snoopin' around," says the beleaguered man.

Frankie lets out a loud laugh. "You shoulda seen yourself! Ya looked like a doe in the headlights."

"Well, yer damned lucky I didn't plug yer ass fulla buckshot," the man returns.

Turning to Stella, Frankie says, "Stella, I'd like you ta meet Denzel Merz—one of the best damn moonshiners on the island. Denzel, this here is the prettiest lady yer ever gonna have the privilege a meetin' in yer whole life. This is Stella, my girlfriend."

Denzel pulls off his flat-billed hat and gives a slight nod. "Nice ta meet ya, ma'am. Yer sure a hell of a lot better lookin' than the sap yer hangin' out with."

"Thank you, sir. That's very kind of you ta say, but I do find him handy at times," chimes Stella.

Frankie turns to Denzel once again. "How we comin'?"

With a slight sparkle in his eyes, a knowing grin, and a swooping hand gesture to invite them inside, Denzel says, "I'd say pretty damned good. This last batch is the best yet, an' ready ta bottle. Come on in an' have a taste."

Taking Stella by the hand, Frankie follows Denzel into the boathouse. Inside, they find a young boy who's not much more than twelve years old. "I'd like ya ta meet Junior, my boy. His name's also Denzel, but me an' the ol' lady jus' call him Junior. He's learnin' the trade." The boy gives them a slight, self-conscious nod of acknowledgment.

The room is a scuffed-up space stacked with cases of empty bottles ready to be filled and shipped to waiting speakeasies. In the corner is a full operating whiskey still with copper tubing and a container with a spigot. Denzel places a pint-sized fruit jar under the spigot and lets it fill. Then he shuts the spigot off and hands the clear liquid to Frankie with a satisfied grin.

Holding it up to the only light in the shed, Frankie says, "Looks damn good." Moving it to his lips, he takes a sip. "Whew! And it tastes damn good, too!"

He passes the jar on to Stella. She takes it without a thought, but now that it's in her hand, she realizes this stuff might not be the Mary Pickford ladies' drink she's used to. She boldly takes a sip anyway. "*Agh!*" It's all she can do to swallow it without snorting it back through her nose. "This stuff ain't nothin' more than a corpse reviver," is her only comment as she wipes her scrunched lips and hands the jar back to Frankie. Both he and Denzel break out in laughter.

"How much ya figure we got here, Denzel?" asks Frankie.

"I figure about twenty-five gallons."

"Sounds good ta me. Lemme know when ya get 'er bottled up, an' I'll be around to take it ta market."

With all the business taken care of, Frankie at last turns to Stella and resumes their date. As far as she's concerned, it's been suspended in midair since he picked her up hours ago.

Frankie says, "You ready for lunch, kid? I got somethin' good planned."

"More than ready, big boy. I thought you was never gonna get around to it," declares Stella. "What d'ya got planned?"

"You'll see soon enough," is Frankie's only reply.

Chugging along the dirt road in Frankie's old truck, they both are silent with their own thoughts. The clouds have moved out, and one of Michigan's beautiful clear blue fall skies is presenting itself in all its glory. Frankie is thinking how he could never grow weary of this kind of connection with Stella. She, in turn, is wondering how long something this good is going to last before the other shoe drops.

The wonder of Harsens Island is the way modern people have civilized small chunks of the island to make it habitable without desecrating its wildness. It's an attempt by contemporary people to make these hallowed grounds into something they can safely adapt themselves to. The opulence of the Old Club is such a place; it's a fine piece of art placed in a rough-cut frame. Another of these oasis against a wilderness is the Riverside Hotel where at this moment Frankie is pulling into. It's a favorite recreational destination for wealthy Detroiters.

"We gonna eat here, or you got yourself more business?" asks Stella. It's clearly said with a sardonic tone.

"So far only recreation, but it's still early," replies Frankie. His reply is a bit lighter in scale but clearly heckling.

They are again silent as they enter the hotel lobby. Suddenly from somewhere a man appears with a voice, "Ah, Mr. Morgansky. We've been expecting you, sir. Everything is arranged." It's obvious he's the hotel's concierge.

Stella looks first at this man dressed in a sport jacket with the hotel monogram sewn on the outside breast pocket, and then back at Frankie. *What is going on here?*

"Follow me, sir, and I'll see you to your accommodation," says this concierge with a voice so smooth it could melt butter. With that said, he leads them to an upper room with a very ornate door. It's now obvious to Stella that this isn't going to be a run-of-the-mill room. With a purposeful flair, the concierge opens the door crosses the room and pulls open the curtains allowing the day light to light up the room. All of the furnishings come alive. They are the best the hotel has to offer including two bottles of French imported wines. They have arrived in the penthouse, with a spectacular view of the water.

Behind them comes a food cart with cloche-covered dishes pushed by a uniformed chef. While the concierge is busy seating them at their private table in front of the window overlooking the harbor, the chef has uncovered their meal: fresh perch, baked potato, and a green salad with walnuts and island-grown blueberries.

Even though Stella has provided such luxuries for many at the Old Club, she is flabbergasted to be on the receiving end of them.

"Is there anything we can get for you, sir?" asks the concierge.

"No, Burt, you've done a great job," says Frankie, slipping him an ample tip.

"Thank you, sir."

Watching the concierge and the chef walk out and close the door behind them, they find themselves alone. They sit silently eating, sipping wine, and staring out the window at the business in the harbor. This is so foreign to their relationship; they aren't quite sure how to handle it. It's difficult to find a context to begin.

Frankie attempts to break the ice, "You look especially beautiful today, Stella. I can hardly keep my eyes off you."

"Thank you, Frankie. It's sweet of you to put all this together. As you can see, I don't know what to say."

"Well, it's not over yet," says Frankie, swirling his goblet of wine with a grin.

"Don't tell me you've ordered a circus to perform, 'cause I can't think of anything better than this."

"No, not quite that extravagant but nice. I think you'll enjoy it."

For the next half hour, they enjoy their dinner, with the wine beginning to have its effects, their conversation is beginning to flow much more easily. They see each other as somebody to talk with, share interests with, and be seen as interesting by. Right now, their relationship feels normal enough to have always been there—or if it hasn't been, it should be. It's comfortable.

With dinner behind them, they find themselves drawn to a beautiful, restful-looking gold brocade couch. Stella slips her pumps off and places her bare feet on Frankie's lap. Instinctively, he begins to massage her feet. Stella can't be more spellbound. This is exactly the way she had hoped their day would go. To her, all this attention is lovemaking. The chains that bind her to her old life are beginning to fall away, and the discovery of something nobler is becoming a reality. Sex isn't the biggest part of this relationship—rather, she's beginning to see sex as a righteous celebration of this truthful bond they are forming, and she's ripe for it. The more Stella and Frankie interact with one another, the more they long for their relationship to deepen. They have come to a place where their hearts are melding into one. They have discovered something in the other they wish to care for. Their conversation has become a soft flow of words with little or no effort behind it.

Stella is not the most intellectual woman Frankie has known. Newspaper headlines don't interest her, but on the other hand, she possesses something many intellectuals lack: a kind of classy earthiness that exhibits an independent spirit. He finds this attractive. She also isn't needy in a sense that cripples either of them. Rather out of necessity, she has built a life of self-sufficiency, and often gives Frankie the impression she doesn't need a man.

Neither of them have ever had a home anyone would describe as lovely. To a great extent, discomfort is much more a part of their normal existence. They share an adapt-and-overcome mindset. This afternoon spent at the Riverside Hotel is the most lavish one either has ever granted themselves. They're both delighted they can share a similar excitement and contentment in these singular comforts. The raw natural beauty of the landscape surrounding the Riverside demands effort to overcome its primitiveness, but this makes its distinctness stand out all the more.

    A right proper fall evening arrives while they sit on their balcony, overlooking the lake. The long red rays of sunset stretch across the still waters. The days are getting noticeably shorter. As the sun sinks below the horizon, a huge harvest moon appears. The night sky builds slowly as each constellation staggers its way into visibility.

    This has been a glorious day for both Frankie and Stella, but there is still some unfinished business Frankie is hesitant to bring to light. Realizing that the day is getting away from him, it's become a now-or-never proposition. He looks at Stella with apprehension as he formulates his next surprise. His heart is beginning to pick up speed with nervousness, and his hands are sweating. He drops to one knee in front of her, and a rather sheepish look wiggles its way across his face.

    Stella looks at him crawling around on the deck like he's had too much to drink. Reaching into his pocket, he produces a box. Swallowing hard in an attempt to remove the growing lump in his craw, he opens the small box. There, sitting in the middle, is a surprise Stella hasn't seen coming: a diamond ring. Clearing his throat, Frankie manages to squeak out the words, "Will you marry me, Stella?"

    It's like all the oxygen has suddenly been pulled from the earth into the stratosphere. Stella sits as though paralyzed, staring dumbfounded before this unseemly overture. She feels her heart swelling in a wild fervor. Stella drops from her chair to the floor and hurls both arms around Frankie's neck, throwing him backwards to the floor.

    With Stella's full weight holding him down, Frankie is still grasping the open ring box. After pulling her arms from around his neck only long enough to push the ring onto her finger, he reclines where he landed and looks up at Stella as she admires the addition to her extended digit, all the while gasping with girlish delight.

"Can I deduce that it's a yes?" asks Frankie, still flat on his back.

"Say it one more time. I wanna hear it one more time," demands Stella with a wide smile. She's beaming from ear to ear, and still admiring the diamond.

Now, with just as big a grin, Frankie repeats his proposal. "Will you marry me?"

Stella places a hand on his forehead as if to check for a fever. Still sitting on him, she replies, "Yes! When?"

"Whenever you say." It's the only answer that fits this circumstance.

Now there is a lot of crying and hugging, and then a lot more crying and hugging.

Soon they are checking out to make their way back into the same world they left earlier in the day. The problems they ignored for a few hours are still there to meet them, but they are coming back into this arena with renewed spirits. Both of them are still basking in the afterglow of their day. For the moment, they are only concerned with each other.

As they make their way back to pick up Carly, Stella is quietly contemplative.

Aristine meets them at the door with Carly, who is all decked out in a pair of pajamas that was once Aristine's, but has now been cut down to sort of fit Carly. Carly has a bewildered look on her face as she sheepishly looks to her mother. It's a look that Stella recognizes. As young as she is, Carly has an eye for her own personal fashion. Stella knows from the look on her daughter's face that these pajamas are not to her taste.

Frankie has other things on his mind. Looking to his mother, he asks, "Vo Ta ist?" (Where is dad?)

"In de salon." (In the living room.) With the grin of a Cheshire cat, Frankie motions his mother and Stella into the living room. Simon is reading something. Now he peeks up over his pince-nez glasses.

"Hello, Frankie. Hello, Stella. How you doingk zees evening?" he asks.

With the same grin, Frankie returns his father's greeting. "You got a minute, Ta? We got something we want to tell you." Something in Frankie's voice and both their uncharacteristically wide grins alerts both parents—something out of the ordinary is afoot. Now they notice the way Stella is hanging on to Frankie's arm with both hands.

"I've asked Stella to marry me, and she's accepted," announces Frankie.

Simon continues to look at both of them. It's as though he's fighting for words to express something—anything. His mouth hangs open like he's a dummy without a ventriloquist. He's obviously lost for words. He sees a young woman in her twenties who has experienced more of the dark side of life than others her age. He's listening to this announcement as a father concerned for a son who might be caught up in something he can't get out of.

On the other hand, Aristine is not. "Mazel tov!" (It's about time!), shouts out Aristine. Realizing her involuntary enthusiasm, both her hands shoot up to cover her mouth. At the same time, the tears begin to well up in her eyes, and she smiles broadly.

Carly's eyes always show her feelings. Along with this particular announcement, her eyes are alight. She's all but forgotten that she's wearing Bubbie's oversized pajamas. Her words are tumbling out at a rate too fast to respond to, she insists on doing an exuberant twirl. Looking up at Frankie, and in an excited voice, she levels a scrutinizing question. "Does this mean you're gonna be me and my mommy's dad?"

Frankie looks down on this pajama-clad minikin. He can't help but chuckle at her exuberance and the innocence of her question.

"You're close, sweetie. I'm gonna be *your* daddy, but your mommy's husband," says Frankie, still carrying the same grin he's had for most of the past hour.

"Does that mean I ain't gotta be a bastard anymore?" she asks, exhibiting the same excitement.

The whole room suddenly goes quiet. The interest that has been directed toward Frankie and Stella is quickly being redirected toward Carly.

Stella is the first to respond to this unforeseen, unsettling probe. She as well as the whole room is taken aback at this six-year-old's comprehension of her situation. "Where on earth did you ever hear that you should be called a bastard?"

"Billy Grimes said so at school. He said, 'Anybody that don't got a dad is a bastard,'" answers Carly, as pure and innocent as the white driven snow.

Stella is dumbstruck.

Frankie's heart goes out to Stella and Carly. He picks up the conversation where Stella has turned quiet. "Don't you worry about that, Carly. We're gonna fix that really quick."

Aristine joins in behind Frankie, squeezing Carly's face between her hands. "I still be you bubbie, zveetie, no matters vat goink on."

Stella reaches down and instinctively picks Carly up as if to rescue her.

There is still one more stop to make. Aware that Alina will be getting home from work about this time, they opt to leave to make their way back to their Harsens Island cottage. Frankie is a bit more hesitant to approach Alina about marrying her daughter, because when Stella's father was alive, he didn't want to have a Jew that close to his family—especially because there was little chance that he would become a Catholic.

When Alina gets back to the cottage, she's surprised to see Stella and Carly return so late. Carly has fallen asleep and is being carried in by Frankie.

"Don't you think it's a bit late to have Carly out? After all, she has to get up for school," says Alina with a trace of grandmotherly dominance.

Ignoring her mother, Stella responds with a question of her own. "Can we speak with you for a minute?"

Alina can tell this is not going to be a run-of-the-mill question. She looks at both Stella and Frankie for a clue as to what this discussion will entail. She sees nothing that will give her a heads up. "Sure. I got nothin' but time. Let's go in and sit down," says Alina, with an unsettled feeling about this mystery talk. *My God, is she pregnant?*

Once they're in the cottage, Stella takes a moment to put Carly in her bed. This leaves Frankie and Alina alone for a couple of uncomfortable minutes. Conscious of Frankie's presence, Alina thinks, *You better step up to the plate this time, big boy!* By the time Stella has made her way back, Alina's impulsive thought has worked its way into her mouth. Without a second thought, she blurts out, "Yer gonna tell me yer pregnant, ain't ya?"

Stopping dead in her tracks, Stella's look of disbelief quickly changes to bemusement. "Mother! Where in the hell did you come up with that?!" is Stella's only response. She tries to force an uncomfortable grin.

When she recognizes the injustice that she's just done her daughter, Alina apologizes, shamefaced. "I don't know where that came from, Stella. Please forgive me. I guess I'm just tired. Let's sit down. I want to hear what's on your mind."

Turning to Frankie, Stella says, "Frankie has something he wants to ask you." Frankie has the wide-eyed look that comes with being put on the spot. Straightening his shoulders and clearing his throat several times, he begins to put some words together.

"Even though Mr. Mazzara is gone, I still want to do this by the book. What we want to know ... uh, um, what I want to know—is it all right if I ask for your daughter's hand in marriage?" Not knowing what else to say, he nervously blinks and swallows a couple times. He looks first to Alina, and then to Stella for support.

Frankie's question totally blindsides Alina. This is the last thing she's prepared herself for. Speechless, she stares at this rather muscular young man and curvy young woman—with an emphasis on *young*. The two of them stare back.

"What did you say, Stella?"

Very much aware he is an integral part of this discussion, Frankie feels compelled to get it right. This question throws him for a moment. Instead of letting Stella answer, he forces out an explanation.

"I know I'm riding the horse before I put the saddle on, but I didn't see much sense in asking you if she wasn't already agreeable," explains Frankie. At this point, Stella is still more connected to her mother than to him, and he feels his intrusion demands an explanation.

Finding her own voice, Stella assures her mother, "I did say yes, Mother."

Alina is becoming more at ease with the struggle she sees within Frankie, and, in an effort to spare him further discomfort, she says, "Francis asked me before he asked my father. Neither of you have to explain."

With a look of puzzlement, as though she has not completed her thought, Alina picks up a package of cigarettes on an end table next to her chair. She pauses to light one and exhales a plume of white smoke. Her gaze becomes much more intense as she looks at her daughter. Stella can sense her mother's uneasiness. Its contagion spreads to her because she knows its root well. A silent, private communication makes its way between mother and daughter.

"Okay, mother! I'll take care of it!" says Stella, agitated.

Frankie says, "What's going on between you two? Somehow, I sense it has to do with me."

Continuing their locked gaze, the two women remain silent.

"When?" Alina asks, somewhere between probing and prodding.

Still confused, Frankie attempts to intrude again. "All right, what the hell is going on between you two?"

Seeing this encounter is taking on a life of its own, Stella attempts to regroup. She's known this day would come, but it presents many difficulties, and she just doesn't want to deal with it right now. Nevertheless, seeing Frankie's steadfastness in getting an answer, she feels she has no choice but to confront the source of her anxiety.

Frankie is sitting right next to her. She takes his hand. It feels large, rough, and strong. Taking in a deep breath, Stella begins, "Frankie, how many children do you want?"

Once again taken aback, he replies, "I don't know. I guess we'd have to discuss it further."

Now Stella looks directly into Frankie's eyes. "What if you already have a child?"

Frankie gazes back at Stella, trying a little forced grin and hoping to understand what she's getting at. Thinking he understands, he readily says, "If you mean Carly, I'll adopt her in a minute."

Taking a deep breath, Stella exhales the words, "You don't have to. She's already yours."

Frankie remains silent, still gazing at Stella, who's less than a foot away. She remains just as silent, with a steadfast stare. The quieter he becomes, the more he feels. At first, he's confused. *What the hell did I just hear her say*? Next is the same kind of nameless delight that usually comes when one is told one has a refund coming. And, for some yet unknown reason, he also feels sorrow. While he feels this muddle of emotions and a hundred other unnamed sentiments, Frankie remains only half convinced that Stella is telling the truth. His other half still has many questions.

Seeing Frankie's confusion, Stella continues to stare directly at him. "Do you remember the last night we spent together?"

She catches him off balance. For a moment, he loses himself in that long-gone time and tries to recapture that moment. He recalls how they vowed to stay in touch no matter what would come between them, how they said they would always love one another, and how the intercourse they had that night was, in a sense, a way to consummate these vows. It's suddenly becoming clear. The reality of that night is still his reality today, and Carly is the result.

To answer Stella's question, Frankie takes her in his arms, holding her close. Joy pours over him. In direct proportion to how sad he was on that night those years back, now, he cannot contain his joy.

Wondering how she could ever have expected anything less of Frankie, Stella cannot believe how long these circumstances have plagued her. Life has suddenly gotten bigger for both of them.

CHAPTER 17
Another Nemesis

It doesn't take but a morning for Ray Burnstein to get the report of the destruction of the Jewish Navy and their loss. It has Frankie Morgansky written all over it. He immediately calls in Axler and Fletcher.

"I gave you schmucks a contract. You told me you could deliver. So far, I ain't seen jack shit of a delivery. What the hell's goin' on? You must think I'm meshegeneh (crazy). This Harsens Island rube is making an ass outta all of us, an' you two putzes ain't done nothin. He's just destroyed fifty thousand dollars' worth of torpedo boats while you two guys spend your time jerkin' off on my dime. Either you get this guy vaporized, or your asses are on the line. You got what I'm sayin'?"

Not waiting for an answer, Burnstein storms off, leaving them alone to contemplate their options. Both know they'll be in a bad place if they don't deliver on this assignment. They can't risk a Harsens victory of any sort before they get this job done.

The remaining contact they have on the island with a direct, day-to-day link to Frankie Morgansky is an eighteen-year-old kid named Lyman Woodard who works at the Old Club as a musician but is secretly subsidized by the Axler and Fletcher.

"That kid's gonna have ta start earnin' his pay. He's gotta do a hell of a lot more than make a phone call once in a while," bemoans a frustrated Axler.

"Yeah, well, how in the hell you proposin' ta have that kid do anythin' else?" responds Fletcher.

"I dunno just yet, but we gotta figure a way of gettin' these schmucks to come to us," says Axler.

Another week has slipped by, and then another is nearly over. Fall is now in full swing. City-dwellers seldom see a change in seasons as much as they feel it. Temperatures are beginning to fall. The humid, sticky summer Great Lakes weather is being replaced with crisp, clean-feeling air.

On Harsens, the duck season has come to a close, so the recreational season is also coming to an end. Some trees have already turned to their fall colors, and some leaves have dropped to the ground. Others have kept their green hues, as if they can serve as a cloak to ward off the freezing winter weather.

In any season other than summer, the liquor business is not for sissies. The winds in Michigan's fall season present special challenges to boats on any body of water, regardless of its size. The Detroit River, Lake St. Clair, the St. Clair River, and Lake Erie are no exceptions. The Harsens Island cottage industries of rum-running are left to the bravest and boldest. Even in the harshest conditions, the Jewish Navy is always watching for any opportunity to pirate a load of liquor.

This takes us back to Denzel Merz and his son Junior at Frankie's hidden boathouse/ liquor still. Denzel is reputed to be the "best damn moonshiner" on the island. Frankie feels fortunate to have him as a partner. Denzel is in charge of the brewing, and Frankie the distribution. They have put together a state-of-the-art, 150-gallon copper still to supply all of Frankie's regulars. They've come up with their own label—Harsens Breeze. Denzel and his son have bottled up enough moonshine to begin selling it. They expect to make fifty dollars a case and know full well it will be cut at least three more times, returning a minimum of a hundred dollars for each cutting.

"How much you got there, Denzel?" inquires Frankie.

"'Nuff ta get ten ta twenty if we get caught," replies Denzel.

"Well, with the Good Lord willin' an' the creek don't rise, we'll get this stuff ta market," proclaims Frankie with an air of confidence.

Frankie has used the organizational skills he learned peddling his father's fish at Detroit's eastern market to create a good liquor market with the Harsens Island hotels and eateries, as well as private citizens. After it's sold, this hoard of bottled liquor will inevitably be cut several times to ensure a good return for the the wholesale buyers.

It's believed that around eighty percent of the country is not in favor of prohibition, while hardcore Prohibition advocates make up the other twenty percent. Those who have not had their views compromised by a promise of a payoff from the estimated 250-million-dollar annual take in trafficking illegal liquor are as dangerous to the business as dogs are to cats. Getting this cargo to market requires a degree of stealth. Even though the Purples are formidable foes, there is another opposition group; it often forms committees with the sole purpose of thwarting the efforts of the local bootleggers in their communities.

Harsens Island has such a group. It's headed by a group calling themselves "Citizens in Favor of Sober Living." They are centered around a temperance group from a local non-denominational church. These like-minded groups of protestant Christians, though small in number, provided a loud voice in favor of passing the Eighteenth Amendment, which prohibited the sale of alcohol across the United States. Their expectations were that the country would willingly give up its thirst for "spirits." Instead, they have discovered this pious endeavor has created an illegal underground market for liquor. Nonetheless, this unexpected phenomenon has not been enough for this group of like-minded citizens to abandon their cause. They have a small group of around a dozen members who meet regularly to discuss techniques to thwart the efforts of the liquor cottage industry on Harsens Island. They are often frustrated by the lackadaisical approach the local law enforcement community takes toward enforcing Prohibition laws, and they realize the significant likelihood that illegal liquor monies have reached the pockets of these so-called guardians of the law.

Norval and Louise Burgess are the primary drivers behind the Harsens committee. Nolan is a deacon and self-proclaimed preacher in a non-denominational church. He feels a particular call from God to put an end to the "devil's brew" everywhere he can.

So far, this group have not been a threat to Frankie, but that's not to say they are leaving him out of their scope. They've certainly been known to harass others for engaging in the same activities. Since Norval has assumed he has a divine calling to destroy anyone involved in the liquor business, he has taken to wearing a sidearm. Along with a number of his disciples, he often targets a hotel or a speakeasy and threatens all involved with "God's judgment."

The group's primary targets are those they believe they can bully into compliance. Their preferred method is to shame people into changing their behavior. If this doesn't work, they threaten violence. Because they are often reluctant to bring any more attention to themselves and their clandestine activities, these victims will swear to comply for no other reason than to shorten the rebuke.

On this particular day, Frankie's old Ford truck is loaded to the gills with bottles of Denzel's primo moonshine whiskey. Frankie is preparing to make his rounds to the various customers he's promised to supply. He's covered his load with the old tarps he used when he was hauling fish to market. The two-track to the main road is full of ruts, so he must carefully maneuver to prevent the load from shifting. Hearing the bottles clang as the truck negotiates a low spot forces Frankie to double clutch to pull it out. In doing so, and with a bit of luck, he keeps his cargo from shifting. The end of the two-track can't come soon enough. With a sigh of relief, he lets out a long-held breath as he manages to pull safely onto the smooth, graveled main road.

He's less than a half mile along when a sedan pulls around him; another remains behind his truck. The sedan in front slows, forcing Frankie to slow to their speed or risk running into their rear end. He's at a crawl when he hears the sound of breaking glass coming from the back of his truck. His military training suddenly kicks in. He has an idea what's happening and who's behind it. He smells the sharp aroma of alcohol wafting into the cab. Stopping as quickly as he can, he climbs out of his truck to see a group of men carrying baseball bats leap from the back of his truck bed to get back into the sedan. Before he can make a move, they are pulling around him.

Through an open car window, they yell, "Satan's advocate! Killer! You're gonna burn in hell!"

Frankie recognizes Norval Burgess and several others as they make their escape.

They've thrown his tarps off in order to smash as much of his cargo as possible, so what's left of his cargo is now exposed. The smell of alcohol is overwhelming. The truck bed is covered with broken glass and wet with liquor, which runs through its slats and down onto the road, making little muddy mounds of dirt. Gathering up his tarps, Frankie recovers what's left of his haul. Deciding to regroup, he makes his way back to the boathouse.

"Ya broke 'er all ta hell, din' ya?" says a clearly disappointed Denzel.

"You're right about all broke ta hell, but it wasn't the drivin' that did it. It was that crazy bunch of temperance people led by that Norval Burgess. They got onto the back of the truck before I could pull over and clubbed the hell outta the whole damn load."

"Looks like they got about a fourth of it. I think we got enough ta replace it 'til we can get the still fired up again."

Within minutes, Denzel has Junior cleaning up the broken glass and hosing off the booze-soaked boards. Within a half hour, the truck has been reloaded and is ready to go.

"I'm gonna ride with ya this time. We can't take a chance of losin' any more ta these holy rollers," says Denzel, biting firmly on the stub of an unlit cigar. Denzel never smokes cigars. Instead, he chews on one until it's gone.

Frankie likes to make his runs alone, but isn't in a position to come up with a convincing argument to support his case. Giving in to Denzel's persistence, they pile into the truck to have it make its way out to the road one more time. Careful not to be as mindless as he was before, Frankie looks one way and then another. Satisfied there isn't a present danger, he lets the clutch out on the old truck. Once more, it struggles under the load and up onto the road. Denzel supports himself with both hands as the truck makes its final lurch and sets out down the same dusty road.

"For any damn fool ta romanticize bootleggin'—thinkin' it's easy money *is* damn foolish. This is damn hard work," acknowledges Frankie as they make their way toward their first stop at the Riverside Hotel.

Before Denzel can agree, they've come within a mile of their destination. Denzel calls out, "Uh-oh. Looks like we might have more trouble."

They both spot a car stopping alongside the road. Slowing down, Frankie takes a hard look at this potential trouble. Suddenly, a man wearing a long white kitchen apron pops out and waves his arms. Frankie recognizes him immediately as the head of the kitchen and bar at the Riverside.

"What's the problem?" asks Frankie, fully expecting it's not going to be good.

The man is obviously distressed. "Mr. Kingsbury sent me out here to warn you the Feds are at the hotel. They went through the whole place lookin' for booze. We been waitin' on you, so we didn't have much left, but they found enough ta make a bust and shut the club down. Now they're hangin' around waitin' ta see if a bootlegger shows up."

Frankie's mind is twirling like a top. Facing the man, he says, "You hang on a minute, hear?"

Turning to Denzel, Frankie continues, "We gotta ditch this load for a while. I know just the place."

Turning back to the hotel's messenger, Frankie says, "Follow me!"

The man is not about to argue. "Okay, sir," is his only reply.

With that, Frankie quickly turns back a few hundred yards and onto a narrow passage that is completely covered with tall swamp grass. Once the truck is a few feet into this hideaway, it can't be seen from the road. In a moment, Frankie and Denzel crawl out of this refuge and motion for the messenger to pick them up. In another moment, they enter the car and order the man to drive them to the hotel.

Still with a taut, anxious look, the man unquestioningly puts the car in gear and obediently begins to make his way toward the hotel. Within a couple minutes, he's pulling between the two small channels that buttress the hotel's entrance. He hasn't spoken a word since Frankie and Denzel entered his sedan, but now he's excitedly pointing at another sedan in the parking lot. It's occupied by with two men wearing fedoras. He blurts out, "There the schnooks are! Right there."

Looking in the direction, Frankie sees the two men, but he finds the older Model-T parked next to them more interesting. Frankie can't recognize the occupant from this distance, but he notices that occupant gesturing toward the car he's in. He doesn't want them to know he's aware of their presence, so he purposely avoids making eye contact.

Frankie says, "Okay, calm down. We want you to look as inconspicuous as we do."

The man drives the car as close as he can to the back door of the hotel. Satisfied they're out of sight of the fedoras, they enter the kitchen, where they're met by Mark Kingsbury. Nodding toward his messenger, he says, "I'm glad Don here was able to stop you guys before ya came chargin' inta the feds' trap. They been hangin' around here for most the day, and they managed ta find enough booze ta fine us and shut us down. I reckon they'll get bored and leave pretty soon."

Frankie says, "Ya know, Mark, I was mullin' over somethin' while were comin' over here. We've been puttin' so much effort in watchin' for them damn Purples that we plum forgot about all these other donkeys. We need our guys ta be on the lookout for all these damn temperance people, too. They're gettin' ta be just as big a pain in the ass as those Purples."

Kingsbury agrees. They make a mental note to bring the issue up at their next meeting. Frankie asks to use the phone to call a few of his regulars to warn them of the fed problem and that he will be around with his delivery as soon as they're off the island. In the meantime, they all sit down to have a nice lunch.

CHAPTER 18
Norval

Axel has been taking his new sleuthing job seriously. He's been spending much of his time shadowing Axler and Fletcher. Since they very seldom are apart, it's been relatively easy to keep an eye on them both. Their main hangout is the Third Street Club. Terry, the bar keep there, has been heard to say, "These two even take a shit together at the same time, an' wipe each other's ass."

When Axel sees a hint of a new development, he's quick to relate the information to Frankie. Today is such a day.

Meeting at Frankie's parents' cottage is the norm for Axel. He has a sense of allegiance to Simon for all the years they spent together in the fishing industry, and likes nothing better than to keep this old relationship alive. After refurbishing his ties to the family with one of Aristine's bagel and lox breakfasts, he gets down to business with the latest scoop on the Purples' activities—especially those dealing with Harsens.

"I heard about your near clash with the feds," says Axel, speaking to Frankie. "Axler has those guys on the take—I found out through the grapevine. They had that kid—Lyman what's-his-name, from the Old Club—fingerin' you. They was hopin' ta bust you with a delivery an' put you outta commission. I wanna tell you, they was not happy when you showed up empty handed." Axel can't help but laugh about the failed ploy.

Frankie doesn't find it so humorous. He's thinking back to his combat days. He should've been more attentive to the old Model-T parked next to those feds. *If this'd been a combat situation, that failure could have been my life. I knew what that little schmuck Lyman was drivin'. I gotta pay more attention.*

The Feds, the Purples, and now the temperance people are all, for their own reasons, attempting to thwart Harsens' cottage liquor business, so they're all on Frankie's list of people to avoid.

The temperance people are becoming more and more of a nuisance. They are confident, despite their often seemingly unholy methods of handling those who disagree with their opinions, that the ends will justify the means. They remain steadfast in the belief that they're doing the Lord's work, and it seems they're willing to put up with any amount of blowback. They have suffered a few beatings of their own because of their vigilance to "never allow liquor to pass our children's lips." All this, despite the fact many of their children have already discovered that alcohol is their culture's rite of passage from a kid to a young adult. It's accessible in every cove and cranny of Harsens Island.

Nevertheless, the island's temperance union continues their vigilance against everyone in the alcohol business. Since Axel is readily sharing his information about the Purples and Feds, Frankie relates the encounter he had with Nolan Burgess and the island's temperance union.

Axel listens with an ear bent on solving the problem. "I think I know a way we can get these critters outta our hair. It's gonna cost a few cases of Harsens Breeze ta get the job done, but I'm sure it'll take care of the problem."

"Well, at least tell me what you got in mind," says Frankie. He's known Axel long enough to know whatever he's got in mind will be well planned out.

"Give me a few days ta get a crew together and do a little scoutin'. I wanna get a few ducks in a row 'fore I show my hand. All I need right now is a couple cases readily available, 'cause once we get goin', I don't wanna have ta stop."

Frankie agrees as they make their way out to the boathouse distillery. Denzel and Junior are busy with another batch. Harsens

Breeze has become a big hit among the hotels thanks to the combination of Denzel's brewing skills and Frankie's sales proficiency.

Axel takes a little time to loosely outline what he has in mind. Part of it involves infiltrating the ranks of the temperance people. Frankie and Denzel are all ears as Axel continues to lay out a plan he believes will be the death of the island's temperance union. "Ta kill a snake, ya gotta cut its head off," says Axel. Taking a couple cases of booze, he leaves them with enough knowledge of his plan to get both their support.

Axel has put together a trusted support group of his own. Many of these individuals are also seasoned veterans of Frankie's resistance movement. They're made up of small-time rumrunners who are more than happy to involve themselves if it rids them of at least one of their adversaries.

Axel is a known island Jew. He needs a Protestant who can play the part of a repentant rumrunner for long enough to gain a foothold in the temperance movement. That man is Edgar Bentley. He's been accosted by the temperance people several times. They always maintain it's out of love for his soul, and they always destroy his cargo. When they bring him to tears over his loss, they imagine his tears are tears of repentance, so they are always praying over him.

When Axel explains his plan, Edgar is anxious to become part of Axel's team. Over a few hours and a few samples of Denzel's "Harsens Breeze," Axel lays out a workable plan. It's to begin this Sunday, when Edgar will attend services at the Island Non-Denominational Church.

Arriving early with hat in hand and gazing at the floor, Edgar makes his entrance. No one has ever matched his ability to appear repentant. As Norval catches a glimpse of this "godless reprobate," his head shoots up like somebody just goosed him.

"Well, I'll be da—" says Norval, catching his own godless verbiage just in time to save him a repentance of his own. He no less than shocked.

Norval can't get to the aisle fast enough. With a satisfied smile, gets his glad hand out fast to welcome this trophy he's sure his efforts have won over.

"God be glorified! If it ain't Edgar Bentley!" exclaims an excited Norval.

Edgar, maintaining his servile demeanor, offers a limp handshake.

Offering Edgar a chair with a satisfied air, Norval says, "Sit right here, Edgar. This here chair's had your name on it for a long time."

Within twenty minutes, the church has accumulated ten congregants—equally split between men and women. They do not appear to be a happy or contented lot. Rather, they are a tenser, more serious sort. The men are suited, and many mustachioed, and their hair has been pomaded and slicked back. Having strapped themselves into their bustles, the women have a tendency to be as tight-lipped as they are tight-waisted. At the appropriate time, Norval approaches the podium carrying a Bible. After welcoming everyone, he immediately breaks into a hymn. The congregation follows along in a hand-printed, mimeographed song book that's been stapled together and placed in folders. The drys use the hymn "Christ Is Calling for His Soldiers" as an anti-drink song:

> Christ is calling for His soldiers,
> Who will bear the battle brunt;
> Those who will in every conflict
> Keep the colors well in front;
> Who will neither shirk nor falter,
> Who will face e'en death and shame,
> Who will keep the banner waving
> For the glory of His name.
>
> There is need for consecration,
> There is need for hearts sincere,

> There is need for hearts courageous
> Who will never have a fear.
> We will take our place as soldiers
> And with shouts of glad acclaim,
> Charge the hosts of sin and Satan,
> For the glory of His name.

Following the hymn, Norval's face takes on an even more expressive look of dismay and sadness as he begins his sermon.

"It's a decisive time for us as Christ's soldiers. God expects each and every one of us to answer the call to duty. You might ask, 'What may that duty be?' It's to charge the hosts of sin and Satan! We have found that sin and Satan lie in the very brew of the Devil: liquor! Liquor in all its forms must be purged from the earth, along with those who are determined to be the very purveyors of sin and are acting as the devil's agents peddling it for him to destroy our children—to destroy hearth and home …"

Norval continues on for an hour, focusing on the evils of alcohol and how it's as bad as treason to sit ideally by and allow these rumrunners and bootleggers to run amok.

Edgar does the best he can to maintain his humble, repentant demeanor and still let his eyes and mind search the building for doors and windows to enter. He is actively working his part of a plan Axel is sure he can put together to get these overzealous drys out of their lives.

Two hours later, Norval dismisses the congregation, but not before he points to Edgar as one who has been "snatched out of Satan's grip and has found his way to the Lord" and how he and some of "Christ's soldiers" had encouraged Edgar to abandon his evil ways, even when it meant chastising him.

Edgar continues his deception perfectly. He's getting a lot of satisfaction in being able to pull the wool over the eyes of these men who have sanctimoniously judged him as evil. He remains the repentant sinner while casing the church for an easy entry to eliminate the risk of getting caught breaking in. When he goes to use the men's room, he discovers exactly what he's been looking for: a window with a rear exposure off to the back of the church basement. Carefully unlocking the window, he returns only to have Norval and several others tell him once again how the Lord answered their prayer by bringing him to his knees.

"I gotta tell ya, Edgar, I prayed hard for the Lord ta knock some sense inta ya. Yer livin' proof the Lord is blessin' our work," crows Norval as he grips Edgar's hand once more. It's the kind of grip an egotist uses when he thinks he's won a round.

Edgar can't quite bring himself to thank Norval and his henchmen for their prayers. After all, they had cost him a couple boatloads of Canadian whiskey. Instead, he remains in character and allows his voice to tremble as he continues to hang his head in a servile way, all the while hoping they'll get tired of congratulating themselves over saving his soul. After another go-around on how they destroyed his rum-running business "out of love," Norval allows him to leave at last. It can't come soon enough. Edgar can't be happier. It's come to an end. He breaks out in a happy whistle as he goes to meet with Axel.

Axel is a pragmatic man. For him to become a part of anything, things have to be on the square. He's wondering how his plot is going to square with himself when he aligns it with the ethical principles of his western tradition. There's no doubt it's truly a genius idea he's bringing to life. Despite its illegality, he feels it's right for this circumstance. It's allowing the people on Harsens Island to remain as autonomous as they possibly can under all these outside circumstances, and rid themselves of this sanctimonious zealot at the same time.

Axel is readily immersing himself into his scheme. He meets with a cousin who is a reporter with the *Detroit Free Press*. As predicted, he's able to catch his cousin's attention by referring to an "upcoming surprise." Not wanting to give him all the details, Axel gives him enough to ensure he'll write the story.

Things are beginning to come together. He calls the group of men he's entrusted together, and they begin to put the final touches on the plot. It's four in the morning. The night sky is moonless night and overcast, and the two cases of Harsens Breeze have been carefully loaded into the back seat of Axel's sedan.

Meanwhile, Edgar has made his way to the church. Satisfied he hasn't been seen, he slides around to the rear of the building. Finding the window that he carefully left unlocked, he cautiously slides it up and slips into the building.

A lit match offers him just enough light to make his way to a side door. Opening it from the inside, he waves the lit match, signaling the team to go to the next phase. Axel and another team member are parked on a side street, where they respond to the signal by carefully unloading the two cases of Harsens Breeze, and carrying them across the lawn to the open door.

Other team members are positioned as lookouts. They've been instructed to start their engines if they see someone getting curious.

Edgar awaits their entry with another lit match and leads them to a closet that's home to a stack of folding chairs. Directing the two to place the cases toward the back of the closet, they quickly cover the booze with a wall of chairs. Finishing the task without a hitch, they make their way out of the building and return to their cars. Happy to have successfully completed this phase without a problem, their enthusiasm is only superseded by their adrenalin surge.

After a few hours of sleep, Axel and Edgar arrange to meet with Frankie to bring him up to speed and to discuss the next phase in their plan.

They meet in the backyard of the Morgansky cottage, where Aristine has planted a small garden of hardy Mums. It's one of those late November fall days that defy reason, with temperatures reaching seventy degrees. The brilliant red and yellow colors of her flowers only to serve to enhance the day.

"I've got the *Free Press* ready ta go. My cousin assured me this is the kind of story he looks forward to breaking."

Frankie muses over this statement for a moment, "How much did you tell him?"

"I merely told him we have a trusted source that has uncovered a cache of liquor in a church that has consistently advocated for prohibition," replies Axel.

Looking to Edgar, Frankie asks, "And how do you feel about moving forward with the next stage?"

"I'm good with it. I can't wait to see the faces of these sweet-talkers when the shoe is on the other foot, and they get their asses handed back on a plate," says Edgar.

They move into the cottage, where the telephone hangs. After a short rehearsal, Edgar begins his next assignment. Placing the phone to his ear, he makes the call. After a short, in-depth conversation with the party on the other end of the line, Edgar says, "Yes sir, I can meet you this afternoon. Yes, sir, at the ferry landing will be fine. Three o'clock is good." With his ear still to the phone, he's looking around as though he's hunting for something. Spotting Aristine's mums, he continues the conversation. "You'll know it's me 'cause I'll have a bouquet of red and yellow flowers." With this final word, Edgar places the phone back in its cradle. After a pensively silent moment, he turns to Axel. "What d'ya think?"

"I think ya done damn good. Couldn't a done it better myself. Came off without a hitch," says Axel, slapping Edgar on the back with a huge grin.

Axel's next move is to phone his cousin at the *Free Press* and inform him of the latest development.

Axel is showing more enthusiasm than usual. He's found that often the quieter he becomes, the more he hears. He's discovered his mind will begin to answer his questions in the quiet of relaxation.

For Axel, along with the residents on Harsens Island, the solitude of being one with the ever-present water is always obtainable. In the backyard of the Morgansky cottage overlooking Lake St. Clair, taking that moment alone, Axel realizes it's *his* move next. Life seems to have an insurmountable number of options, while death never does. He doesn't always have a firm theological grip on what he considers to be his next move, but he does seem to possess an inherent ability to discern what he perceives to be righteous. This has become his aim: to merely do what he perceives to be the next right thing.

Axel's community on Harsens is his world. The people he shares a life with are an ultimate concern for him. He thinks about how these good people make their living, and how those few neighbors who oppose their methods might have gained enough power to be considered enemies.

There are those who have painted alcohol use with a single brush. They allow the abusers to influence the laws enough to set standards for its use among the non-abusers. In Axel's world, alcohol has seldom been a negative, but now the islanders are dealing with this group of teetotalers who not only choose abstinence for themselves, but feel they are directed by divine guidance to use violence to keep it from every human being. To many islanders, these people are violent nemeses.

Axel prefers life to be like a waltz—creative and well organized. Today he's dealing with what has re-formed itself from a waltz into a polka; things are moving much faster. The hour has been set to deal with these unhappy people. This evening happens to be the weekly meeting of Norval's group to negotiate how they are, "out of love for the sinner," going to make their fellow islanders comply with their own ideals.

Frankie has become quite interested in Axel's scheme, and has invited himself along to view its outcome. By three o'clock in the afternoon, they have arrived at the ferry, and are prepared to see Axel's trap come to fruition. The temperature is beginning to cool from the earlier highs, and it's suddenly feeling like a late November day. With the shorter days, it's nearly dark by five p.m. The waves are kicking up on the river as the ferryboat makes another of its thousands of crossings. Axel and Frankie have opted to remain in the background so Edgar can appear to act alone.

Edgar has a rather awkward look as he stands holding the agreed-upon signal: a bouquet of red and yellow Mums. It's as though this self-conscious man wearing work clothing were expecting a paramour to arrive. He's conscious of what he must look like, and all the while wondering *Why in the hell did I choose this symbol?*

The ferry is unloading. Car after car passes him by. The last one is a dark sedan with two dark-suited, fedora-wearing men inside. "Get in," says the driver through a lowered window. Relieved to at last toss the bouquet aside, Edgar enters the rear seat. With Edgar in tow, they pull over out of the way alongside the road. "So what kind of bullshit you got ta tell us?" asks the man in the passenger's seat.

Not wanting to be totally at the mercy of these mainlanders, Edgar pulls out a nugget he saw in a moving picture show. "Who wants ta know?"

Both men look mystified. "Don't be a smartass, kid. You know damn well who we are!" says the passenger.

Edgar sticks to his guns because he really doesn't care for these men any more than he cares for Norval and his ilk.

Letting this Harsens Island hick know they're put out, they each let out a sigh and pull out their badges to prove they're US federal officers.

Satisfied he's let them know he may be a scrubby-looking hick but he is, nevertheless, a citizen, Edgar begins to tell them of this church he's been attending, and how they have been deceiving everyone with how they are fighting for prohibition, but are secretly selling moonshine. He goes on to tell them how he discovered the cache of what he believes to be illegal liquor in a closet, and how they will be having another meeting in just a short time.

The two agents are scrambling to keep up their note-taking through Edgar's exuberant verbosity. He's enjoying watching them personify themselves as the vultures he's always known them to be. They're about to swoop down on unsuspecting prey. As much as he dislikes Norval and his breed, he has a slight tinge of sympathy for what he can tell the miserable bastard will soon endure. Edgar is also noticing how much these agents are swallowing throughout this interview; it tells him they truly do salivate over the prospect of catching an unsuspecting rumrunner.

The time has come for Edgar to take them to the church site. As one would suspect, they cautiously drive by the address to survey the conditions that will ultimately confront them. This is the very type of behavior a real rumrunner knows is typical of a Fed. The agents are merely going by the bureau's handbook for sleuthing.

In close proximity to the church, they spot a summer cottage with a driveway. Using their most official-looking personas, they do their next bit of surveillance by knocking at the door to establish if the owner is present or absent. There is no answer, so they assume the cottage is deserted. This, in turn, tells them they have decreased their chances of being noticed by the owners. They make this driveway the headquarters for their surveillance operation.

At last, the agents have established an arrangement they feel secure with. They feel reassured because no one is paying any particular attention to them. With this potential problem out of the way, they begin to focus on the men and women who are making their way to a meeting of a group that supposedly supports prohibition but is purported to be selling liquor. Edgar knows many of them as those who have often dogged him in his efforts to deliver a load of liquor to a market. Of course, he's keeping these incidents a silent secret as he continues to embellish his account of how appalled he was with their deception when he accidently came across the hidden cache of illegal liquor.

As expected, the agents aren't interested in Edgar's allegations without proof. They're putting together their own procedure to investigate his claim. Since this is apparently a public anti-liquor meeting, they are plotting to determine the best way to confront the situation. They have decided to make an entrance as interested citizens and attempt to assess the surroundings much more closely once they're inside and can get a look at the closet.

With the meeting about to begin, the two agents, who have identified themselves as Agent Bronson and Agent Sorensen, are on their way across the lawn to the church basement's side door. After entering the church basement where the meeting and the suspect closet are said to be in close proximity, Norval is to his feet in a second to greet these two new hopefuls. He's overjoyed to have more interested citizens join his get-together. Shaking their hands, Norval eagerly leads them to a couple of vacant chairs.

Trying not to overplay their inclination to notice everything, the agents find the storeroom door where Edgar said it would be. Since Agent Bronson is placed on an end chair, he can nearly reach out and touch the door to this mystery room. The next step plaguing each of these agents is how to gain access to its interior. This procedure is not in the agents' manual. They are going to have to improvise.

Norval begins his chairmanship of this meeting by delivering a reading from Proverbs 23: 29–35, describing the problems a drunkard has with managing his drinking. After his reading, he is more than willing to share his thoughts. His tendency is to paint all drinkers as drunks whose sole function is to endanger women, children, and the rest of the community. The core of this prohibition assembly is here because they are of one mind with Norval, so he is preaching to the choir.

Without warning, the door opens one more time. A man enters carrying an oversized camera with a huge flash attachment and wearing a fedora. A press credential casually stuck in his hat band indicates he's a reporter for the *Detroit Free Press*. Norval is dumbfounded. He has no idea what would bring this man to his small, independent church clear out on Harsens Island. Two strangers wearing suits, and now a reporter. The man is looking around for a place to sit. The chairs all seem to be taken.

Noticeably annoyed, Norval says, "Would someone please get this gentleman a chair?" Recognizing an opportunity when he sees one, Agent Bronson gets out of his chair. He isn't fast enough, as Norval's wife has already opened the door and retrieved a chair for the reporter. The open door reveals a wall of chairs stacked right to the opening. Straining to see around them without removing them one at a time, Agent Bronson opts to return to his seat without a complete search. The pietistic, amateurish ranting of this self-proclaimed "soldier of God" on the need to follow Divine ordinances in ridding the community of the sinful influence of evil imbibers is beginning to annoy him.

With the intention of locking the door, Norval casually walks across the room and places his hand on the doorknob, only to have it turn. Who should be entering? It's none other than Edgar. With this seeming sudden interest in his movement, Norval is overcome with an assuring conviction that he has at last broke through the barriers of resistance.

"Please get Mr. Bentley a chair," says Norval to anyone who can hear him. The pleased look on his face can't be missed. *People are at last truly beginning to realize the importance of joining forces with me in fighting this plague on our society.*

This time, Agent Bronson is on his feet. Edgar has practically sprinted to the closet door, nearly pushing the agent out of the way as he clumsily tears at the stack of chairs. It comes crashing to the floor, resulting in a half dozen of Norval's regulars racing to lend a hand to these befuddled guests. Instead, they themselves become befuddled. Instead of facing just a pile of disrupted chairs, there is an accompanying resonance of clanging bottles as they escape the confines of the closet and slide across the painted church basement floor. There is not much doubt in anyone's mind that these are liquor bottles. Norval stands dumbfounded. For the first time in anyone's memory, he is left speechless.

With the suddenness of greased lightening, both federal agents have abruptly changed from obsequious guests to men in command. Each has directly brandished his badge and identification with an accompanying order. "No one is to leave! Sit back down in your chairs and be prepared to show your identification."

The room is stunned, to say the least. Norval is not responding very well. He can't grasp his role in this debacle. The Federal agents have placed him in handcuffs and have ordered him to sit on the floor to minimize his ability to escape.

Edgar is processed along with the others so as not to single him out and reveal his key role in bringing this whole farce to its end. The *Free Press* reporter is snapping pictures as quickly as his spent flash bulbs can be replaced. People are trying their best not to be the subject of his attention. Some are turning away, and others are covering their faces with their hats, their hands, a coat pulled up—anything to not have their picture appear on the front page of the paper for being involved in such an ignoble state of affairs. The few who are willing to talk with him insist on their innocence.

"I feel like I've walked into a hornet's nest," reports a stunned attendee.

Another is a lady who claims she came to hear Norval says she was there, "because he seemed to have proven himself a stalwart soldier of God in fighting the cause of demon rum."

Within an hour, the attendees have all been given citations and instructions to appear in court.

A small crowd of neighbors are gathering outside, curious about all the hubbub going on at the church. As in all small communities, it doesn't take long for a curious event to acquire several different explanations. Axel and Frankie are doing their level best to direct the rumors toward Norval and the irrefutable evidence exposing his supposed hypocrisy. Trying as best he can to cover his face, Norval is led out in handcuffs to be seated in the rear seat of the federal agents' sedan.

There is no doubt he's devastated by this sudden reversal in his structured life. It's the kind of incident men like Norval either collapse under or come back from roaring like a wounded lion. In this case, it's too early to make a prediction.

Undoubtedly, the saga of Norval Burgess among the drys has been, at least for the present time, stifled by this awkward event.

When a movement can boast of even one hero, they feel energized. This turn of events is going to knock the wind out of the sails of this crusade for some time.

Frankie has nothing but praise for Axel. He's always admired Axel's ability to calmly, patiently plan an incident like this and pull it off. If he didn't have so much admiration and respect for the man, his admiration could step over the line and become envy.

CHAPTER 19

The Diver

Every way of life has its heroes, and often for reasons that are not universal. More often than not, our judgments of heroism are only compatible with a particular type. In the case of Frankie, he perceives Axel's composure while under fire to be admirable. Frankie was a student of this kind of repose while he was in the military, but fears he has lost much now that he isn't living under the same intense discipline in his civilian life. His hope is that as he matures, he will grow to have more of Axel's forbearance.

Another group of young men have chosen a couple of their peers as heroes less because of their forbearance and more on the merits of their explosive violence. There are two such men. These current heroes are admired because of their vicious nature. The recipients of these laureates are Abe Axler and his ever-present partner in crime, Eddie Fletcher. These two are forever embellishing their criminal lives by surrendering more and more of their civility to even more heinous offenses. They will kill just as readily for a thoughtless purpose as for a thoughtful motive—either way, their admirers are junior members of the Purple gang who hope to be noticed for emulating their champions.

As of late, there have been news headlines in the *Free Press* lamenting the killings of several racketeers from Chicago. The suspicions continue to circle around the Purple gang, which is suspected of taking exception to Chicago racketeers invading its turf. Specifically, the story involves these two New Yorkers, Axler and Fletcher, as the triggermen. What is glorified among the gangster ranks is the method used to kill these men; the Thompson machine gun was the modus operando.

Because of Frankie's organizational skills and continuing successes against these big-city mobsters, those island residents who openly took money for cooperating in the Purples' campaign to shakedown island businesses have become fearful of retaliation by their island neighbors. Many of those who profited from the Purples for supplying information on businesses ripe for a shakedown are becoming much more reticent in their cooperation with the Detroit mobsters.

This has been a major reason Axler and Fletcher have placed Lyman Woodard inside the Old Club as a mole. His presence is crucial to access the island's resistance movement, which is driven by Frankie Morgansky. The two mobsters are unaware that their mole has been compromised by Stella's careful shadowing his every move, and in particular her diligence in monitoring his telephone conversations.

Even though the recreational season has come to an end, the duck season has also concluded, and the need for a piano player has lessened, Lyman has opted to stay on to work only on weekends and the promise of a busy holiday season, but he doesn't seem to be short on cash. What had once been suspected is now silently accepted: he has an outside interest underwriting the cost of his room and board.

These are all matters that remain within the view of Frankie's periscope. He has managed to accumulate a small fortune with his various interests in rum-running and bootlegging, so he's now able to support his parents as well as putting Axel on his payroll. The illegal liquor business is proving to be the cash cow the fish business had never been. A major reason for Frankie's success is his uncanny ability to seize opportunities.

One such opportunity has made its way into his area of interest. William Barnes, the owner of the Harsens Island ferry service and a member of Frankie's inner circle of confidants, brings it to his attention a truck loaded with a hundred cases of French champagne went through the ice the previous winter, and no attempts have been made to recover it.

"That's a good five thousand dollars' worth of good selling booze doin' nothin' for nobody," says William.

"Maybe so, but it ain't gonna jump up outta the water and land in our boat. What d'ya think it's gonna take to find it? And once that's done, we gotta determine if it's gone skunky layin' down there in the bottom of the river for a year," says Frankie.

"The story is that this truck loaded with champagne was comin' across the ice at night with a couple a Burnstein's goons drivin' it. Since most of these Detroit city slickers should never venture outta town, these two guys got twisted up like they always do an' ended up goin' through the ice. Nobody knew where that place was they went through 'til me an' my kid was out ice fishin' last winter an' found the spot. There it was, big as life in twenty feet a clear water. All's we need ta do now is to drag a few lines with hooks across the bottom. Once we locate it, we'll mark it, then send a diver down and have a look. At the same time, I know for certain it can be determined from one bottle, the condition of the other nighty-nine," reports William with the air of one in the know.

"What makes you so certain you know the condition of this stuff? And more so, what makes you so sure that was the same truck? And furthermore, what makes you think you can find this spot again? And who's this diver we're gonna trust ta bring on board?" asks Frankie, more than a little curious.

William reaches into a bag he's been carrying. What he pulls out brings Frankie's interest to a new high. It's a corked bottle. Holding it in his hand, he exclaims, "This is why I know it's the same truck! I snagged this and another with my fishin' net an' brought 'em up. I uncorked the other one, and it's damn sure a high-grade champagne."

Handing the bottle over to Frankie to examine, he further adds, "I got a good idea the general location she went down. Once we run the hooks, we'll get a better idea. As far as the diver—that'll be me."

"You?!" says Frankie. rolling the bottle around in his hand.

"Yeah, me. After see'n all that money layin' down there, I got a divin' suit. I been tryin' it out ta see if I can handle goin' down in it. Once I done 'er a few times, I got the hang of it. Works pretty good. All's I'll need is somebody up above runnin the boat and pumpin' air."

Still holding the bottle, Frankie continues staring at William in disbelief. With more than a little reservation, Frankie asks, "When ya wanna do all this?"

"The sooner the better. If we can rig a boat up to give the impression we're just fishin', I think we can pull this off without drawin' a lot of attention," says William in the same confident tone he's used all along. "The less hubbub we make over this, the less we have to worry that somebody's gonna figure out what we're up to."

Frankie is sure William is not going to easily abandon his game plan, regardless of the hassle. As far as William is concerned, it's already written in rock. With or without Frankie, he's on a mission. If nothing else, Frankie needs to figure out a way to feel more comfortable with this escapade.

With the same reservation in his voice, he makes a request. "Not to doubt your expertise with this diving caper you want to pull off, but I'd like to have a practice session so I know what to expect."

William couldn't be happier. "I know you're nervous about this, an' probably think of it as a bunch a tomfoolery. I did too, 'til I tried it, and now I'm hooked," rejoices William.

Frankie is still mulling this whole gambit over in his head. "Tell me something, William, are you more excited about the dive, or finding the booze?"

"To tell the truth, both got me goin'," admits William.

At this point, Frankie is willing to let it rest. Uncorking William's rescued bottle, he offers a toast to their exploit and agrees to go along for this wild venture. Besides, if there is anything he can be a part of that makes life a little harder for the Burnsteins, he's interested. If they're successful, it will mean a small fortune in the rum-running business. There's no question the burgeoning stock market is creating a new kind of buyer who's generally young and adventurous. There are more than enough high-rollers in Detroit alone—not to mention those as far away as Chicago—who are willing to pay a handsome price not only for the champagne, but also for the story that goes along with it. It's been said by one notorious Chicago gangster by the name of Alphonse Capone that "Prohibition is a business; all I do is supply a public demand." Many on Harsens Island agree with this sentiment. As far as the Burnsteins attempting to make a recovery, that's not their style. They're more inclined to let someone else put forth the effort and then attempt to hijack the load.

They set a date for a practice run in the middle of Lake St. Clair. Frankie has brought Axel along because his trustworthiness is unquestioned, and he possesses years of boating skills. The temperatures are in the low forties, and the waves are at a minimum. They're using a fishing boat with an enclosed cabin from William's fleet. It's outfitted as a commercial fishing boat in the hope it will be ignored by the coast guard and the Jewish Navy alike. To envelop the diving operation in as much secrecy as possible, William will make use of the cabin to don the "heavy gear" he needs to make the dive.

Lying on the cabin floor is a state-of-the-art diving suit comprised of a copper diving helmet, a waterproof canvas suit, weighted shoes, air hoses, a pump to supply the air line with life-sustaining oxygen, and an attached rope to pull a diver to safety, should he need it.

On Harsens Island, secrecy is forever sought, but nearly nonexistent. The population is small enough that someone always pays attention to someone else's business. Getting all the equipment on board without being noticed by some curious onlooker takes some doing. The shoreline is also dotted with peeping Toms paid by the Purples; they're all equipped with telescopes and watching every move that's made on the water.

With enough effort, the team manages to gather all the equipment they need, put it together, and make their journey to the center of the lake. They hope to be seen only as a routine fishing expedition. William has spent the previous afternoon acquainting Frankie and Axel with how to negotiate the hand pump he'll need to sustain his life. Other than that, he expects it to be a routine dive.

They have successfully anchored the boat and are busy arranging fishing lines while they prepare for William's practice dive. This time of the year, the water temperatures are beginning to drop, but as yet, not too significantly. It's been prearranged for William to remain submerged for twenty minutes, providing all goes well.

Watching William emerge in his dive gear brings about a curious expression that can only spring from noting something particularly bizarre. It prompts Frankie to say, "Man, you look like some kinda alien in that outfit."

The copper helmet has been screwed on, bolted, and sealed onto the receptors. Once he's inside, William can't hear anything but the sound of his own breathing, accompanied by a sensation of isolation that increases his concentration. All the emergency signals—"give me more line" and "pull me up"—have been thoroughly rehearsed. He can't help but have a mixed sense of excitement and reservation about this whole procedure.

Not yet in the water, but still on board, he wrestles with the tremendous heaviness of the weighted boots and the fifty-pound headpiece. All of this paraphernalia is compromising William's balance with each step. Frankie and Axel are there to aid him: Frankie to mind the hand pump providing the air supply, Axel to mind the anchor and the general stabilizing maintenance about the boat, and both to help him get safely into the water.

With a few assisted steps, William finds himself at the rear of the boat, where a rope ladder has been lowered off the deck. His next maneuver is to position himself to make his descent as safely as he can. With a little more assistance from his crew, he manages to lower himself with the full expectation that a few more underwater rungs will completely submerge him.

The water level is making its way up his body. Suddenly, a flicker of panic makes its way into his consciousness. His first response is to resist by climbing back up the ladder, but his second response is a conditioned one of trusting his equipment to keep him safe in this normally hostile setting for non-gilled creatures. The canvas diving suit is beginning to compress around his arms and legs; it feels like a gentle hug. It's not until his head is completely submerged and he takes his first breath totally underwater that he begins to trust Frankie's ability to supply him with oxygen.

Once William has reached the bottom rung of the twenty-foot ladder, he is surprised at how remarkably clear the lake is. His first step onto the lake bottom changes things dramatically as the silt rises up around him. He's also surprised at just how light his equipment has become. Desiring to test things out a bit more stringently, and instead of taking a step, he leaps forward, allowing himself to drift down a little. It's an experience he initially had when he was testing the equipment to buy it, and he's been looking forward to initiating it once again. It's also practice so he won't land face first on the lake bottom and have to struggle his way back upright.

William discovers this particular spot is littered with debris—everything from empty cans and bottles to dead-heads left over from the logging days. After all, it's not unusual for the sight-seeing ship *Tashmoo* to dump its garbage overboard, just like every other ship that passes through the lake.

With only a few steps, William unexpectedly comes eye to eye with an elusive muskellunge. *This monster has to be at least a four-footer* is his silent thought. It pays little heed to his presence as it glides by. These are places these underwater creatures pay little attention to as long as they can feed, breed, and poop. They swim around all this stuff with the expectation of coming across a food source growing amongst it all.

Up above, Frankie and Axel are hoping to give the impression they are busy setting a fishing net while making certain William is getting enough air and remains safe. While he's pumping the air machine, Frankie gazes across the lake at the Old Club. He knows Stella is working and wonders if she's aware of his whereabouts. Little does he know that their every move is being followed with telescopes supplied by the hotel for a group of aquatic birdwatchers. Coming in for a lunch, the birdwatchers' discussion is centering around the fishing boat with a person in a diving suit. This activity becomes the buzz, since this type of endeavor is rarely—if ever—seen on the lake.

Stella is quite aware of Frankie's and Axel's reasons for being out in the middle of this body of water at this time. All this business about the truck laden with expensive champagne going through the ice the year before is not hidden history, but as things go, something else nudged this event to the sidelines, so it's been forgotten by most people on Harsens. Stella listens with interest at the different theories each of these patrons have.

"I'll bet they're lookin ta find one a them sunken ships with gold on 'em," says an elderly man with an adventurous lilt.

"Where in hell you gonna find gold around Michigan?" asks another man.

"I heard a boat caught on fire and burnt a few years back. They cut it loose so's it wouldn't catch all the island grass on fire. It ended up sinkin' somewhere out there," says another with the hope that he's adding another piece to the puzzle.

Stella notices Lyman has deserted his piano and taken a position behind one of the telescopes. He seems to have it fixed on a particular part of the lake. Taking a moment to search the horizon, she realizes he has also pointed his glass at the boat. She's not sure what he might know or not know about the champagne truck accident the year before, but she is certain she needs to take extra care in noticing his reactions to what he's viewing.

What he is fixed on is the diver coming on board and the fact Frankie and this oddity are on the same boat. He has no idea what this might mean, but keeping true to his commitment to Axler and Fletcher to give a full report all of Frankie's goings-on, he is hell-bent on getting this information into their hands.

Lyman has grown up around ambitious men. The quickest way to success he's learned is not to leave things to chance when you're given a task, and instead to be thorough in whatever it is you're asked to do. He is resolved to believe that he needs to map out a strategy and stick with it. Transmitting this information in a timely fashion is to eliminate the chance some important aspect will be overlooked. He realizes that what he is looking at but doesn't understand could be significant to those who might be able to decipher what he is seeing. After spending the next half-hour watching the activities of Frankie's crew, he's satisfied he can give a comprehensive description of the happenings going on between this bunch.

The Purples' influence on the island has diminished precipitously since the islanders have aligned themselves with Frankie. There is no question he has become the Purples' most sought-after nemesis. To the world, Frankie is only one person, but to these mobsters, he's becoming the world. They're ready to go to any length to defeat him—including paying Axler and Fletcher thousands of dollars' reward for his head on a platter. Considering he's costing them thousands of dollars every day in lost revenues, this is chicken feed.

These telephone calls from Lyman have become most important because of the nearly impenetrable line of defense the islanders have set up in defending themselves against personal visits by these gangster intruders. Since this has denied the Purples the luxury of personally assessing what their next move should be, they're relying on these calls from Lyman to keep them updated. Axler and Fletcher are not happy with this seemingly fragile telephone arrangement, but are curtailed in doing anything else. At least for now, they are begrudgingly relying on their trustworthiness.

True to his resolve, Lyman is on a mission to get to a telephone. Suspecting this would be his next move, Stella gives him enough time to become absorbed in his task before she slips into the accompanying phone booth. It's obvious to Stella he's conversing with the same contacts he's spoken with in the past. Never suspecting his conversations are anything less than private, Lyman pours out the details of his probe.

These details are quickly deciphered by Axler and Fletcher, who connect this activity with the lost champagne truck. Both these men recognize they can quickly redeem themselves with the Burnsteins if they can successfully recover that vanished load of expensive booze.

Listening carefully to Lyman's account, Axler is torn between an agitation that he is having to depend on an eighteen-year-old kid to give him a full account of what amounts to a grand discovery and an excitement that this opportunity could reap huge benefits if they play their cards right.

"Listen kid, your on ta somethin' big. Tell me: where they were positioned, and did ya see that diver bring anything up?"

Lyman can't be happier to hear these words from Axler. In an effort to be as concise as possible, he reports, "They're just south of the Old Club, more in the middle of the lake, and no sir, I didn't see them bringing anything up—only them helping the guy outta the water and getting him outta his suit."

Axler is quiet on the other end of the line. It's obvious he's digesting Lyman's observations. Realizing it's going to be his move next, Axler further instructs Lyman to stay on this endeavor and to report back immediately with any new developments.

After hanging up, Lyman takes a brisk trot back to the window, eager to validate his resourcefulness. The horizon is clear of Frankie's venture. Satisfied he's dotted all his i's and crossed all his t's, he returns to his piano-playing with renewed vigor.

Stella is begrudgingly inclined to inform Frankie about what has transpired. She has been preoccupied with her wedding plans, and it's disconcerting to have this disruption. She's as ready to blame Frankie for "forever stirring the pot" as she is to blame the unforgivable charlatans who are getting stirred. Well aware that Frankie is not going to heed her pleas to stop this war with the Purples, she reluctantly gives herself over to the reality that no one can stop him. So here she is once again, hearing just one side of the conversation between Lyman and his handler on the other end of the line.

After Frankie patiently listens to her objections to his involvement in challenging the Purples for possession of the lost truck, Stella finally gets around to giving her account of Lyman's conversation.

Frankie says, "I'm not surprised, Stella. That little shit of a piano player is going to have to be dealt with. Sooner would be better." Giving his words a second thought, he realizes it might be a blessing in disguise to have this mole think he's doing all this spying without being noticed.

Not wanting to upset Stella any further, Frankie thanks her for her diligence and earnestly asks her to continue to shadow Lyman.

With more than a little reluctance, she promises to do so. Not willing to let Frankie have the last word, Stella then adds a request in the form of a plea. "Frankie, please don't do anything stupid that's gonna get us killed. Carly and I moved out here 'cause you promised we'd be rid of all these problems, and now you're dragging them in behind us."

Not wanting to carry this unease of Stella's to another level by attempting to explain his behavior, Frankie assures her, "We can make a different ending to all this if we persevere. I promise, I ain't gonna do anything that's gonna hurt you and Carly."

Stella hasn't gotten this far in life because she lacked insight. Much of her discontent begins with a propensity to crucify herself between two thieves; shame because of her past, and worry concerning her future. On the other hand, she has been blessed with an innate sense that she cannot allow herself to be a product of her circumstances; rather, she must be a product of her decisions in spite of her circumstances. She also realizes Frankie is not going to become anything other than who he is. To say this is not troubling is certainly an understatement. Frankie has attempted to reason with her that the life she hopes to have is going to have to be fought for. This surrender of her security is only temporary. Sitting alone with her thoughts, Stella wishes she could be more certain.

CHAPTER 20
Madge

Since Stella's revelation that Lyman has compromised their dredging effort, Frankie has taken some extra precautions by alerting his defense team to be prepared to respond to a possible interruption of their exploration. This team continues to be a select group of the island citizenry. Those with a military background are especially competent; it's like they have a third eye to perceive what they might be seeing and respond accordingly. They, in turn, have selected confidants of their own to assist where needed.

All in all, things are going along smoothly. It's the chilly end of November. The lake has lost some of its warmth, having given in to the endless change of seasons. This morning, a mist rises off the water. Nonetheless, the tiny crew are diligently pursuing their goal to locate the lost hoard of sunken champagne. Continuing to outfit the boat as a fishing trawler, they have dropped lines with hooks to drag along the bottom with the hopes of discovering the elusive sunken truck. So far, they have snagged everything from immersed logs to barrels containing God only knows what stuff they've appreciatively left where they found it. It's not been a secret that the burgeoning auto industry are using the waterways as their private dumping grounds and more than likely much of this debris has come from this source.

William has a good idea where this truck went through the ice. To him, locating it is merely a matter of persistence. He's already donned his diving suit this morning, going to the bottom on a promising snag with the hook, only to discover a sunken skiff. These reversals don't seem to daunt the resolve this team has in bringing this mission to a fruitful end. They each know it's a fact the truck is down in a region where the current doesn't allow the ice to freeze very thick; now it's just a matter of time before they hit the jackpot.

Much of Frankie's challenge out here on the water is to remain secret in purpose toward the average islander, whose life revolves around snoopy gossip in its many forms. Since Stella overheard Lyman's phone conversation with Axler, the idea that they are keeping something secret from the Purples is nonsensical. But the islanders are a different breed. It's not so much that they wish to purposely harm Frankie—it's that if they become aware of the nature of Frankie's quest, the waterways would become a free-for-all. Everyone would be floating some type of a device in hopes of finding the mother lode. For that reason, every day Frankie's crew removes one attachable insignia naming the boat and screw on a different name plate bearing another insignia the following day. They also have placed spotters with signal flags to warn of any unwanted guests. The name of this game is not only to remain obscured in intent but to find the prized hoard.

Axel has also been replaced with Frankie at the helm, Ezra Church and Jacob Freebold as deck hands. Ezra is in charge of pumping air to William's dive helmet while Jacob watches for signals from the spotters. This leaves Axel free to go onto the mainland and hang around the gangster haunts to discover any fresh chatter concerning Frankie's doings on the water.

Axel has teamed up with Albie Lieberman. Albie has become a trusted ally, after all, he was quite instrumental in discovering the hidden mooring used by the Jewish Navy to berth a half-dozen of the torpedo boats that Frankie and Dave Schindler later destroyed by firebombing. Albie has acquainted himself with many of the haunts where these mobsters hang out, and is especially willing to join with Axel to seek out any evidence where the mob might be planning to play a role in the recovery of their sunken champagne truck.

One recent adjustment made by the Purples is to no longer place all the Torpedo boats in one berth, but rather to place them separately in different locations. This means their crews aren't centralized making it more difficult to locate all of them. Both Axel and Albie have some reservations on how to get a firm hold on a good comprehensive search plan that will be effective, and at the same time won't show their hand.

Accordingly, another drawback to these scattered crews is finding a central watering hole used by all of them. It's not looking too promising. Nevertheless, they need to begin somewhere. They decide the best place to begin is in a restaurant where the clientele is made up of blue collar workers. These individuals tend to be less suspicious of their own kind even if they are strangers. Axel and Albie have no problem fitting in since 'blue collar' is exactly what they are.

The duo begins their investigation in a locale eatery in Algonac on the mainland across the north channel from Harsens. The waitress is a young, stylish twenty-something woman whose seeming goal is to single-handedly present her age group as the foremost in the new upcoming flapper style. Her hair is bobbed and thickly marcelled. Her apron is tied in such a way as to showcase a knee length skirt with a tight little roll at the top of her stockings. Her lavishly applied lipstick and freshly painted nails are of the same bright red hue. The only item that sets her apart from a speakeasy sugar baby is her pencil, order pad, and a name tag identifying her as "Madge."

"What can I get ya?" is her only greeting along with the little snapping sound her chewing gum delivers.

"I'd like a plate of scrambled eggs, toast and coffee," replies Axel.

Still chewing her gum and without a word, she writes the order. Turning to Albie she still says nothing, only communicating with a fixed stare, raising her eyebrows, slightly nodding to acknowledge she's prepared to take his order.

"I'll have the same," pronounces Albie.

Axel watches as she swishes her way back to the kitchen. Shaking his head, he exclaims, "It sure as hell ain't my world anymore."

Albie, being the younger man, and with a purposely orchestrated grin says, "Maybe not yours, but hers don't look all that bad."

Still shaking his head, Axel's only response is a little, "Humph!"

"You ain't ever gonna get married with your way of thinkin'," says a still grinning Albie.

"Who in hell says I wanna be married," responds Axel with a rather severe expression.

"I dunno, I thought every man needs a good woman," says Albie a bit more serious than he's been.

Axel gives a little pause as though he's contemplating Albie's certainty. "Lemme ask you, Albie: if I were ta leave a woman and a dog home alone all day, which one da you believe is gonna be happy ta see me when I get back?"

Before Albie can answer a young man swaggers through the front door. Immediately, Albie recognizes him as the same man "Bob" who showed him the location of the Purples Torpedo boats. With a reflex action, Albie pulls his hat down in the hopes this man won't recognize him. It soon becomes apparent the last thing on this young man's mind is who might be sitting around the restaurant. His interest is definitely in another direction. It quickly becomes obvious he has his eye on Madge. Taking a seat at the counter, he orders a coffee. Hardly able to take his eyes off her, his gaze follows her every move. From where Axel and Albie are sitting, they can't hear the exchange going on between these two and don't want to blow their cover by acting too intrusively.

Soon Madge is clumsily plopping their order in front of them. She appears to be a bit more harried than she was when she initially took their order. Axel decides to take a chance and say something. "Ma'am, are you okay?" Not waiting for her to answer, and nodding toward the man at the counter, he quickly adds, "Your boyfriend over there givin' you a hard time?"

Just as quick to reply, she says, "Boyfriend?! He ain't my boyfriend. He just wishes!" With that abrupt answer, she turns on her heel and marches back to the kitchen.

It's becoming evident that the attraction between this duo is one sided. Soon the young man, who Albie remembers as Bob, finishes his coffee. He makes his way back out through the same door through which he had made his self-assured appearance with a certain buoyance only minutes before, but he now has an unmistakably doleful disposition.

The eggs prove to be short-lived as they devour everything on their plates. Soon these two are at the counter, where Madge adds their bills.

Axel is willing to take the lead once again. "You said that fellow ain't your boyfriend, he seemed damned interested in you for not bein' more than a customer."

This waitress owing neither this other guy nor himself any more than a goodbye, suddenly becomes loquacious. "He's been buggin' me ta go out with him every day for two weeks, but he's one a them damn gangsters from Detroit, an' I don't wanna thing ta do with 'em. They kilt my dad for more than a rowboat load a booze."

Both Axel and Albie glance at each other for no more than a split second. Both recognize a potential ally standing right before them and both begin to speak at the same time. Looking at one another again, Axel lets Albie take the lead on this. "Madge, I want you to know how bad we both feel about you losing your dad to these pigs. We've also had our moments with them." Pausing long enough to regroup his thoughts and permit Madge to also have a moment, he continues. "We also know that guy who's perturbin' you." Pausing once again to get a read on Madge's countenance. Seeing that she may be receptive to his next offer, Albie continues, "He's bad news all the way around. You're doin' the right thing not ta get mixed up with the likes of him. But I'm gonna ask you ta do with this guy. How'd you like ta make fifty bucks in the next few days?"

Madge's face takes on disbelieving twist. She finally manages to say, "What kind a bull crap you guys tryin' ta pull anyway?"

Holding back while Albie makes the initial offer, Axel jumps in, saying, "We need some info an' we're sure this guy knows the answers. You get what we need outta him in the next few days an' we'll willingly pay you the fifty bucks."

She's beginning to relax a little saying, "You guys are serious about this ain't ya? How do I know yer on the level?"

"We're dead serious," adds Albie. He spends the next few minutes taking her into their confidence enough to let her know only enough about their resistance group to gain her confidence, but nothing about their diving project.

Enthusiastically wiggling her pencil between her fingers and looking at them with new eyes, Madge says, "I've heard of you guys. My dad would wanna be part of somethin' like that. What do I gotta do?"

Albie continues while handing her twenty-five dollars with the promise to pay the rest after she gets what information she is able to glean. "We need ta know where he keeps his boat and a few other minor things like what he's lookin' out for in the next few days."

"I'll do what I can. How do I get a hold of you?" she further enquires.

"I'll check in with you here every day for the next few days. Just give me the restaurant phone number," says Albie.

With an agreement made between the three of them, Axel and Albie leave satisfied Madge is just the ticket to get them what they need.

CHAPTER 21
Jackpot

Meanwhile, back at the lake, the diving crew are continuing to methodically drag the bottom with long drag lines connected to hooks fastened to and extending out from the back of the boat. The charted parcel is over an approximate ten-acre area. They are suffering no lack of false snags—mostly sunken crafts of various sorts. The lake proves to be a time capsule; it's not uncommon to discover some long-lost artifact from a previous century tangled up in their lines. Usually something of a curious nature rather than anything of value. Nonetheless, each time, William has to suit up and to go to the bottom to inspect. If nothing else, William is gaining much more diving experience and is gaining a vast knowledge of the lake's other sunken resources.

It's well into their third day of operation when the lines grow taunt, indicating they have hooked something once again. This is not a new development, nor is it surprising, as it has happened so many times already. They shut the engine down and drop the anchor, only to discover how unforgiving the lake had been to some nineteenth-century sailing vessel lying peacefully at the bottom of the lake. Regardless of the number of false indicators, William sits prepared with the same ready resolve as he had from the start; Readied once more to have his helmet and air lines attached. The crew's optimism is mixed with a healthy dose of possibilities; to say they aren't excited each time is to misread this crew's resolve. With a bit of luck, this could be the jackpot. On the other hand, it might be just another unfruitful dive.

The number of unrewarding dives are proving to be directly proportional to the number of rewarding practice sessions the crew undergoes in preparing William for yet, another safe descent. The result of all this practice is they have cut their readying time in half. In this instance, in just a matter of a very few minutes, his helmet and airline are in place, and he's in the water.

With this added sense of proficiency comes a sense of professionalism. With a steady hand and trained eye, each of the attendants are faithful to their posts, ready to respond to any sudden calls of responsibility.

Watching William disappear with nothing but swirling water covering his head, is something that each of these deck hands deal with in his own way. For many reasons—all considered to be practical—there isn't one of them who would willingly change places with him. They're thankful to be doing any task on board, rather than what William has chosen.

It's only a matter of minutes before William is sending a signal to be brought to the surface. The crew is extremely responsive since it's not clear if William is in a life-threatening situation or has made contact with something important. With the reflex of a well-oiled machine, they begin the process of hoisting him and his hundred-pound diving suit back to the surface. The copper-colored helmet is the first piece of the package to emerge. The next is an appendage thrusting through the surface with a bottle of sorts in its gloved hand.

Frankie is momentarily taken aback. At this point, things are taking on a different light. There is a definite need to get this diver back on board and speak to him. Has he uncovered the Holy Grail, or is this just another random souvenir? With Frankie handing off the recovered bottle to Ezra, along with Jacob, they manage to get William on board. Anxious to be freed from his screwed-on helmet, William begins the unwinding process himself. With extra hands helping, they finally finish. With the helmet off, William takes a moment to clear his throat. "JACKPOT!" he finally manages to shout.

The first reaction is to let out a walloping whoop celebrating their success, but since they're certain they're being viewed by spotters who are ready to take note of any type of celebration, they've decided to curtail any outward festivity.

"I been seein' that truck layin' down there below the ice in my sleep for damn near a year, it's still settin' exactly the way I and my kid left it," adds William with the same exuberance he's demonstrated since he began this escapade.

Frankie wants to avoid setting any kind of surface marker that could reveal this location. Instead, he takes notice of their position by making use of markers from both shorelines. Next, he draws a crude but satisfactory treasure map with an X marking the spot.

William is absolutely elated beyond description. He's chattering about everything he saw and thought of when he made the discovery.

"You can't believe how good a shape all that stuff is in. Other than a few cases breaking loose, the rest is still all tied up, an' still in the truck," he shouts in his excitement. With a lot of help and a generous amount of congratulations, they finally get him out of his gear.

"I gotta hand it to ya, William, ya done good, but right now, I suggest we take a break. We know them damn Purples got spotters watchin' every move we're makin'. What we need ta do now is check with Axel. He may have some new info we can use to make this recovery happen without I' our asses caught up in an unnecessary shit storm with them and their damnable Navy," says Frankie. For the time being Frankie is happy to take this break. Meantime, Stella has another project she can't do without Frankie's help.

William continues to chomp at the bit. He wants nothing more than to get back in the water and pull this load of champagne up from its watery haven. Nonetheless, he has consented to wait and give Axel and Albie their speculation that Madge will come up with some more helpful information. Axel and Albie, on the other hand, don't regard this wait as a gamble, they're certain she can come up with something helpful.

Albie has been willing to allow her a day or two guaranteeing her a reasonable amount of time to fulfill her end of their bargain, now it's come time to make contact and review her progress. In keeping true to his word to stay in touch, he phones the restaurant and asks to speak to Madge. In just the short time it takes for her to get to the phone, when considering the significance of the information she's been able to provide, they hope they were correct in their assessment of Madge's ability to come through.

"Hello. This is Madge," comes the husky voice over the line. It's clear it's a female cigarette smoker on the other end. She could be described as a bit edgy, or maybe indelicate, but definitely female.

"Hello Madge, this is Albie Lieberman. I'm calling to check if you had any luck with our friend and possibly some information that can interest me?"

"As a matter of fact, I do. Can I meet you some place where we won't be seen together?" she asks.

Placing his hand over the mouthpiece, Albie turns to Axel. "She wants to know if she can meet with us alone, where nobody's gonna see us?"

Axel immediate reply is, "Yeah, tell her ta meet us on the island side of the ferry landing in an hour. We'll let her follow us out to an old fishin' shack I know about. Tell her ta make sure no one's followin' her."

Albie relays the message back to Madge, emphasizing the need to be sure no one is tailing her.

Making their way to the ferry landing, Axel remembers how obsessed William is about recovering that load of champagne, especially now that he's discovered its location. He decides to make a stop at William's office and bring him up to date. Finding him sitting alone behind his desk, he tells him the latest development and how it's beginning to look promising; like how it can all come together. William can't be more pleased. After his immediate response of cheering their efforts, he asks to become part of this reconnaissance team. He's far from feeling thrilled to have his project put on hold by people he feels he brought into the venture to aid him.

"I want to meet with this babe and personally hear what information she's got ta give."

Knowing William, the way he does, Axel had half way expected this. He also realizes how William can be when he has his mind set.

Living up to many similar challenges and overcoming them, Axel believes he can control William; he sees no good reason to leave him out of the mix.

Agreeing to bring him in, Axel instructs him as to where he plans to meet with this woman. "You remember the old fishing shack we took that weaselin' Squeaky Schwartz to? Meet us there."

Within the hour everyone is in place. Madge is the last car off the ferry. Axel and Albie deduce that it's unlikely anyone is following her. Sitting stiff behind the wheel of her sedan, she has a lost, bewildered look. With a quick glance through her car window, she spots the familiar physiognomy of her two seeming guides. In recognition, both parties give a subtle signal of detection. This ensures they're still altogether, and on the same page.

Leaving the ferry landing with Madge directly behind him, Axel makes a right turn to head toward the fishing shack. Within ten minutes, they're at the turnoff that takes them down a two-track road quickly concealed by a wall of six-foot-tall marsh grasses. William is already there and waiting. Knowing what he knows about this fortune in champagne lying only a few feet below the water line makes it difficult for him to take on the demeanor of a patient man.

Aware of the negative force William's impetuous attitude can have on this meeting, Axel pulls William aside, making a point very clear to him, "I ain't real sure what this woman has ta offer yet, but I know one thing damn certain, everyone involved in this puzzle has a place to fit in gettin' that champagne out of the lake. What we gotta do is make real certain we ain't destroyin' a piece of this jigsaw by scarin' this woman off. A hunnerd percent of the success of this liaison with this woman is gonna depend on our careful reactions. Don' say nothin' that's gonna make her wanna run."

William is taken back at Axel's forthrightness for the moment, but having a second thought he quickly comes to agree. Introductions are made between Madge and William. Noticeably, William is taking on a calmer character as he smiles and shakes her hand. Axel leads the troupe into the shack with the flair of a confident negotiator. As soon as the door is opens what is in plain view are the chair and bindings used to shackle Squeaky just months before. Seeing this, Madge freezes in her tracks. The look on her face is one of near terror as she attempts to grasp the meaning of this set up.

Sensing what this must appear to look like to Madge, Axel quickly pushes these items to the side with the words, "This ain't got nothin' ta do with our meeting. You ain't got nothin' ta be concerned with 'cept the other twenty-five bucks you gotta earn."

Still not certain what she has gotten herself into, and after all is said and done, she finds herself standing inside some old shack with three strange men, a chair, and a bunch of rope. She is certain that she's more than willing to share whatever she knows, if for no other reason than to get this meeting over with and be on her way.

Remembering what Madge had told them of how the Purples had murdered her father, Albie steps in. "Madge, the only reason all of us are here is because we got the same hate you got for these brutes. They killed your father, and they should have ta pay for that. All we want is for the same payment to be made for the wrongs they've done in our lives. You're here to help us begin."

As Madge listens to Albie's words, an ease gradually makes its way across her face and replaces the strained, worried look she had a minute ago. There's something in his voice she finds trusting. In another moment, she settles down enough to share what she believes they wanted her to uncover.

After rummaging around in her purse until she finds the package of cigarettes she's sure is in there, she places one between her lips. In the next moment, Albie produces a lighter. After taking a deep drag and exhaling a stream of smoke, she's prepared to begin.

"After you left, Bob came back later that afternoon. He was insistin' that I was gonna go out with him to the point I knew that he ain't gonna leave 'til I agreed. I finally gave in, but I told him I'd only go if he took me to the Blue Bird nightclub. The reason I insisted we go there is 'cause the bartender is my cousin an' I figured he'd help me out if I needed it."

All three men have, as if on cue, lit cigarettes of their own and are content to listen quietly and as a further gesture of this being a friendly encounter, Axel passes a flask between them; it contains an unnamed sort of moonshine. Madge pauses long enough to take her turn with the flask and then continues. "He agreed ta take me there. After a few drinks, he started to brag about how important he is in the Purple Gang and how they run these boats out on the water ta run down rumrunners around Harsens Island. I asked him if he had one of these boats. He said he not only had one, he'd take me for a ride. It's too damn cold for me ta be goin' out on the lake this time of the year, but like you asked me ta find out where he kept the boat so I told him I'd do it. We left the Blue Bird an' went about a mile east outta Algonac to a little group of cabins on the St. Clair river. He drove down behind 'em to a boat house, then showed me the boat sittin' inside."

"Did you happen to get the name of the cabins?" asks William, who until now has been restraining himself and let Axel and Albie do all questioning.

"Yeah. It was on a big swingin' sign. I think it said 'Mike's Deluxe' cabins," replies Madge. She's much more relaxed now as she recounts the events of this date with Bob; maybe because of the alcohol, maybe because she has undergone a transition from fear of these three to one of trust—or some of each.

William is listening, but is also lapsing back into being on edge. His next question is a bit more forceful. "Did the son-of-a-bitch say anything about what the hell they're up to now?"

When William becomes worked up, he has a way of attempting to suck those around him into his vortex of tenseness. In reaction to William's behavior, Madge's face suddenly paralyzes with an awkward look of uneasiness. Seeing a need to intervene before Madge locks up completely, Axel steps in and gives William a hard look of disapproval. Then, turning to Madge, he says, "William is getting ahead of your story. You just continue to tell it the way you feel it needs to be told."

Madge takes a moment to give each of these men one more intense look of suspicion. This is all done to satisfy herself that she is still avoiding the chance things are going to get ugly for her. This extra scrutiny is made by most women of her age for good reasons. Only in the past few years have women been granted the same legal rights as men, and men still have a tendency to regard women as underlings. Undoubtedly what separates her from other women is her tendency to get involved with this kind of caper to begin with.

Satisfied with Axel's patient way, she continues, "Once I got a good look at the boat and where it was located, I stuck to my decision about it bein' too damn cold ta be takin' a boat ride. I then asked him if he still goes out in weather like this. He said that he and another guy were probably gonna be goin' out in a few days. I asked him 'Why is that?' He said it was 'cause some weird guy in a divers suit was out on the lake tryin' ta locate a sunken load of champagne that belongs to his boss."

There is a sudden intense interest in this last statement. William is chomping at the bit to get his two-cents worth in again as Axel gives him a subtle hand motion to calm down, then once again turns to Madge, giving her a little patient nod indicating she should continue.

Regaining her thought pattern, Madge continues. "I asked what he was plannin' on doin' about it an' he said, 'Oh we got plans that'll make yer hair stand on end.' I told him that I like a good thriller and wanted ta hear about it. He said that they had spotters watchin' every move these guys are makin'. As soon as they make their find and feel comfortable enough to bring the booty on board, he and another guy are gonna hijack their boat, leavin' the crew at the bottom of the lake."

Pausing for a moment to regroup her thoughts, Madge begins again, "He said, since they knew whose boat this is and most of the people on board an' that they was gonna wait 'til the boat returned to its marina before they give them Reubens the surprise of their lives."

With this last statement, Madge indicates that's all the information she has. Letting things settle down a bit, they all light another cigarette and pass the flask one more time to celebrate a fruitful meeting. Madge has proven to be a resource they could not have done without.

"You don't know how much you've helped us," says Albie while he's peeling out another twenty-five dollars and handing it to Madge. A smile comes across her lips. Even if she has no idea how this information is to be used, somehow, she is vindicating her father's murder—if only a little.

Relieved to have this chore behind them, they all return to their previous tasks delighted they have the kind of information that will, once more, allow them to have a 'heads up' in dealing with these adversaries. Axel agrees to bring Frankie up to date as quickly as possible and get back to the project.

CHAPTER 22
Now or Never

To her credit, even though Stella has had some reservations about Frankie's resistance movement, she has been a steady advocate for him in his ongoing clash with the Purples. In spite of their rocky start, Alina has also come to grow quite fond of Frankie and has known about Carly's relationship to him since her daughter discovered she was pregnant. Neither of them ever found a way to share that information with Stella's father. He never could have reconciled the idea of a granddaughter fathered by a Jew. As things are with Frankie now days, Alina couldn't be more pleased.

But lately, Stella has other things on her mind. She has a wedding to plan. The closest female confidant she has way out here on the island is her mother. Today, the two are planning a trip to the mainland to visit the priest at St. Anthony church about wedding plans.

It's shortly after noon when they arrive. Sister Dina Bosatta, the parish secretary, greets them. Stella remembers her as her school principle. She has since retired and has taken a less demanding position working in the parish office on the day to day affairs. Back in high school, she was far from being Stella's favorite nun. Sister "D," as she was referred to back then, still possesses the demeanor of one who remains guarded against anything or anyone from the outside world.

"Please tell me the nature of your visit so Father can be prepared to meet with you," probes Sister D.

What Stella notices immediately is the way Sister D presents this request, it's the same voice she used to intimidate her students. Taking only a second to assess her situation, Stella arises and boldly approaches Sister D's desk. By this show of confidence, Stella is hoping she can overcome the lingering fear she still has of this woman.

"I want to speak to Father about a wedding," she says, she's also very surprised at how easily she's responding to this woman's manners. She recalls how she and her friends would go out of their way to make Sisters life a little more stressful—especially when they insisted on smoking cigarettes. Sister looked upon women smoking as a mortal sin.

Not looking up from her desk, Sister D continues her interrogation, "And what is your name?"

Without a hesitation, Stella declares in as clear and bold a voice as she can muster, "My name is Stella Mazzara."

Sister D, without looking up, halts briefly. It's the kind of a pause that accompanies a recollection of sorts. In a moment, she pulls herself together once again, and continues to enter this information into an official-looking, hardcover dossier.

With a small, forced smile, she invites them to have a seat while she delivers this information to Father. Disappearing behind a closed door for a few minutes, she reappears with the message, "Father will see you now."

Both Stella and Alina are out of their seats making their way to the inner sanctum of St. Anthony Catholic church. Father Michael Dana is pastor at St. Anthony. He's a middle-aged man of Italian descent. He's served here for a couple of decades. Like many other

Italian Roman Catholic clergy, he is of the opinion that the church belongs to them. Irish, German, Polish: any Catholics other than Italians are considered an off brand. The Italians rarely—if ever—allow these other clergy members to serve a mass in any of their parishes.

Stella knows what she is up against with Father Dana. Frankie being a non-Catholic, even more so as a Jew, she is going to be put on the receiving end of Father Dana's denunciations. This is the very reason she didn't insist Frankie come with her, instead, she brought her mother leaving Frankie to tend to Carly. She has a good idea what they'll be in for. After the introductions are finished and Stella has explained why she's here, he holds true to his need to denounce Jews, Protestants, and any other non-Catholic institution that comes to his mind. All these, in his mind, are teetering on the very edge of perdition.

"I can bring this matter up to the Bishop, but I can tell you that since your marriage will not be a sacramental union, and in order for you to get a dispensation, you would need to have a reason so desperate it would mean you were on your deathbed before he would agree to it—and probably not even then. He will demand a 'just and reasonable cause.' Even then, he will denounce anything you present in the case of a non-Christian as 'the impediment of disparity of cult.'"

These are the last words Stella hears before she and her mother walk out of the church. With all the pretty words to explain the church's reason to remain stoic in its pronouncement, it can only can be considered as a loveless decree. Like so many parishioners over the years, she and Alina have heard of these things happening to others, but until it's happened to them, they had never felt the full impact of its loveless bite.

"I don't care if I never set foot into this church again as long as I live," deplores Stella.

Alina can hear the hurt in her daughter's voice, and like all mothers, it pains her.

Stella can't wait to get out of the city and back to her new home on Harsens. Every street, store, or persons she sees only serves to bring back her pain filled past, and now to have had the rejection of her church is making her departure even more urgent.

Within an hour, they are back at Algonac making their way across the channel. William is working the deck when he sees Stella. Taking her hand, he turns it over to view her ring. "That Frankie should get right down on his hands and knees and kiss your ass every day for a woman like you." With that he kisses her hand.

"Oh, thank you, William. You're such a flirt." This kind of encounter with the island people only serves to reinforce how sure she is that coming to the island was the best thing she could have done for herself, her mother, and Carly. All that's left to do now is to meet with Frankie and explain to him what has transpired.

Meeting at the Morgansky cottage, Stella replays her miserable day for Frankie. He listens with an understanding ear. His thoughts wander to what he knows about Jewish weddings.

"Stella, I want you to know that with you being Catholic doesn't mean your people have the corner on this kind of practice. I can't think of a Rabbi who would marry us in a synagogue, with you being a gentile."

They sit for a minute looking at each other. With the choice of crying or laughing, they finally begin to laugh a little, then a little more, and finally a lot.

"Oh, Frankie, now I know why I love you. You're crazy," says Stella, still laughing. In a moment, her smile begins to fade as the reality of their situation begins to creep back into her being. Her eyes begin to fill. She struggles to get words out without crying. "What're we gonna do, Frankie?"

"We're gonna get married. That's what we're gonna do," says Frankie with the assurance of one determined to overcome this debacle.

She gazes straight into his eyes; his assuring words only serve to bowl her over once again. Her smile, having once again been vanquished by his compassion, returns. "Where? How?"

"I'll bet you we can ask Jerry to make room for us at the Old Club, and we can ask my dad's old friend Judge Lindenbaum ta do the ceremony," says Frankie with the same reassurance he has held up through this whole fiasco. "Besides, he's a cantor at the synagogue."

A light is suddenly coming on in Stella's head. Her smile is getting bigger. "Yer damn tootin', Frankie, that's what we're gonna do. We're gonna get married. When you wanna do this?"

"How 'bout this time next month?"

Stella is more than ready, suddenly flying as high as a kite on a windy day over all the possibilities. Her head is immediately swirling with plans. "I gotta get a dress. And shoes."

"Well, get 'em," says Frankie with the same matter-of-fact attitude he uses to approach most of life's kinks.

"And you gotta get a suit. I ain't marryin' a guy who ain't wearin' a suit. And polished shoes," adds Stella. After all, isn't she planning a ceremony that is intended to bring her and her leading soul mate into a lifelong bond? Besides this, she also gets to showcase her feminine qualities in making this a special day for both to remember and celebrate every year for the rest of their lives.

She knows exactly what she is going to wear. She saw it in a boutique window in downtown Detroit. It's a low-cut, form-fitting pink brocade dress. She'll wear it with full-length white stockings, a pair of white pumps, and long white gloves.

Later that day, Stella presents her request to Jerry at the Old Club. He's delighted to play a role in this union.

"Hell yes, Stella! We'll make a party out of this," says Jerry. Word soon flies throughout the club. Everyone is wishing Stella well and very willing to help make it a gala event. Lyman also joins the well-wishers. Stella accepts his congratulations as nonchalantly as she can.

****

While all this is taking place out at the Old Club, Frankie has rejoined his compatriots. Axel has spent the last half-hour catching him up on the information Madge has provided. The weather is quickly closing any opportunity to finish this salvage mission. It's into December already—anything can happen with ice and snow this time of year to hinder their moving forward. Adding the Jewish Navy into the equation makes it even more imperative to get this mission behind them.

Everyone present has an idea. Facing Frankie, Ezra makes a suggestion. "We can put your Torpedo boat with the .50-caliber back into service." His memory of watching the Purples speedboat fly into a million pieces is still fresh enough to believe it can be done again.

"That's an option, but a last resort option. Where that truck went down is two damn close to year around residents. That .50-caliber could rip up too many good neighbors," says Frankie with enough negativity that to bring it up again will be to no avail.

With his attention drawn to William, Frankie addresses him, "I've been studyin' some about these newfangled water proof magnesium lights they're usin' under water. What do you think about sneakin' out there at night usin' one of those gizmos ta light up the truck?"

With the kind of silence that comes with William when he is hashing something over in his thoughts, he finally explodes like he has just had an epiphany, "That's a damn good thought. I've heard a little bit about them. Some say they're pretty good, others say they tend to explode. Lemme do a little research on them."

"We ain't got a lot a time ta be wastin'. If we're gonna get this done, we gotta do it in the next few days. They're forcastin' a snowstorm later on in the week," says Frankie, with the air of one who's on top of things.

"Gimme 'til tomorrow. I just gotta do a little checkin' on this idea," says William.

Meanwhile at the Old Club, things are beginning to take shape. Stella is still doing her job in putting arrangements together for the various doings that are on the schedule for the month of December. Harsens Old Club remains a favorite destination for the Detroit and Pontiac corporate people for their Christmas and New Year's parties. Along with this, she continues to make her wedding arrangements.

Because Stella's schedule is so hectic, she has been remiss in keeping an eye on Lyman's comings and goings. She has noticed him leaving the phone booth several times when she was busy and unable to monitor his conversations. This has given her pause. She has learned from overhearing many of his prior phone conversation, the kind of information Frankie and the resistance group have needed to ward off vulnerabilities that would ultimately have been catastrophic had they not had her information.

Lyman's been making it a point to discover as much of Stella's wedding schedule as he is able under the guise of offering his services free of charge, and nearly making himself a nuisance by insisting on hanging around conversations centered around her and Frankie's doings.

Stella's not sure of what he would do with the information he's been a party to, and certainly not wanting to cast any suspicions on herself, she plays along thanking him for his generous offer, but remaining cautious and staying aware of the kind of material she's feeding him. Besides, as far as she's concerned, she can't imagine how Lyman could interest his bosses in her wedding plans.

As previously planned, William sought out the information he needed concerning the viability of using underwater dive lights for this salvage operation. He's called a meeting to discuss his finding.

"We have all agreed that speed and efficiency are what we need to get in and out of our site and make the recovery without detection, this is paramount in the success of this operation. "I got my hands on a set of lights. They're dry battery-powered sodium—brand new, state-of-the-art lamps. I wanna give 'em a good try out before we take 'em out for real," reveals William.

■ ■

Frankie, along with the crew are listening attentively as William goes through his litany of tests he thinks he has to complete before he'll feel proficient enough to get in and out of their salvage site as quickly as they need.

"If we're gonna do it, we gotta do it now. This weather ain't gonna hold much longer," pronounces Frankie.

"I agree," says Axel, "we ain't got the luxury of a lotta time. We gotta quit chewin' the rag an' get our ass in gear and get it done. I know from the info Albie and I got from our waitress friend that we might not be seein' them, but they sure as hell been seein' us. They know every damn move we're makin', jus waitin' ta pounce on us like a bunch a sittin' ducks."

Like many former military men, Frankie falls back on some of his war time training. "We gotta do somethin' ta outsmart 'em. Chances are they got somebody on this side watchin' us load up, then reportin' what they see. From what we've learned from Madge in the past few days is they haven't figured out we already located the wreck. They still think we're searchin' for it. We gotta get a decoy boat out in the water in order ta take 'em off in another direction—just ta throw 'em off awhile, then as soon as it gets dark, we'll bring the boat back in, unload like we're all done for the day, give it a few hours, then load back up an' head out ta the site an' pick up the goods."

William is nodding his head in agreement. "You remember I didn't want this delay an' I know you're right about gettin' goin', but I ain't sure about these lights. I'd feel a lot better if I were a little more comfortable with how they was gonna work out."

Not wanting to waste any more time, Axel's thoughts are forming into words as he begins to pick up equipment that needs to be loaded into the boat. "I think Frankie's right. Them goons think 'cause they live in the city they got the jump on us when it comes ta bein' smart. So far they've proved they ain't nothin' more than a bunch of dumb-ass punks. I wanna keep it that way. So, let's just quit flappin' our jaws an' get this job done."

Once again, with a singleness of purpose and a resolve to get this mission completed, they're soon back out on the water. They have positioned a spotter along the channel with signal flags to warn them of any Purples making their way in the direction of their boat. A Harsens Islander can quickly decipher the difference between one of their own making a liquor run and some Jewish Navy boat looking for easy prey.

Once positioned at a previous dive site where William had discovered the remains of a nineteenth-century schooner, they give in to William's insistence to make a test dive using the lights—providing he doesn't do anything to alert any unwanted guests.

Axel is being his usual fuss-budget self. "William, keep them damn lamps off 'til you get down ta the bottom. There ain't no sense in lettin' our tail know how were gonna bust their balls all over again."

William is nervously involved with hooking all the wires to the right receptors and searching out places he can hang them on his diving suit and still be in a position to use both hands. He's worked with Axel often enough to come to grips with his seeming obsession to have all his i's dotted and t's crossed.

William is half listening as he continues to sort through his hodge-podge of leading-edge equipment. Realizing the dangers of getting things wrong, with more than a little impatience, William snaps, "Axel, for the moment I have no clue what these Palookas can see and can't see. All's I know is we gotta know what we're doin' with all these new-fangled gadgets so's they don't turn on us an' kill us all."

Frankie is too busy positioning the boat to get involved with these petty disputes. His mind is on their subterfuge plans. He also is keeping his eye on the sky. The big dark snow clouds are beginning to swirl over head with plenty more threatening to come in behind them. The sun is nowhere to be seen. This time of year, the afternoons turn into night time by five o'clock. With the imminent warning of rough seas, it's all Frankie can do to arrange the boat so William can finish his practice run with the new equipment.

All eyes are on William as the dark waters swirl in to replace the vacancy left by his disappearing form. Suddenly the waters below them take on a yellow glow. The crew break into smiles and a war whoop. They know for sure at this point they are closer to fulfilling their goal then they have to date. They're also sure this kind of festivity is not going to go on undetected.

Jacob is on watch duty when he lets out with, "Oh, oh! We might be gettin' some visitors."

The spotter on shore has signaled there is a fast boat making its way toward them. William is already back on board in the process of removing his diving equipment when the boat comes into view. It doesn't appear to be one of the Jewish Navy crafts, and soon proves to be none other than a Coast Guard vessel. Coming within shouting distance, they recognize the craft as one of William's. They know William as a capable captain, but are concerned as to why he would be out in this kind of weather. They have also been monitoring his diving and are curious as to what he might be attempting to do. Without going into any detail, William informs them he has taken up a new hobby. That his diving is merely a form of recreation. Their concern now turns to whether he has salvaged anything without a permit.

Without warning, the captain on the Coast Guard vessel suddenly shouts, "Heave to, we are preparing to come aboard to make an inspection."

In a moment they have secured a line, and are beginning to board. Once on board, it soon becomes clear who is in command of this vessel. In between shouting orders to his men, the captain is throwing questions toward all the crew members. As the interrogation continues, it soon becomes clear that the Coast Guard has also been aware of the sunken truckload of champagne. Without making any direct accusations, their captain makes it quite clear that any information concerning the location of illegal alcohol would be needed to be turned over to the authorities immediately.

William assures them, "I will certainly do my civil duty and contact the authorities should I come across anything illegal. Yes, sir, I surely will do that."

Frankie, as well as the rest of the crew are taking little knowing glances at one another. Although this encounter is disrupting, it certainly beats the Jewish Navy. After a thorough search, the captain has satisfied himself that William's boat has no illegal contraband and he and his underlings make their way back to their own vessel and soon on another mission.

With William's crew left to go free, the daylight coming to an end, and a looming snow storm already spitting snow, the question is how they are going to make the rest of this endeavor play out.

The last thing William wants is to have another delay, so he is the first to make his judgments known. "We got a storm comin' on fast, if we go back to the launch now, with the blowin' snow, we may not be able to see the lights on shore ta get our land and water co-ordinates over our dive location."

Axel is next to voice his concerns. "We don't know if them damnable Purples are still doggin' us or not. The whole idea of coming back to port is to make them think we're done for the day, an' sneak back out in the dark."

Frankie calculates the situation with yet another angle to consider. "If them Purples was watchin', they seen the Coast Guard give us a thorough search and come up with nothin'. I don't think they're gonna waste any time searchin' us again. I believe they've already called it a day. I say we risk it an' head to the mother lode and get it on board. Even in a storm, I can navigate this tub to our launch and hide it there 'til we can get it to market."

The circumstances are quickly weighed among the crew. It becomes clear everyone is willing to get to the site and hope for the best. With this option no longer, an option, but a preference, they high tail it to the other side of the island. The blowing snow is increasing by the minute as well as larger swells. Frankie takes his hand drawn treasure map from his pocket sanctuary. He slowly maneuvers the

Boston Whaler to satisfy his co-ordinates. Certain he has the location correct, he orders the anchor set.

In the time it has taken to relocate, William has struggled back into his dive suit. He's nervous about this. Much of the success he's going to need is to have everything go perfect. He needs Ezra to maintain a steady hand on the air pump, he needs the boat to remain in the same location as when he disembarks, and he needs the lights to continue to work.

They have hooked up a block and tackle pulley system with a large basket that can be readily lowered to facilitate the loading process. Satisfied that all systems are ready, William makes his descent down the rope ladder secured to the starboard side of the vessel. Haste cannot be akin to waste in this situation. Every move must produce the proper result. The work must be planned and the plan must be worked. These life lessons are the same ones these men employed to bring the Kaiser to his knees in the European theater.

Once again, the above water crew can see the light come on below the surface. The surface of the water is twisting these light beams into warped rays flashing them in a willy-nilly pattern. They had their moment of celebration earlier, now is the time for a more restrained excitement. The payoff for all the time spent in search of this elusive treasure lays at their feet. It's only a matter of time before they are able to calculate the risk verses payoff factor.

In a few minutes the signal for the pulley to bring the first load to the surface is executed. All hands are eager to play a role in its success. The boat is rocking as the water strains in individual streams through the swaying sea basket. The snow and water are freezing cold as it strikes the raw skin of these buccaneers. They barely feel it as the first load lands successfully on board, holding the promise of many more to come.

Down below, William is purposely dissecting the carefully stacked crates still held taunt by hemp ropes, each attempting to tighten its grip on this mound of tipped over bottles—all held hostage by its murky master. The truck has settled on its side showcasing the cargo like a huge wine rack. William has jerry-rigged his lamp to his dive helmet in such a fashion to allow him to use both hands. Each time his light hits a crate, he uses his dive knife to slash the bindings, and sensing the weightlessness and freedom each crate is demonstrating as he effortlessly fills the basket.

The truck bed is soon emptied. For a final inspection, he decides to make a walk around the area for any retrievable booty. Using the exposed parts on the underside of the truck to climb to the cab for a look-see, he pulls himself across the now horizontal door. Shining his light against the still closed window, there pressed against the inside glass staring back, is the pale face of a corpse still held by the force of the water against the door. A sense of dread crawls up his back. It overtakes him as he holds before his view, the sight of this stilled, dead member of his race, with his hopeless dead stare, helplessly witnessing William loot his tomb.

The result of this unnerving sight has thrown him into a disarray. It's put an immediate damper on any previous desires to do any further surveying. Without looking any closer, he's willing to end the chapter on this escapade and get to the surface, out of his cold suit, and into his warm dry clothing.

On top, the crew is fighting to stay balanced as they battle the elements to secure a viable arrangement for this most prized cargo. The intensity of the storm and the darkness of the evening is creating a working ambience that none have often experienced. But then, each crate handled without the Purples knowledge is giving each of these attendants a boost of energy.

William needs special assistance as he grapples with the undulating motion of the rope ladder still tightly secured to the starboard side of the boat. Unable to advance himself up the corded rungs and not getting a response from the crew on the top side as they're busying themselves with not losing a single case of champagne back to Davy Jones's Locker, he manages to cross under the boat to the port side in view of the pulley system. Once there, he's able to roll himself into the basket, give the proper signal that rings a bell up top.

Expecting yet another load from below, they're flabbergasted to find William being hauled to the surface like part of the cache.

Surprised and amused to see William make his final retirement in this way, they immediately haul him aboard and begin his dismantling. Looking around his boat, he's shocked to see the result of his below efforts being fitted into every crack and cranny of his small ship. Never has this much alcohol been dispersed on his boat at one time—not only has this never happened before, it more than likely will never be repeated.

With Frankie's navigational skills now being put to a life and death test, he begins his sightless trek to the other side of the island in hopes of finding what's left of the Morgansky Fishery launch. The pelting snow and the rough seas are relentless as they mix into an icy brew to beat against the windshield of the Boston Whaler. There is barely room for the entire crew along with the several dozen cases of recovered champagne and William's bulky diving suit crammed inside—much less Frankie's challenge to keep the boat afloat.

Rounding the southern corner of the island, Frankie can barely make out a glow. His suspicion is that it's the lights emanating from the Old Club. It's a welcome and inviting glow. The choices he has are to continue on his course in an attempt to locate his father's fishery launch in the blinding storm or take advantage of the miraculous appearance of this obvious safe port. As he turns the wheel from a southerly direction to head east, a burst of wind forces a large wave to come pounding against the starboard side, nearly capsizing the entire boat along with the crew and cargo. In a split second, this convinces him to announce, "We ain't gonna last out here, the way this storm's comin' at us. I'm taken 'er in, boys!"

William has had as much experience navigating these waters as Frankie, and is more than willing to trust Frankie's judgment under these extreme conditions as if it were his own. His silence is the only affirmation Frankie needs as he begins the effort to bring them safely to this welcomed port in the storm. Changing directions only serves to find the seas change once again. They now find the wind and seas whipping at their backs with no regards to Frankie's effort to thwart the storm's attempt to swamp the boat along with all of them.

With the crew realizing their lives are on the line, they trust they will not become victims of their circumstances, but rather to how they react to these circumstances by not doing something stupid—like panicking. They unanimously remain quiet but pensive, allowing Frankie to focus his full attention on bringing the boat safely to port. The balance between the power produced by the boat motor and the power produced by the storm can only be calculated by the hand of experience. Frankie's steady hand and mind soon pay off as they find themselves entering the relative calmness of the lagoon alongside the Old Club.

None of the crew have to be told what to do. With each of their minds still keenly focused on the understood peril surrounding them, within minutes, they have fastened the boat with several tethers to secure it to the dock. The idea of celebrating a safe arrival, hasn't entered their minds until they enter the warmth of the Old Club. It's only now, with a sigh of relief they begin to feel the dominance the storm has had over each of them begin to subside.

First on the scene to greet them is Stella, who is working her shift. A look of surprise would be to understate her reaction. To have this many men, suddenly come charging in, in the middle of a storm is unnerving to say the least. For a moment, she stands looking at this wet shivering group of seeming reprobates. Her first reaction is to get a male co-worker to handle this sudden, unexpected mayhem. It's not until she begins to take a closer look to see the first familiar face appear.

"Frankie? What the hell is goin' on? You scared the crap outta me!" Stella barks.

"Oh, we was just out for a boat ride and decided to drop in for a drink," says Frankie with a little smirk.

"Don't mess with me, Frankie. What the hell are you up to?" asks Stella with the same intense tone. The rest of the crew can tell this confrontation is taking on a domestic tone. They independently begin to separate themselves. One by one they drift off in the direction of the bar to leave these two to work out this seeming mystery.

Realizing he has crossed a line where Stella is not going to readily give him a leave to attempt to use humor to duck her question. Clearing his throat to give himself a moment to shape a more feasible reply, he says in a more whispered tone, "Remember the cache of sunken champagne we've been searching for? Well, we found it and recovered it."

"Well, ain't that dandy. Now maybe you can start helpin' with our wedding plans," says Stella.

A familiar form crossing the room brings their conversation to a sudden halt. What neither of them have expected is to see Lyman leaving the phone booth. He evidently had overheard the men talking at the bar and promptly reported what he had learned. Frankie and Stella give one another an uncertain glance. As unnerving as it may be, they're not sure what to do next; they can only play the hand they're dealt. In such matters, they have no way of knowing who, when, where, how, or what other attachments will come along with the cards they can still play.

CHAPTER 23
The Doodlebug

Abe Axler and Eddie Fletcher have received the news from their planted mole, Lyman Woodard, regarding their navy's botched effort to keep track of Frankie's work. Both these thugs originally hail from New York. Fletcher, the lightweight fighter who had discovered there's more money in beating people up for the mob than there is in the ring, and Axler a born killer who takes great pleasure in watching a mark suffer and beg before he heartlessly takes their life.

These two, as demonstrated throughout their Detroit career have been successful in capturing the attention of the Purple Gang upper echelon as being able to deliver on a contract. Then there are those mob bosses too, who prefer to have underlings with a professional bent like these two do their dirty work, thus providing layers between themselves and any corruption or wrongdoing.

They've had time to digest this failure as a disappointing fact. This is not the way this was supposed to end. They had in mind how they were going to boldly present themselves to the Burnsteins as the champions who were able to successfully retrieve the lost load of French champagne. If this were accomplished, at least in the eyes of their crime bosses, it would have covered over all their other bungling efforts to bring Harsens Islanders into compliance.

"Those dumb-ass juniors runnin those boats oughta be rubbed out. They ain't much better than those rubes we're dealin' with on that goddam island. Now we got no other choice 'en ta start tightenin' the screws on these hicks," grumbles Axler. As is typical with these mugs, it's always someone else's fault when there's a failure.

"What ideas you got goin'?" asks Fletcher. They both know if they want any kind of a future continuing on the Burnstein payroll they have to produce with no excuses.

"We gotta get that goddam load of champagne before they get it to a market," says Axler without an idea as to how he's going to prevent it from happening, "or fer sure our asses gonna be hangin' on a Burnstein pike pole."

This is not the answer Fletcher had hoped for, although he is well aware of the tight rope they're both trying to walk, especially in what the Burnsteins expect him and Axler to deliver and the continual failures they're suffering in these efforts at the hand of one Frankie Morgansky. Scowling at the less than satisfactory reply his cohort Axler is providing, Fletcher doesn't hesitate to voice his displeasure'.

"We gotta come up with somethin' quick. We can't risk havin' Burnstein call us in again and not deliver. We gotta get on that goddam island and make a snatch before they know what's happenin'."

Axler is suddenly attentive. As usual when he and Fletcher conspire, their minds travel to the same dreadful page. This has been the glue that's held these two criminals together since they began working together.

"Yeah, so tell what ya got in mind," says Axler.

The two of them pour themselves a large glass of Canadian whiskey to spend the rest of the afternoon endeavoring to work out a plan of action.

****

The freezing days of December on Harsens Island bring a sudden halt to the big ships making their way through the narrow river channels. These shipping lanes are beginning to freeze over with a steady unrestricted, serpentine flow of light blowing snow making its way across a glare of new ice. To the Islanders this begins the transfer of housing units from the mainland to the ice in the form of fish shanties. Beginning with a hardy few who defy the chance of breaking through the newly formed freeze over, the shanty village begins. Within the week there is an ever-growing population of anglers positioning themselves to begin the age-old Harsens Island tradition of ice fishing.

Another phenomenon is the ice cutters resupplying their all but exhausted stock of last years ice. Every household ice box on the island depends on these resources.

There is also a new adjustment among the island's rumrunners from boats to anything that will traverse across these frozen waters, this includes hand drawn sleds to motorized trucks. Frankie is also making adjustments. He's retiring his trusty torpedo boat in making his deliveries to the mainland of his and Denzel's 'Harsens Breeze' to using an ice boat with ice skate like runners and a motor. He is confident he knows the river currents well enough allowing him to significantly reduce the risk of breaking through its surface.

Frankie has discovered he thrives on these risky maneuvers much like he did in his past sniper days during the Great War. He has willingly taken over this share of his and Denzel's rum-running business. The challenges come daily—from avoiding thin ice to avoiding federal agents and the Purples who have left the frozen channels to the more daring in favor of monitoring the various ports for liquor activity. They are definitely up for thieving anyone's cargo that have little or no defense against their ruthless tactics. Those that attempt to put up a fight are quickly compromised and disappear to some kind of watery grave.

Madge doesn't hesitate to get in touch with Axel when she has some new information she feels will help her with her resolve to wreak out her revenge upon the Purples. This is all done to avenge her father's untimely death at the hand of the Burnsteins. To satisfy this resolution, she has found a willing vindicator in the 'resistance group' led by Frankie Morgansky out on Harsens Island. They are willing to help her satisfy her desire to get even providing the 'resistance' can find a reason they need to get involved. Madge believes she has the kind of information she needs to compel the group to take action.

Speaking with Axel, her ready contact, she brings to light her new evidence of the Purples changing their tactics.

"Axel, you remember that guy Bob who ran a torpedo boat for the Jewish Navy?" Not waiting for an answer, Madge continues, "He an' two other guys come in the restaurant for lunch today. They came in a contraption they called a track truck. The damn thing was a big truck with a caterpillar track. They was talkin' how they was gonna use these ta pick off the 'Rubes' on the island. They was sayin' they ain't gonna wait 'til them hicks out on Harsens come ashore before they hijack their liquor, now they're gonna go right out on the ice an' pick 'em off."

Axel listens to Madge go on with more details about the Purples' decision to change tactics. It seems the local Harsens Island rumrunners have found too many waterfront entries not known to the Purples. These ever-ingenious gangsters have all but abandoned these waterfront hijackings in favor of employing four-wheeled drive two-ton trucks to intercept these unsuspecting rumrunners while they are still on the ice, struggling to find a safe port. Neither the Coast Guard, nor the federal agents have no such budgets to compete with these ever-up dating machines afforded the Purple Gang by the lucrative liquor business. Consequently, the frozen waterways are left mostly unattended by law enforcement.

The Purples are not the only ones searching out ingenious ways of guaranteeing themselves an edge in the ever-demanding liquor business. Frankie has been working on a plan to develop a motorized ice boat. Like most days in Frankie's life, this one promises to be eventful. This afternoon, he contacted his old friend Dave Schindler. He and Dave have had little reason to get together since their joint bombing effort in destroying the majority of the Jewish Navy a month or so back, but Frankie has found a new reason to bring Dave back into his life once again. He insists Dave is the only one he can trust to bring his design to fruition. They've chosen to meet at Dave's home, since this device would come to life in Dave's state-of-the-art machine shop.

Meeting Frankie at the door, Dave grabs his hand, half shaking it and half pulling him through the opening. Once inside, Frankie can smell the aromatic odor of smoked fish.

"Come in! Come in, my friend. You're just in time to help me sample these smoked white fish," says Dave, pulling on Frankie's arm.

He has set a table of freshly smoked fish, hard cheese, and beer. They spend the next half hour eating and having another laugh over the havoc they spread among the Purples with their bombing escapade.

"It's too damn bad we can only imagine what their faces looked like when they discovered they'd been snookered once again by a couple Harsens rubes," says Frankie. The glint in his eye tells that despite the look on the faces of these adversaries, the look on his and Dave's was one of great satisfaction.

With lunch over, their focus changes to the business which has brought them together once again. Frankie wastes no time in laying out on the cleared table a rough drawing of a gasoline powered ice boat.

"If you haven't already noticed, I've used the same concept the military used to develop your plane—except this contraption will travel on ice and water instead of the air and water," directs Frankie as Dave examines the drawing.

Dave's interest is piquing. What he is looking at is a boat with runners beneath it and a motor behind operating an airplane prop designed to drive the contraption forward.

Frankie gives him a minute to digest what he is looking at. A smile begins to broaden across his face. "I think you've come up with a crazy idea that will definitely put you at an advantage against anything them silk suits can come up with," says Dave.

Seeing Dave's broad faced grin, Frankie gleefully joins in with his own, asking only one question, "So you wanna build this thing?"

Reexamining the rough drawing once again, Dave responds with a resounding, "Hell yeah, man, providing you stick around and give me a hand."

With a continuing grin, Frankie rewards Dave with a huge hug, saying, "I'll be here 'til the cows come home!"

With a boat Frankie has supplied and a spare motor Dave garnered from a military surplus store, they begin the project. Dave has taken the eighteen-foot duck boat, added runners and a rear motor with an airplane prop in the rear giving this contraption the potential of being the fastest ice boat on the water. They work feverishly, around the clock, and by the time the Christmas and Hanukah season is over, the ice boat is ready to test. They've loaded several hundred pounds of sand bags to simulate a load of liquor. All that's left is to drag it out onto the ice, fire it up, and put it through its paces.

The days have remained cold, with temperatures plummeting to single digits and leaving less and less open water in the channels and rivers. This is perfect to give this newborn contraption a fair test. Frankie insist Dave accompany him on this maiden voyage—as much for moral support as for a ready mechanic in the event of some unforeseen break down. In giving this new creation one last going over before starting it, Frankie says, "I wanna run 'er on the ice downriver, where it hasn't frozen over, and see what she can do in open water."

Dave is just as intent on making certain Frankie keeps this contraption a float as he is in making sure the mechanics hold together. To ensure this, he's giving Frankie a few last-minute instructions, "Keep the engine rpm's high enough to be sure all the weight this contraption is carrying continues to skim over the water rather than trying to float 'er 'cause when you come off the water an' hit the ice again, this'll help the runners get back up on top."

Frankie responds with an assuring nod. Despite the cold, Frankie's arm pits are wet with a nervous sweat. He had the same type of reaction before a sniper mission when he was in the military. Disregarding the fact that he has been a part of this project from its inception, he has an uncomfortable reaction to the idea of ultimately being the one in charge of running this machine. Without a doubt, its design will prove to be intimidating. The propeller is mounted off the back of the engine in such a way that it is capable of pushing the boat, fully loaded at fifty-miles per hour across the ice, and if performed correctly it will reach close to the same speed across the open water.

With a deep breath, Frankie fills his lungs in anticipation. With a nervous excitement, he approaches the prop. Exhaling the air, he spins the propeller once, and then again. The second time the engine comes alive with a roar. With Dave already seated, Frankie swiftly takes his position. When he releases the brake, the contraption begins its maiden voyage by pushing sideways rather than straight ahead. In a second, Frankie corrects the steering as the speed also begins to regulate itself to these freezing conditions on nearly frictionless ice.

With a bit of testing the steering apparatus, Frankie increases the speed. There is no way of knowing how much is too much until that speed is exceeded. They are quickly exceeding speeds of first thirty miles per hour, then forty, then forty-five. At fifty, the steering can't compensate for the speed and the boat refuses to turn easily promising that this will get worse if pushed beyond this speed.

Frankie is satisfied he can't push the envelope further, so he maintains this speed as he heads for a part of the river with open water. Seeing the water rushing toward him forces his adrenalin, breathing, and nerves into an all-too-familiar concert, assuring him that he will continue to push ahead.

As the boat leaves the ice and hits the open water, there is a slight drag indicating the runners have changed materials, but there is no doubt this contraption will power its way to the next ledge of ice. Without hesitation—only a slight bump—the runners catch the lip of a frozen surface. Frankie quickly adjusts the steering from the denser water back to the slick ice. A few more maneuvers promise him he has a dependable machine he can use to successfully transport more of his and Denzel's burgeoning private label "Harsens Breeze," along with Denzel's latest addition, "Harsens Gold."

****

Both new labels and their success has definitely caught the attention of the Burnsteins. Calling Axler and Fletcher in for an update on their progress in getting this Harsens Island fiasco back under control, Ray Burnstein turns his attention to the in-roads this 'rube' Morgansky is continuing to make.

"What's a matter with you two schmucks? You can't get this job done? I've given you more time than either of you deserve. I ain't waitin' no more! You got 'til the end of January an' not a goddam day longer ta get this "meshegeneh" (crazy person) dead!" shouts Burnstein hammering his fist on his desk all the time clinching a half-smoked cigar off to the side of his mouth.

Well aware they are on their last leg with the Ray Burnstein, the first thing Axler and Fletcher do after they leave Burnstein's hotel room is to make a stop at Squeaky's speakeasy. They're well aware of Squeaky's bad experience with Frankie Morgansky's Harsens Island resistance group and his reluctance to have anyone bring the incidence up. Nonetheless, he's the only one readily available to have had firsthand experience in dealing with the specifics of this clandestine and sly alliance.

"You guys are gettin' inta somethin' you ain't never had dealin's with before in your life. This Morgansky guy is crazy. That island ain't nothin' I ever want ta deal with again. Those guys appear outta nowhere wearin' hoods 'at make 'em look scarier 'en one a them Klu Kluxers." Squeaky reports this account between gulps from a bottle randomly grabbed from his back bar.

Fletcher is the first to interrupt Squeaky. "Well, they ain't dealt with us yet then have they?" he says referring to himself and Axler.

Axler follows Fletchers line of thought with another question for Squeaky, "This guy ain't a god, he's gotta have an Achilles heel somewhere. What d'*you* think it might be?"

Squeaky gets a little wry grin at this question. Setting the bottle back on the shelf with the assurance of one who feels he has the ready answer to this pointed question. "Hell, that's easy," he says, "it's that wop whore he's stuck on. She used ta work here. Damn good lay, too. Hated ta lose her."

Axler makes a knowing glance at Fletcher. They both know this is the same woman their inside man, Lyman, has been working with at the Old Club.

Thanking Squeaky for the information, they leave. They're confident they know where to strike to get Frankie's attention.

Frankie and Dave have parted ways once again with Frankie more than sure he has the ultimate in rum-running machinery. He's anxious to put his creation to work. Making his way around to the other side of the island where he and Denzel have their distillery, Frankie introduces this new piece of equipment to Denzel.

Standing with one hand on his hip while the other hand holds his hat with a portion of his fingers left to scratch his head, he exclaims, "What in the hell kind of doodle-bug do ya call this thing?"

"Well, now, I haven't thought much about what I am gonna call it—I think 'Doodlebug' is as good a name as any," says Frankie satisfied his machine has a moniker. "The best part is we can get as many cases in this thing as it can hold and get 'em delivered in no time flat."

"Me and the boy just got another batch bottled and ready ta go if you wanna start loadin' 'er up," states Denzel. Frankie is excited not only at the prospect of making deliveries, but also at the opportunity to easily out run the Jewish Navy's new addition of track driven trucks capable of overtaking any other contrivance rum-running between the United States. and Canada.

Like all the other liquor operations that are taking place in and around Harsens, the spotters from the Jewish Navy reported to the drivers of these new "track trucks" what they have witnessed during Frankie's test run. Madge has been a Godsend in supplying information on these hot-shot drivers sitting about her restaurant bragging about how they are going to take down Frankie Morgansky once and for all. Since the spotters have no idea all that transpired during Frankie's test run, they missed an important segment where the ice boat went from ice to open water and back to ice. From the vantage point of these voyeurs, they had no way of discerning open water from ice in this all-important portion of the trial. Notwithstanding, driver Bob, who has a lustful eye on Madge, has also made this restaurant his new headquarters, bringing along with him a number of other repugnant, arrogant brothers in exploitation. They have spent much of their time discussing the information the spotters have given them on the funny looking contraption Frankie Morgansky is driving across the ice. To them it is just another challenge. Since Frankie spoiled driver Bob's opportunity to be the hero in recovering the champagne, he has inaugurated himself as the one to be notified of any activity involving Frankie and his contraption. It isn't long before a spotter makes the call to the restaurant payphone alerting Bob of Frankie preparing his ice boat for a delivery.

After finishing his conversation, Bob hangs the phone back on its hook, returning to his table of reprobates, he announces, "Get ready boys, I just got word our pigeon is loadin' up with what looks ta be a bonanza load." A look of delight sweeps through Bob's brigade as though they had just been told they had won a big sweepstakes prize.

"I think we need ta clip his wings!" states one of Bob's compatriots already up, anxiously putting on his coat.

Within minutes this contingency of debased menaces is on their way to raise havoc with this so-called "Harsens Island resistance group." The Purples regard them as little more than troublemaking agitators who need to be brought to their knees. The problem with this thinking is so far everything they've thrown at this group has done nothing but come back to bite them.

Not being the brightest bulb in the room, Bob is sure if given a fair chance, he will bring this opposition to rue the day they were born. Along with his goon squad, they have prepared themselves with enough weaponry to supply a small army. As the self-proclaimed leader of the pack, Bob has decided to employ every track truck at their disposal in order to present an impenetrable show of force.

"When that rube sees this armada comin' at 'im, he's gonna shit bricks," declares Bob as he gives a hand signal to begin making their way to the object of their hostilities. To personally view this squadron of a half-dozen ominous trucks making their way down the frozen river is to be unquestionably happy they don't have you in their sights.

Downriver, Denzel and his boy have all but finished carrying the last of their hoard out to the dock. Frankie is there to personally and very carefully place each case of liquor into the ice boat so they all will fit and not throw the boat off balance. It's not long before, Frankie is satisfied with his compacting job and ready to fire up the "Doodlebug" and be off to make his deliveries.

Being somewhat of an adrenalin junkie, Frankie is beside himself to get back out on the frozen waterways and open this contraption up with a real load of liquor rather than a few bags of sand. Saying his goodbyes to Denzel, he gives the prop a good downward thrust. The motor gives a little chugging noise as if to clear its throat. Not to be dissuaded, Frankie gives it another try. This time the engine barks to life with the roar of a wounded bear. In a flash, he's on board releasing the break. The craft begins to creep letting him know it needs more gas. Gradually increasing the throttle produces the effect this beast is hoping to bring about. Suddenly there is a big enough burst of power to get this heavy load on its way. With little warning, Frankie is experiencing a speed he had hoped for.

Without a timetable, by the time all is finished and ready to go, it's late in the afternoon. The daylight is quickly giving way to the gray color of dusk this time of the year. Frankie switches on his head light. It gives an interesting yellowish hue to the ordinary drabness of the ice. Within the first mile, he is given ample opportunity to test his steering skills as he weaves his way through the hundreds of fish shanties and ice cutters dotting nearly every inch of the frozen water. So far, he is satisfied with the performance of his Doodlebug.

Breaking around a bend in the river, Frankie finds himself, suddenly, and without warning, being flanked on each side with what appears to be an armored cavalry of sorts. They are Model T trucks fashioned with what appears to him to be the same type of tracks used on military tanks. There is no question in his mind that he is the object of their concern.

At this point, they're having no problem staying abreast. What he sees next is the most disconcerting sight he has experienced since his military days—it's the flash from a discharged weapon—and it's aimed at him. This is not exactly the way he had envisioned this inevitable encounter with this group. In his imagination, he was never at a disadvantage, rather he always had the upper hand. Discovering he is in no position to return fire, Frankie begins to weave in a snake like trail, giving himself an enhanced advantage along with the hopes of not being struck with all the lead they're throwing his way.

His next step is to increase his speed in the hopes of outrunning them. *Damn, these guys are gaining on me. I gotta do somethin' damn quick, or they're gonna get me.*

What flashes across his mind is how he's outfitted to cross open water. *"I've gotta get to some open water quick!"*

With what is left on his throttle, Frankie opens this last little bit as wide open as it will permit. Feeling a little extra surge, it's enough to put a little more distance between them; at least it's enough to manage to stay out of range of their guns. Nevertheless, this is hardly enough to dissuade these scoundrels from accelerating along with him. The gap he had managed to put between them is narrowing once again.

The only place Frankie recalls there is enough open water to prevent these rogues from further pursuing him is where he and Dave had done a test run the day before. It's clear on the other side of the island, at least ten minutes away. His only prayer is to continue to stay in the lead long enough to reach this place before they manage to close in on him. The daylight has given way to enough darkness to enable him to judge where they are in relation to himself by their headlamps. At the speeds they are traveling, he knows once he reaches the open water, they will hardly notice his immediate transformation from ice to water and follow him to their demise.

His head light is indicating that he has arrived at the previous day's test site. The Doodlebug's light beam has changed from a smooth beam refracting off the solid, slick ice to the ripples of open water. With hardly a change, other than the engine giving a slight straining sound as it struggles to maintain enough speed to keep the runners on top of the water, he storms across much like he did the day before. In a matter of seconds, he's to the other side to successfully have the runners leave the water's edge and find their way to solid ice. With this much extra weight, the variation effecting the runners from water to ice is hardly noticed.

Cutting the throttle back with one hand and the other on the break lever, Frankie manages to bring his Doodlebug to a stop. Immediately, he turns back toward the trail he has just blazed in time to watch, one by one, as each of these malefactors along with their track trucks, make a surprised splash and an even bigger surprise to find themselves at the mercy of the river's death chilling waters. Within seconds, the waters have swallowed everything that couldn't float, leaving no sign or proof that anything out of the ordinary has just taken place.

Frankie takes another minute to reflect on how the events over the past quarter hour have transpired, but much as he was able to do after a successful war time sniper shot, he puts it behind him only to ready himself for the next assignment. In the meantime, he has a boat load of liquor to deliver.

CHAPTER 24
The Snatch

Rumors have spread through the island concerning the disappearance of the Jewish Navy's fleet of track trucks along with their drivers. The Purple Gang with their network of paid spotters sporting binoculars to monitor Harsens Islanders making rum runs, were the last to see Bob and his merry band of scoundrels. Because of the brightness of their head lamps, they had been easy to follow. But as one of these men reported to Ray Burnstein, "I was spot on watchin' 'em chasin' 'at Morgansky fella when they just plain disappeared off the face of the earth, an' leavin' Morgansky sittin' on his machine all by hisself."

Burnstein is beyond any chance of being humored. His face turns to the deep red of one beyond rage. He's way past reason over this news of yet another failure to rein in the Harsens Island rebels. He wastes no time to recall Axler and Fletcher. With his hotel door closed and armed guards outside, he begins to berate the two men. "You two schlemiels been schleppin' around on my money long enough. I changed my mind, I ain't givin' you 'til the end of January to get this job done—you got 'til the end of this week or you're gonna join the rest a them like the goddam fish bait you deserve to be."

Neither Axler nor Fletcher are in any way prepared for this absolute castigation of any of their efforts to date. Their failure thus far is a blatant fact in the eyes of Ray Burnstein. Both leave with a renewed sense of desperation to get this contract fulfilled.

"We gotta get a plan inta action, Abe, or our ass is grass and Burnstein's the goddam lawn mower," says Fletcher in a near panic.

Axler is in no position to argue. He, along with Fletcher have depended on Lyman to feed them information, but now they realize there are going to have to act on this information themselves.

"You're right, Eddie. We gotta get on that island and take care of this ourselves," says Axler. At this point, it's clear they have no plan.

"You remember a few days ago we talked 'bout makin' a snatch with one of them guys Lyman's been tellin' us about. I still think that's gonna be the only way we can draw that Morgansky guy out. We gotta make a snatch on somebody he's willin' ta make a move ta get back," says a confident Fletcher. "I say we take that whore an' her kid. From what we know, she and Morgansky are gettin' married soon."

Axler is listening intently. The wheels are beginning to turn in his brain. The idea of actually achieving an action to make someone's life a living hell appeals to his base nature.

Fletcher continues, "Ten ta one says she's gonna be comin' back on the mainland for somethin' ta do with this stuff she's plannin'."

"I'm with you, Eddie. We gotta make this work. I say we get a hold of that Lyman kid and get him to pay more attention to the whore—like what she's doin', where, and when. We don't need ta tell him anything more," says Axler. It's becoming obvious that both these degenerates are becoming much more animated as they continue to deepen their plan. The way this plan is beginning to excite them is all but made them forget the very sentence hanging over themselves should they fail. They are already enjoying the misery they will bring to this family.

****

The old year has already given way to the new, but Stella is relieved work at the Old Club has slowed enough after the Christmas season to put a bit more effort into her wedding plans. It's still early

January, and there's a week or so left before she and Frankie will finally tie the knot.

There seems to be an endless supply of loose ends that need to be brought together. With all these details swimming around in her head, Stella has paid little attention to Lyman's doings, although she has noticed he seems to be making frequent calls. Not being in a position to monitor these, she brushes this circumstance aside; the details of the upcoming wedding are taking over all her thoughts and energy.

Lyman is aware that his role is to supply information to Axler and Fletcher. What they do with it afterward is not something they have shared with him. Despite his young age and naiveté about what the Purple Gang might be doing with the data he supplies, he also has a selfish reason to continue supplying these gangsters with material, it's because they are supporting him in a life style he could never afford to duplicate. It's becoming more difficult to give details to these rancorous benefactors when he suspects they will use them to the detriment of people he's growing to care about.

Nevertheless, he's beginning to feel trapped. As a hardworking staff member, Lyman continues to be caught up in his double life as a caring associate of the Old Club's working personnel and a simultaneous affiliate of the Purple Gang. He's beginning to sense there is more to the information he is supplying than he's being told. He's an affiliate, but he remains an outsider and is unaware they are hell-bent on destroying any and all resistance standing in the way of their takeover plans, including those he's come to regard as a workplace family.

Much to the chagrin of Stella, through the several months Lyman has been employed by the Old Club, he has developed quite a relationship with Carly. Stella has tried leaving her with Aristine or her own mother, but from time to time, she finds she must bring her to work with her. At every opportunity, she beguiles Lyman with her little girl charm to play music allowing her to practice her new dance moves. He willingly obliges, captivated by her unique artistic ability to choreograph dance moves way beyond her age.

"Carly, what are we going to do with you. You continue to amaze me," says Lyman after a marathon of non-stop dancing.

With her face all red from the exertion, Carly says, "Why don't you hire me, Mr. Lyman?" her exuberance and innocent demeanor are captivating to all who've come across her path. Her smile alone is enough to win over most hearts. She has a passion for whatever task she has given herself, thus giving even the hardest hearts an opportunity to experience the unbridled fury of this new age of women—be it for her cat, her mother, her passion for dancing, or merely her innocent, transparently readable expression.

Despite the advent of the women's rights movement, many still believe that children should be seen and not heard, and would look at Carly's behavior disapprovingly, but none of this negativity has spoiled her healthy outlook on life, nor squelched her zest for expressing herself through her passions.

Frankie arrives in time to review the better part of her effort. It makes him smile.

"Carly, that was wonderful. Did you make that all up by yourself?" asks Frankie.

Taken aback at his surprise visit, Carly throws out her arms as she leaps into his.

"Mr. Lyman says he might hire me!" she exclaims, not losing a beat. Turning back to Lyman, she makes a further announcement, "Mr. Frankie's gonna be my daddy." With that, she turns back to Frankie, giving him a big kiss.

"I already am your daddy, but now your mom and me are gonna make it official," reiterates Frankie for the hundredth time. In her mind, the only way you have a mom and dad is if they are married.

Lyman can't help but be moved by this display of affection this little girl has for the very man he has been attempting to have exterminated since he arrived last summer. Frankie is also moved by a disdainful awareness this young man is not much more than a wolf in sheep's clothing. It's a disdain he's managed to keep covered using the old Semitic adage that one should always keep his friends close, but his enemies even closer.

Frankie is always interested in Lyman's latest phone conversations, so he seeks out Stella to bring him up to speed, only to find an agitated fiancée who's making it perfectly clear she has no time for his concerns.

Nearly exploding, she shouts loud enough to be heard across the room, "You been off gallivantin' all over this island stirrin' up another hornet's nest with them damn gangsters. You do anything to make them wreck my wedding, an' I'll never forgive you! I've still gotta get into Detroit yet today and get Carly and my dress from the seamstress."

Realizing that his presence is doing neither of them any good, only making a stressful bride more stressful, he opts to leave. But not before his mind turns his eye toward Lyman who is across the lobby making small talk with Carly, but who has also heard all that is going on between himself and Stella. He can't help but wonder what this infiltrator has in mind to do next. Staring at him entertaining Carly gives him pause. *He looks to be a genuinely decent kid. I can't help but wonder about him. He doesn't appear to be the villain he actually is. So far, we've been able to stay one step ahead by never taking a victory to mean there is no more work to be done.* With this thought finding no good conclusion, Frankie makes his exit.

Along with a million other details, Stella is also preparing herself and Carly to make the hour-long trek into Detroit for their final fitting before the wedding. Finally, at a point where she declares herself ready to go, she and Carly are waiting on Simon and Aristine to pick them up here at the Old Club, to drive them to their appointment. It will be the first time either Simon or Aristine have been back in the city since they left months ago. They are looking forward to visiting with some old acquaintances while Stella and Carly are getting fitted with the seamstress.

"Bubbie, Bubbie!" is Carly's sudden bubbly shout as Simon and Aristine make their way into the lobby.

"Oh, da est mein bisl feygela! (Oh, there is my cute little girl!) exclaims Aristine with her arms wide open. Carly is always excited to have her grandmother's attention. She has grown quite fond of her bubbie's kindness and particularly her soft hands that always wear a faint odor of garlic and onions.

Bearing up under Stella's over developed energetic hyperactivity to get things done, they are soon on the road. It's a blustery day with snow blowing and crafting itself into small drifts along the sides of the plowed roads. Aristine has provided blankets and has heated several bricks and wrapped them in newspaper to hold the heat, placing them at their feet. Simon is doing the driving. Carly is talking nonstop. As much as a devoted grandmother can be, Aristine is being attentive to Carly's every question and her long, drawn-out stories about her school and school friends. This leaves Stella to carefully go over and over in her mind how she is to arrange every aspect of her upcoming wedding, down to the last detail.

Because of the less than desirable road conditions, it's taking longer than usual to arrive in the city. Carly has soon tired and fallen asleep against her bubbie. This allows Aristine and Stella to have a conversation that's not centered around Carly's never-ending loquaciousness.

"I vantz you know, ve luff you like tokhter (daughter)," says Aristine, squeezing her hand. "You makes gootz froy (wife) und mutter (mother) for my Frankie and Carly."

Stella slips out from under her blanket long enough to give Aristine a big hug. "I couldn't ask for a better mother and father-in-law than you and Simon. Do you mind if I call you muttie and tate?" she asks with a bit of a happy grin.

"Zat makes me happy. You do zat," says Aristine. Simon looks over from his driving long enough to give an approving smile.

The Telegraph road address of the seamstress is suddenly before them. The traffic is light because of the weather conditions allowing Simon to stop in the street to let Stella and Carly out of the car. "Ve come back in two hours pickz you up, okay?" asks Simon.

"That should give us plenty of time," agrees Stella giving them both a kiss.

Leaving them on the street in front of the seamstress's residence, Simon pulls away and disappears around a corner. Just as Stella and Carly begin their trek across the snow-packed road, a large sedan makes its way in front of them causing Stella to grab Carly and jump back. The rear door suddenly swings open and Stella feel the cold steel of a gun barrel against her neck.

"Get yer ass in the car, and be quick about it!" It's the gruff, mean voice she remembers dealing with some months ago.

Still hanging on to Carly with all the strength she can muster, Stella feels herself being pushed onto the backseat floor of the sedan. Just as quickly as this car had stopped, it speeds off once again.

Trying to catch a glimpse of her captors, Stella attempts to turn her head and look up, only to be met with a foot to the back of her neck with a further reprimand: "Keep yer goddam head down, or I'll kick it off yer neck."

The remembrance of this voice brings on a sick feeling as Stella recalls how she had taken a beating while this person was raping and beating her. *This can't be happening to us. I have to protect Carly, even if I have to sacrifice myself.* She feels Carly begin to cry. Whispering in her ear, Stella comforts her with the words, "Everything's gonna be all right. Momma will take care of you."

After what seems like an eternity, the sedan finally stops. The driver exits. Unable to see, Stella must remain content to allow the sound to give her clues. The next sound is that of a door being slid along a track—like large garage door. In a few seconds, the driver is back in the car behind the wheel, seemingly driving into the inside of this building.

The car stops once again. Their door is jerked open with the result of her and Carly being jerked, pushed, and manhandled out of the car and into a room with a single light bulb, a bed, a small coal-burning stove, a slop pail, and a bucket of water. It appears to be a garage of sorts.

Turning to her captives, Stella tenses for a moment. She remembers exactly who they are—particularly Abe Axler. The other is his companion in corruption, Eddie Fletcher. When accounts of these two men tell of nearly unheard-of methods of torture and death, their reputations are wisely considered accurate, and neither is to be taken lightly. To be fooled by their diminutive heights into thinking either of them incapable of being vicious is a deadly miscalculation. Stella had made that mistake once in trying to reason with Axler as a client, and she nearly lost her life because of it.

That damned Squeaky is behind this. I just know it. He's still hopin' ta get his pound of flesh for me bailin' out on him and for what the boys on Harsens did ta him and Louie. At this point, Stella is not willing to risk the ire of these two cretins for fear of them harming Carly. She continues her silence.

Both Axler and Fletcher wear the satisfied looks of those who have just captured a fly and are preparing to tear its wings, legs, and head off. They're just not sure where to begin. Stella can smell the all too familiar nauseating breath of Axler as he leans into her face. It's a mixture of the rancorous odors of whisky and cigar. His words are just as foul. "The only reason you and that brat of yours ain't out of the frame is 'cause you're worth a dollar more alive than dead. That schmuck boyfriend of yours is gonna have ta pay big bucks ta get your worthless ass—providin' he even wants it," says Axler. "You better pray he does." With that said, he pushes her out of the way.

The last sound Stella hears is a key as it locks the door. She sits down on the bed. With a forlorn gaze, Carly lays her head on her mother's lap. The waiting begins. They have no other options.

CHAPTER 25
Hangin' Out Together

Simon and Aristine have finished their visiting and are happily making their way back to the Telegraph Road address where they had agreed to come by and pick up Stella and Carly after their fittings. Instead of these two waiting along the road, there is a young boy. Simon, in an effort to avoid hitting the kid, pulls the car around him before he makes his stop. The boy follows. Approaching the window, he says, "Hey, mister, yer name Simon Morgansky?"

Simon looks to the boy with a suspicious eye and says, "Who vantz know?"

Reaching into his pocket, the kid produces an envelope and says, "I don' know. A guy gave me a quarter ta stand here an' give a guy named Simon Morgansky this here envelope."

Still giving the kid a suspicious eye, Simon grabs the envelope and rolls up his car's window. Satisfied he has done his job, the boy runs off down the road, disappearing around the nearest corner.

Cautious to do anything more, Simon and Aristine spend a moment, staring first at the envelope, then to one another. "Vatz in hell goingk on here?" asks Simon. Still peering down at the envelope, Aristine shrugs her shoulders, answering back, "Open eet an' zee."

Finally succumbing to their curiosity, Simon slowly begins to tear open the mystery envelope. The letters forming the words are torn from magazines and newspapers and glued to a folded piece of typing paper. First Simon takes a turn at staring at the paper, handing it to Aristine, she also takes a turn. Since neither of these two are literate in English, they fold the paper back up and place it back in the envelope.

Still as confused, Simon makes a decision to approach the seamstress and inquire about Stella and Carly. Knocking at her door, a smallish lady with spectacles perched on the end of her nose comes peeking around the door. The lady explains to Simon that the two people he's enquiring about never made it to their appointment.

Returning to the car, Aristine can tell by the look on Simon's face things are not going well. With no other options, Simon turns the car in the direction of Harsens Island.

With this sudden, unforeseen turn of events, there is nothing left to do other than to get back to the island. The road travels north and then turns to the east. Much of the east portion of this trip makes its way through areas where very few homes are found. The region is as desolate as their thoughts. For them, the world has lost its color. With the blowing and drifting snow in these outlying regions portraying the world as a black and white cinema, Simon and Aristine's world takes on a similarly grey, lifeless mood. This was not supposed to happen in America. When they left the Czar's world and came to America, they were full of hope that catastrophe would not follow them. But along with their new world circumstances have come new hardships. It's as though the devil has followed them to the new world and thrown all manner of deprivations and heartbreaks on them.

The ferry trip is hardly noted by either Simon or Aristine. Their thoughts have become dark and foreboding. Returning without Stella and Carly is increasingly taking its toll on each of them. By the time they find Frankie at the Old Club conferring with Jerry, both feel bankrupt emotionally and physically. They are at a complete loss as to how to manage anything like this. As older parents, they are finding they are placing more and more of their well-being in Frankie's decisions. Only a slight reprieve comes as they share the information with Frankie.

After Simon has given the envelope containing the strange note over to Frankie, he takes a good five minutes to examine and reexamine every word pasted on this paper. Seemingly completed, he lays the paper on the table. Lighting a cigarette, and letting the smoke escape through his words, he says, "They're holding them hostage. They want a hundred thousand dollars in cash for their release, plus the load of champagne we salvaged."

Aristine lets out a gasp, and Simon exclaims, "Dirty momzer! A meesa mashee af deer! (May the dirty bastard suffer a horrible death.)"

Just as these epitaphs are being cast on these unknown lives, Alina appears, as she is just coming on her shift. When she hears the news of her daughter and granddaughter, she instantly turns a pale grey and nearly collapses.

All of this is coming at Frankie. He's trying to make use of his military training where he removes himself emotionally from the matter. Since this is happening in his own backyard, he finds it more difficult to step back. Still, he knows he has to suck it up and take the lead in getting Stella and Carly back safely.

With all the pluck he can muster, he says, "Try not to worry about this. We still have the champagne they're askin' for, and I have the money." Looking back at the ransom note to be sure he's read it correctly, he continues, "They've stated in their ransom note they'll be callin' me with the details."

Butting his cigarette, Frankie does what he always does when things get dicey—he decides to contact Axel. Excusing himself, he prepares to leave giving everyone a hug and a kiss and the assurance this will be taken care of. Loading himself into his old truck, his thoughts are beginning to race out of control. He's nearly to Axel's cottage when he has a sinking feeling. *What the hell has just happened?* This turn of events is something his military training didn't address. He's suddenly overcome with sadness and feels very much alone and helpless.

It's almost five-thirty. These are the shortest days of the year for the northern states. It's going to be dark in just a few minutes, but not anything close to the darkness Frankie's soul is wearing. He's had a number of wins over the Purples, but not in his wildest dreams did he expect them to retaliate in this way. This is the one scenario he hadn't anticipated. When he arrives at Axel's, Frankie shows him the ransom note warning what is to become of Stella and Carly if their demands are not met to the letter.

... and if every demand is not met, you can expect your whore and her bastard kid are going to pay the price for your screw-up ...

Axel spends a minute going over the Ransom note much as Frankie had. Putting the note on the table, he says, "I know who we're dealing with. It's those two New York thugs Ray Burnstein brought in ta take care of a bunch of dirty work he don't wanna be connected to. Abe Axler is one of 'em an' the other one is Eddie Fletcher."

Axel pauses for a minute to let Frankie catch up, then adds, "If yer wonderin' how I know all this, it's 'cause I been makin' it my business ta keep tabs on these big shot schmucks since they arrived. I can tell you this much, I've learned through the grapevine that Burnsteins ain't happy with all the screw-ups these two been havin' with you. They brought these guys in ta get Harsens Island back under their control an' you been a great big pain in their ass in preventin' 'em from gettin' it taken care of."

Frankie listens with a patient ear. He always feels better when Axel puts things into a perspective he can get his head around. "I know what you're tellin' me is so, but I guess I wanna ask you what you think I oughta do about it?" asks Frankie. A lot of his desperation is already leaving as Axel continues on with even more advice.

Pulling a bottle from a nearby shelf along with two glasses, Axel pours them each a drink of his own private stock of moonshine. After taking a hardy sample and making the gasping sound of approval, he continues, "I think you oughta make arrangements with them ta get Stella and her daughter back under their terms, but after that, I believe we can put together a plan ta let them know they ain't dealin' with the rubes they think we are." When Axel talks with an air of assurance like he's doing at the moment, it gives Frankie hope.

For the rest of the evening Axel pours out all he knows about these two reprobates; their habits, where they stay, where they drink, and most of all how the only person either of them are dedicated to is each other. "I don't know if they're queer for each other or not, but I know one thing about 'em—they don't take a shit 'nless the other is there ta wipe his ass," adds Axel, drawing on the same assured air of authority he's used of all evening.

Frankie is all ears. "Axel, you sure as hell been doin' your homework on these guys. I'm willin' ta go along with whatever you say is our next move."

"There ain't no doubt in my mind 'at we can't take these guys ta task. They ain't no damn different 'n any a them other silk suit city kikes," says Axel. "Oh, and by the way, we need ta call Jerry at the Old Club and have him disable that kid, Lyman's car ta prevent him from tryin' ta leave. From what you've told me, he needs ta stay here 'til we sort through all this."

Frankie is listening to Axel with the same intensity he had any of his superiors while in the military. He recognizes in Axel's humble demeanor a man of great insight.

Within this meeting there has been an agreement between the two of them to wait until the kidnappers call with further instructions. Axel asks for one more request, "As much as you want to get this over with, see if you can't stall them a bit while I get a few things in place." In the meantime, Axel will continue his surveillance of Axler and Fletcher on the mainland.

The night has turned to morning, Frankie has no other choice other than to resign himself to sit near the phone. Not having much of an appetite, he drinks coffee and smokes cigarettes. He's desperately trying to set aside his personal stake in this debacle, and resume his sniper demeanor and separate himself from the circumstances. He finds it nearly, if not completely, impossible under these perspectives. His mind is consumed with how Stella and Carly are holding up under these conditions.

With no other options left, he falls on his knees to the floor with a heartfelt prayer for their safety and wellbeing, begging God to be merciful to them. No sooner does he arise, the phone rings. It sends a chill down his back. With the anticipation of one suffering in the hopes of finding a beginning of relief, he answers. "Hello."

The voice on the other end is one containing a boldness spawned from advantage. "Tell me you got the money an' the booze an' we'll go to the next step, otherwise we stop right here and you can prepare their funerals."

This kind of heartlessness is easily understood by Frankie. As a sniper, he spent several years of his life emotionally removed from his targets. He realizes now what he is going to have to become to successfully defeat these monsters. The demands of this beast on the other end of the line cause him to realize he needs to become a bully to defeat a bully. Strength and force are the only way one can deal with these types. But for the moment, he is willing to become the obsequious victim for the sake of waiting like a cobra for the right time to strike.

The demands are laid out where he alone is to bring the money and champagne to a particular address. Frankie listens until all the demands are laid out, then impulsively makes one of his own, "How do I know this ain't a set up just ta get the money? How do I know they're still alive?"

The voice on the other end is noticeably agitated over this demand. "Listen, schmuck, you ain't in no position ta be callin' any shots. You bring the money, an' we give you back your whore an' your bastard kid! You got that?"

Remembering how Axel had asked to create a delay, Frankie presses one more time, "I ain't gonna be your sucker without knowin' the goods are available. You let me hear their voices, an' you got a deal. Otherwise, you can kiss the money and booze goodbye."

There is a silence on the other end over his unexpected boldness. In a few moments of some kind of contemplation, the voice resumes. "Okay, asshole. You got a deal, but don't be pushin' yer luck. Tomorrow at noon, you'll get a call." With that said the caller slams the phone down, leaving a dead air sound in Frankie's ear.

Satisfied things are moving along, and Axel will have the time he's asked for, Frankie spends the rest of the day organizing the hundred grand into thousand-dollar packs. There is a sense of relief in having something to do to move things forward, even if it's as mundane as counting out the cash to meet the demands of this dreadful ransom.

Meanwhile, Axel is doing due diligence in Detroit. The extra time allows Axel to organize a crew of his own, to position himself to keep an eye on Axler and Fletcher. He's stationed himself down the street from the Melthorpe apartments, Axler and Fletcher's apartment complex. He and Mark Kingsbury are taking shifts to assure they don't miss anyone coming or going. It's the end of Axel's shift when he recognizes a couple Purple juniors making a stop at the apartment. He sees them enter the building very briefly before leaving very quickly. It's eleven-thirty and Mark has just arrived. Leaving Mark to continue doing the surveillance at the Melthorpe apartments, Axel elects to tail the two juniors. Less than a mile away, they stop in front of a large garage structure. He quickly takes note of the address of this building. One of these men gets out of the sedan, unlocks a large door, slides it open, continues to drive into the building, and slides the door closed behind them.

No sooner has Axel butted his first cigarette on this watch, when the door slides open with the same two men, except now the passenger is riding in the back seat. Putting his car in gear, not wanting to be seen, Axel waits until these men have put a reasonable distance between himself and them before he moves forward. To his surprise, they head directly back to the Melthorpe apartments.

What he sees next causes his heart to race and his breathing to increase. The two juniors are escorting Stella and Carly into the apartment building. "Jackpot!" he says out loud putting down his field glasses. Mark has also viewed the same phenomenon. Axel elects to wait a while to watch if they take their two hostages back to the same address. Within fifteen minutes they're loading the two back into the backseat area of the sedan. Since they can't be seen, and the passenger is riding in the backseat it's obvious they have placed their captives on the backseat floor of the sedan. Clearly, he's the guard preventing them from making an escape.

Unable to do anything to free these two hapless victims at this time, Axel's mind is working out some details that will be useful in the near future. For now, he is willing to patiently bide his time.

****

Back on Harsens, and fifteen minutes before this exodus at the Melthorpe—at noon—Frankie is trying hard not to be overly anxious. He's waiting with the phone within reaching distance. The phone bell resonates right on time.

"Hello," says Frankie, attempting to remain cool.

"Hello, Frankie!" says the voice on the other end of the line. It's clearly an anxious voice.

"Stella, are you and Carly all right?" Frankie manages to question.

"Yes, but get us out of here!" Stella says, nearly shouting.

Before she can say another word, the phone is snatched from her hand with the same voice from the day before replacing hers with the message, "Tomorrow night, asshole, you be in front of Squeaky's at 9 p.m. You make damn sure you come alone with the booze an' money. Any funny business, and you'll never see your whore and her kid again—you get what I'm sayin'?"

This voice is enough to make Frankie wish he could reach through the line and grab its throat.

Nonetheless, realizing he is in no position to sabotage the arrangement to satisfy his anger, he recomposes himself long enough to give the impression they are dealing with a servile dupe.

"Yes, sir. I understand thoroughly. Just don't harm them. I have everything you want," says Frankie, using the humblest tone he can marshal. The next sound he hears is the click of the receiver on the other end.

Back on the main line, Axel has instructed Mark to take note of any movement by anyone coming or going from the apartment. Heading back to Harsens, he drives directly to meet with Frankie. He relates all he observed. "From what I could see of them they appeared to be all right physically, but I know damn well they ain't doin' that good mentally," says Axel with a tone that suggests he might have had a similar experience at one time in his life.

Frankie also relays what little he can add with the limited exposure they allowed him with Stella. "I think she and Carly are probably more than anxious to have all this come to an end." Pausing with an afterthought, Frankie adds, "I don't get how they plan on making this exchange in front of Squeaky's place. Hell, there's more people hangin' around there than I would think they would want to deal with."

"You're more than right about that. My feeling is, that ain't gonna be where this exchange takes place," says Axel with his usual firm opinion. He then adds, "Just be ready and alert from that point on. I know the address of the building Stella's being held in. They, more'n likely, will take you from Squeaky's place to that building. I believe we can put something together to give them a hell of a surprise." After discussing a plan with Axel, this is the first time since this whole devastation has begun that Frankie believes they can have the upper hand before this whole debacle comes to a conclusion.

The past few days, the Melthorpe apartment has been a demanding place. Axler and Fletcher have had their hands full in their attempt to wound the Harsens Island resistance leadership enough to bring it down. They have depended on their plant Lyman Woodard to give them the information they need to put this kidnapping scheme together. They're not celebrating yet, but they're both displaying a degree of cockiness as they bark out orders to the juniors they've entrusted to guard and feed their hostages. The juniors, in turn, are playing up the importance and the power this task has given them over this helpless woman and her child.

One of the juniors in particular, named Irving Feldman, considers himself a ladies' man. He had heard of Stella when she worked at Squeaky's, and he'd wanted to get around to making use of her services, but she left before he was able. He considers this an opportune time to gratify this unfulfilled lust.

He's arranged things this morning where he's in charge of making sure the two have food enough to last through the day. He's put on an extra dab of cologne to ensure he'll have a receptive partner.

"Hey, Feldman, what's the deal? Ya smell like a French whore," pronounces a fellow junior, Mickey Selik.

"Yeah, well, I'm lookin forward ta havin' breakfast in bed with our little nafka (whore)," answers Feldman, spitting in his hands and applying it to smooth out his hair.

Selik has been guarding the even now locked door holding their prisoner. His guarding is more to prevent someone attempting to spring them from the outside than to prevent them from breaking through a locked heavy wooden door. To say that he too had not had thoughts of entertaining himself with this "nafka" would be a lie, but he also has had a sobering second thought. It's been an unspoken reality that if anybody were to have "breakfast in bed" with Stella, it would be Abe Axler, their boss. To assume the rights to Axler's property would amount to asking to be fitted with a pair of specialized concrete boots and dumped overboard in the middle of Lake St. Clair.

Nonetheless, Feldman didn't get where he is today by listening to someone else's drummer, he has enough weird beats of his own. Many of them off beat. This beat he's listening to this morning is convincing him that when she lays eyes on him, she'll be so overcome with desire that it'll be a cakewalk getting her in bed.

Carrying a basket filled with enough provisions to get their hostages to the exchange hour, Feldman waits until Selik unlocks the door and then saunters through. He expects he'll be able to negotiate a quick lay and be out the door before anyone is the wiser.

He finds Stella cradling her very distraught daughter. This kind of confinement is proving to be taking its toll on Carly. She's used to being free to dance and play without these frightening restrictions.

Feldman stands staring at the circumstances he's faced with. He decides the best approach is a direct one, so he says, "Put the goddam kid down, and get on yer back."

Stella gives him the same protective stare a mother grizzly gives in defending her cub just before she charges. In a second, Stella lays Carly on the bed behind her. In the next, she grabs the slop pail from under the bed, thrusting its contents at Feldman and covering him from head to toe with two days' worth of excrement. All he has to answer back with is a gasp as Stella swings the empty bucket, beating him on the head. In less than sixty seconds, Feldman has gone from a debonair "oysshteler" (egotist) to a guy getting hammered by a hostage wielding a slop pail.

All the commotion brings Selik through the door as fast as a scalded cat, where he sees a compatriot cowering in the corner, covered with poop, and a woman relentlessly beating him while her child jumps up and down on the bed, screaming for her mother. What had been a fairly simple operation has now become mayhem. Grabbing Stella, Selik throws her off Feldman, who is completely discombobulated as he slips and lands back on the floor. In the meantime, Stella has returned to her now even more distraught daughter, rocking her with the determination of a mother tigress.

Once Selik has determined what the mess is made up of, he's torn between running out and leaving the door unguarded or getting Feldman out and relocking the door. He makes funny little whimper noises as he realizes his own shoes are covered. His gag reflex is taking over, so he makes his way to the door.

For the present moment, Feldman is too overwhelmed with humiliation to get violent. For now, he's content to crawl across the floor and get free of this mortifying incident. As soon as they are out the door, Selik slams the it shut and throws the bolt in place, locking Stella and Carly in with their fears of retaliation.

Ignorant of all this pandemonium at the makeshift impound, Axler and Fletcher continue to go over their plans.

"I think we're gonna be in a good position to get rid of that whore and her kid for the real prize, Frankie Morgansky himself," says Axler, addressing a new stage in their seeming triumph.

Fletcher face lights up as though someone has just announced he's an heir to the British throne. "Yeah, and then we can turn that goddam rube over ta Burnstein. Ten ta one says he'll give us the chance ta off the schmuck," says Fletcher.

"That'll for sure get Burnstein off our ass!" adds Fletcher, satisfied Axler has come up with the redemptive plan they need to get back in the good graces of the Purples' higher echelon. They spend the rest of the day preparing for their 9 p.m. deadline.

****

Axel has done an excellent job in rallying the troops. Defeat at the hands of these silk suit kikes is not something any of these Harsens Island patriots are willing to swallow. They all have their stories about how they've been bullied and harassed at the hands of these gangsters. They have all become aware of an old truth applied to their own lives: life shrinks or expands in proportion with one's courage. Alone, their futures are wrapped up in the hands of these monsters, but together, they have the ability to liberate their future. They know from their past triumphs over these seeming unbeatable foes that they had found success when they were able to leave their comfort zones behind—as one of them, in an offhand statement once was heard to say, "Nothin' ever grows there." What each of these resistance fighters has gotten for the benefit of the island as a result of their collective achievements is not nearly as important as what they've become individually. These types of convictions are the fuel that compels them to action. They are all of one mind and know they must get Stella and Carly back to the safety of their beloved island.

The time is winding down. Axel has his plan activated. Frankie, with all his efforts, has not been able to do much—his worry continues to plague his thoughts. He is so grateful he has Axel's cool head to fill the gaps he's incapable of dealing with.

"Axel, I wish I could tell you how much I appreciate all the time and effort you've put into this task. I just wish I could be more help, but my mind won't stay in one place long enough to stay on track with what I know has to be done."

"Things are pretty well covered. I'll say you trained our core group well enough that I have no doubt we can come out on top of this mission," echoes Axel.

"Don't thank me. These guys have all been in the Great War. The United States military trained each one of them," says Frankie with a great deal of pride.

"That's good to know 'cause we're gonna need every break we can get. Theses Purples might be nothin' more than a bunch of city slickers, but we gotta remember they're city slickers with guns. Even though, when they're obliged to face the full brunt of the Harsens Island militia, they'll be dumbfounded," says Axel, "Oh, and by the way, you must have considered that there might have been a reason why Axler and Fletcher wanted only you to deliver the money, it's my belief from what I've heard through the grapevine it's not only the money they want—it's your sorry ass they need ta redeem themselves with the Burnsteins."

With a sigh, Frankie says, "I already figured that out. I'm somewhat prepared, but I'm gonna have ta play that one by ear. I don't know how many of their guys are gonna be hangin' around."

Axel is convinced along with Frankie that his group possesses the desire to win and the emotion and confidence to bring it to a reality.

"That's the problem, we're all gonna have ta play this by ear. Not knowin' their plan in total puts a limit on what we can expect. But I believe our guys can adapt and overcome. They know how to do something well. I see a good end for Harsens," reiterates Axel.

This is the kind of encouragement Frankie needs at this point. He's always known that his source of strength doesn't come from just himself, and rather from encouragers like Axel, who inspires him to look inside at what his creator has left him with. He also has a slightly different plan regarding how the money will be exchanged for the hostages. He spends the next few minutes discussing it with Axel to give him a heads up.

With every angle that can be discussed coming to a conclusion, Axel's crew begin their trek to the city. They each know what assignments they need to perform and from where they need to be to complete them.

"To map out a course of action and follow it to an end requires courage," said Ralph Waldo Emerson at one time. In that spirit, each one of these participants is well aware that their overall success will be directly proportional as to how they each apply their individual effort.

It's eight forty-five when Frankie arrives at Squeaky's. There is nothing unusual about the number of cars and people coming and going for this time of the evening. With the exception of Frankie, it's a run-of-the-mill cold January evening in Detroit. He parks his car where it can be noticed, lights a cigarette and prepares to wait. Taking a final drag, he butts the fag and at the same time notices a car pulling up alongside his car. It's two young men around his own age. He recognizes them both: Irving Feldman and Mickey Selik. They were all at the Old Bishop vocational school at the same time. The men are giving him a stare that says they want Frankie's attention. Rolling down his window, Frankie returns the stare waiting for one of them to speak. "Follow me," are Feldman's only words as he puts his car in gear and abruptly pulls away. Frankie responds by putting his own vehicle in gear, pressing on the accelerator, following a few car links behind.

Not having a complete picture of what to expect, Frankie's eyes cautiously dart up, down, and side to side as they meander their way through Detroit's lower east side. With the degree of secrecy Axel has maintained, and unbeknown to Axler and Fletcher, their improvised prison location has been compromised enough to allow Axel's forces to fill the area. Frankie spots a utility truck working on a lamp post. Another is a seemingly abandoned truck with a full load of something covered with heavy tarps and parked within a block of the target location, and another is a taxi that appears to be searching for an address. Frankie is feeling a lot better as he realizes he's not alone in this venture.

The sedan carrying the two men comes to a halt in front of what appears to be a garage of sorts. The men make an exit and approach Frankie's truck with the words, "The boss says he wants ta know you got the money and the booze 'fore we go any further—so let's see what ya got."

"I may be a rube from Harsens, but I didn't just fall off the turnip truck—no way in hell am I gonna produce money without seein' my goods," states Frankie with an air of finality.

"Listen punk, the boss ain't gonna like us comin' back ta tell him you ain't co-operatin'. If you got any brains left in that bean bag settin' on yer shoulders, you'll show me the goddam money now!" says Feldman.

"With you guys holdin' all the cards, what makes you think I'd be carryin' the money ta just let you mugs snatch it with me left holdin' my dick. You show me both my ladies and I'll produce the money," says Frankie. The sarcasm is noticed by both men. They considered their job done. All they can do at this point is to report back to Axler and Fletcher.

Within a few minutes of them entering the garage, the big door slides to one side, and a big Buick sedan inches through the opening. Frankie's eyes are straining as he focuses on the sedan's rear windows. *There they are!* Stella is in the backseat, holding Carly on her lap. Frankie can't remember the last time his heart beat like this.

The sedan stops. Axler is behind the wheel, and Fletcher holds the two in the backseat. Axler makes the first move by exiting the Buick. Making his way toward Frankie, Frankie can see the sullen look of displeasure on Axler's face. "Okay, shtick drek (shithead), ya better make damn certain you ain't tryin' ta pull a fast one."

"No, sir. You let them out, and I'll get you the money," says Frankie in a matter-of-fact tone.

"Mickey was right, you ain't nothin' but a smart-ass rube!"

Frankie has played this card as far as he can without inviting these thugs to use Carly or Stella's present wellbeing as poker chips. Realizing his back is against the wall, Frankie makes a hand signal to the seeming abandoned truck parked down the street—the same one he passed on the way in. Its headlights suddenly illuminate the street as it slowly begins to make its way toward them. The driver is none other than Mark Kingsbury. Mark has overcome his initial fears, proving himself over and over to becoming more an essential asset to the Harsens resistance. For this endeavor, he has volunteered to play a role in this much hoped-for exchange by carrying the money needed to make the switch.

Seeing a truck approaching that had not been introduced in the initial deal, Axler's first reaction is to grab Frankie and put a gun to his head. "What kinda shit you tryin' ta pull?" he shouts as he twists Frankie around enough to place him squarely between himself and the oncoming sedan. Seeing the predicament, he's created, Frankie shouts, "Relax, he's haulin' the booze and the money!"

Axler responds by tightening his grip on Frankie and continues his mistrust of anything he is saying until proven otherwise.

Mark is also cognitive as to what is beginning to transpire. Recognizing the situation must be handled another way, he stops his truck, exiting with both hands in the air. All the while one hand is gripping the bag containing the money, the other is waving a hand full of cash. Fully visible and as transparent as he can be, he continues to move forward.

Axler is watching Mark's every move. Having another person to deal with in this encounter is visibly annoying him. "Screwin' up our negotiations like this is the kind of shit that's gonna get you two assholes dead," says a clearly frustrated Axler. Mark is now within ten feet of Axler as he slowly lowers his hands, bending down, he places the bag and the loose cash on the ground directly in front of Axler, then rises to put his hands back above his head. Frankie can begin to feel Axler's grip beginning to relax as his trust level rises.

Making one more pronouncement directed at Axler, Mark says, "The champagne is on the truck bed."

Now waving the pistol at Mark, Axler orders him to pick the money up from the ground and to join Frankie. The two are now at the total mercy of Axler as he leads them both back to the sedan carrying Stella and Carly as well as Axler's accomplice, Eddie Fletcher. As all plans go, especially when some unexpected incident enters into the scheme, things have to be changed. In this case Mark is going to fulfill a part of this assignment that had been designated to Feldman and Selik.

Reaching the Buick, Fletcher makes an exit with a hold on Stella. Frankie has not taken his eyes off neither her nor Carly since they began the walk back.

"Say hello and good-by," says Fletcher continuing his grasp on Stella. She looks at him with a distrustful stare.

Axler brings Frankie and Mark to a halt on the other side of the sedan. "I got some good news and some bad news for you two dipshits. The good news is one of you gets to win, the bad news is the other gets to lose," says Axler with a truly evil grin accompanying his verbose. With an even more diabolical laugh Axler continues his torment as a cat does playing with the life of a mouse and says, "Morgansky, you win, you get to stay here with us." Looking at Mark, he lingers for a moment, then says, "As for you, you lose. You take the whore and her bastard kid, and get the hell outta here."

Sure enough, this is all playing out the way Axel predicted: "They don't want Stella and Carly. They'll just be a burden to get along with. What they want is you, Frankie. Burnstein has paid them big money to bring you in dead or alive."

Frankie sees Mark leading Stella and Carly safely away and feels a great sense of relief. His unflappable demeanor returns. Within minutes, things are changing again. Frankie is being shoved; he stumbles back toward the garage. He finds himself in the hands of

Feldman and Selik; they have been given the opportunity to be the cat that chases the Morgansky mouse. Like all bullies, they don't mind demonstrating how tough they believe they are, provided their prey is at a definite disadvantage.

Axler follows, leaving Fletcher to tend to the champagne truck. No sooner do they re-enter the garage than all hell breaks loose. Before the entourage can react, at least two dozen men with hoods and shotguns suddenly appear out of the shadows and surround them. Every gun points directly at Axler, Feldman, and Selik. While the men were busy with Frankie, Axel and his militia snuck into the building.

Faced with the shock of disbelief, they find themselves at a moment of indecisiveness; they are faced with a surprise and must make a decision. The wrong choice will be deadly. Taking advantage of this stalled moment in time, Axel pulls Frankie out of Feldman's grasp. In a momentary reaction that could change Feldman's life forever, he makes an involuntary effort to grip his stolen quarry. He immediately feels the full brunt of the stock of a shotgun on the back of his head, which knocks him to the floor. This action helped the remaining three quickly assess the new terms of life.

With his shotgun pointed within three inches of Axler's head, Axel asks the question, "Mr. Axler, have you ever seen someone's head after it was shot with a gun like this?"

Axler is speechless; he's still in shock. After a moment of silence from Axler, Axel speaks. "Let me answer that question for you, sir. The answer is no, because there is no head left to see."
Axler's Adam's apple moves as he swallows hard; defeat is always bitter when it's swallowed.

The other two are being gang stormed resulting in them being disarmed, lying on the floor. In a moment, a disheveled Fletcher is being dragged in. He's not in any better condition than his accomplices. Fletcher lifts the canvas from the truck bed, expecting to find cases of champagne, he's met by an avalanche of men armed with shotguns.

Axel has one more surprise. From out of the crowd, one hoodless person is brought forward. It's none other than Lyman. He doesn't look to be enjoying this party in the least.

This unexpected new reality is quickly having a much fuller impact on these five gangsters. Facing this overwhelming show of force, they know they are defeated. Their bullying boldness is suddenly replaced with obsequiousness. With no fight left in them, they are pulled back to their feet and placed in the center of the room.

Following this action, Axel takes a spot facing them. "Gentlemen—and I use the word loosely—the Harsens Island citizens have filed criminal charges against you. They have given this committee full authority to hold a trial and decide your innocence or guilt. The charges are kidnapping, aggravated assault, racketeering, theft, and generally pissing people off. How do you plead?"

The five appear stupefied. This change of events has come on them so swiftly. They are left with no mental capacity to make any kind of defense, so they remain confused, stunned, and befuddled.

Recognizing his defendants are not making an effort to comply with the course of events, Axel states in their behalf, "We will accept the defendants' silence as an admission of guilt." Turning to the hooded men surrounding the room, he continues, "All in favor, say 'aye.'"

"AYE!"

"Now, to be fair," Axel continues, "all those who oppose this decision, say 'nay.'"

The room is silent.

The faces of these men give the impression that the entire universe is against them. At this moment, in the deep recesses of their beings, their futures promise to be very bleak.

With little attention to the response this vote has on the five defendants, Axel quickly moves to the next phase, "I believe we can accept their guilty plea." Turning to the five beleaguered defendants, Axel declares in a very strong and precise voice, "Therefore, we also find you guilty and sentence you to hang 'til you're dead, or somebody comes to your rescue."

In that instance five ropes are brought to the forefront. The next segment of this ordeal is to get these men herded outside. There is a yard arm jutting out from the peak of the garage. Normally it's used to support a pulley system to lift heavy auto parts to the second floor. But today it's being put to use to support five hanging ropes—one for each of Burnsteins goons. Next, the coats of these men are stripped off leaving them in their expensive white dress shirt, then their hands are tied behind their back. Someone comes forward with an inkwell, dipping his finger into the black liquid, and inscribes their convictions across their shirts. The label of kidnapper goes to Selik, extortionist goes to Fletcher, *Shmendrik* (stupid jerk) goes to Feldman, collaborator goes to Lyman, and last—but far from least—rapist goes to Axler.

With no ceremony, the ropes are brought out and draped over the highest wooden beam in the barn. The men are now showing signs of fear. They watch as the nooses are tied, the other portion thrown over the barn's accessory, and then each rope is tied to the bumper of their Buick. The idea is that once the ropes are fastened to each of the condemned men, the Buick will be used to pull the ropes, lifting them from the ground and leaving them in the air to dangle.

Axler is the first to be brought forward. In spite of the cold, he is sweating and shaking profusely. Next is Fletcher. His expensive black and white Spectator shoes are filling with water as urine flows down his leg. Selik follows, he's retching his guts as he's put in place for his rope attachment. Feldman isn't in any better shape than the other three as he's bawling like a baby. Lyman is so terrified, he can only babble incoherently.

The wind has ceased, and a light snow begins to fall. Each of the men are made to sit. The ropes are strung in place; the signal is given. Someone puts the Buick in gear, and all five men are simultaneously lifted off the ground and left to dangle ... by their ankles.

Frankie studies each of them as their faces begin to redden as blood pools in their heads. Given the gravity of the situation, he speaks to each as they struggle against this demeaning and totally demoralizing position, "From my understanding of the Burnstein brothers, they're gonna be real disappointed in you boys. You might wish you'd had these ropes around yer necks." With that said, and the return of his hundred thousand dollars, he's relieved to say goodbye to this chapter of his life.

Things have gotten very quiet. The men walk by their handiwork as it hangs in the cold for everyone to see. Satisfied they've accomplished their objective, they return to the ordinary lives they're willing to fight for—something the Burnsteins will never understand.

CHAPTER 26

After assuring Simon and Aristine of his wellbeing, Frankie spends the night with Stella and Carly rather than remain at home. The next day, both, Stella and Carly are uncommonly quiet and reflective for most of the day. After all, it hasn't even been twenty-four hours since their rescue.

Noticing their morose behavior, Frankie takes a moment to engage them both in conversation. "I want to tell each of you that I believe you two to be the most valuable people in my life. I didn't know just how valuable until I feared I had lost you. Now I know I'll go to hell and back again to guarantee your safety and wellbeing. I love you both beyond words."

Frankie's pronouncement stirs Stella to tears. She also feels the need to express the feelings she has for Frankie. "Frankie, since we were those kids playin' house every chance we could, I always felt safe with you. You were always able to take a difficult situation and see things I never could. You can always see deep stuff that I never could, and still can't."

Frankie has returned to his normal pragmatic self and is ready to move on. "I think we need a good, steady purpose to get our heads back on straight. What say we get married?" asks Frankie.

Stella is slowly coming out of her funk. With a little laugh among tears, she says, "That's another thing I hate about you, Frankie. You never let me just piss and moan about things. Sometimes a girl just needs a good cry and ta feel bad. Then you come along and ruin it all with all that positive confidence. You just make me wanna cry sometimes."

Carly is paying close attention to what the adults are saying. Like most children, her resilience is encouraged by being secure. Hearing Frankie say the things a child needs to hear to bring the best of themselves to the surface, she responds, "Can we get married now, Mamma? I wanna wear my new dress and dance."

"Oh, my sweet child. We can get married, and you will be a beautiful dancer in your new dress," declares Stella. Tears stream down her cheeks, and then she laughs.

EPILOGUE

While entering a beer distribution office, Gus Winkler was cut down by several shotgun blasts. He died within the hour after gasping out the Lord's Prayer.

Fred "Killer" Burke died as an obese diabetic in prison.

Abe Axler and Eddie Fletcher, known as the "Siamese Twins" for their constant and eerie kinship, were found riddled with bullets at the corner of Telegraph and Quarton Roads. The bodies were sitting side by side in the backseat of a new Chrysler Coupe with their hands entwined—the pair lived and died as a duo. No one has ever been charged with their murders.

Ray Burnstein and his brothers Abe, Izzy, and Joe were sentenced to Jackson Prison, which they controlled. Ray was released from prison in 1964, and he died soon thereafter.

Squeaky Schwartz contracted syphilis and shot himself in the head.

Lyman Woodard soon left the Purple Gang and went on to become one of Detroit's foremost Jazz musicians. He died at age sixty-seven.

As a young adult, Carly made her way to New York to become a dancer on Broadway.

Frankie and Stella went on to have seven children. They never left the island. To this day, their independent spirit continues to live within the hearts of Harsens residents, who know that what you get by achieving your goals is not as important as what you become by achieving your goals.

The Detroit News, July 15, 1999

Detroit's lower east side was a breeding ground for poverty, crime, and violence during the early part of the twentieth century. It was in the chaotic streets of this ethnic melting pot that the Purple Gang was born in the years just preceding World War I.

Like-minded groups of protestant Christians, though small in number, were loudly in favor of passing the Eighteenth Amendment, which prohibited the sale of alcohol across the United States. Their expectations were that the country would willingly give up its thirst for "spirits." Instead, the amendment created a burgeoning underground alcohol market.

This is one of the great ironies of the twentieth century. Prohibition was expected to bring about a perfect society. Instead, it fostered one of the most lawless and violent periods in American history.

This is the story of Detroit's Purple Gang and their clandestine designs on Harsens Island.